P'ungmul

P'ungmul

South Korean Drumming and Dance

Nathan Hesselink

The University of Chicago Press
Chicago and London

Nathan Hesselink is assistant professor of ethnomusicology at the University of British Columbia. He is the editor of *Contemporary Directions: Korean Folk Music Engaging the Twentieth Century and Beyond.*

The University of Chicago Press, Chicago 60637
The University of Chicago Press, Ltd., London
© 2006 by The University of Chicago
All rights reserved. Published 2006
Printed in the United States of America
15 14 13 12 11 10 09 08 07 06   5 4 3 2 1

ISBN (cloth): 0-226-33093-1
ISBN (paper): 0-226-33095-8

The University of Chicago Press gratefully acknowledges support of the publication of this book by the Korea Foundation, Seoul, Korea.

Library of Congress Cataloging-in-Publication Data

Hesselink, Nathan.
　　P'ungmul : South Korean drumming and dance / Nathan Hesselink.
　　　　p.　　cm. — (Chicago studies in ethnomusicology)
　　Includes bibliographical references (p.　), and index.
　　ISBN 0-226-33093-1 (cloth : alk. paper) — ISBN 0-226-33095-8 (pbk. : alk. paper)
　　1. Folk music—Korea (South)—Chŏlla-pukto—History and criticism.　2. Folk dance music—Korea (South)—Chŏlla-pukto—History and criticism.　3. Farmers—Korea (South)—Songs and music—History and criticism.　4. Percussion music—Korea (South)—History and criticism.　I. Title.　II. Series.
　　ML3752.7.C5 H47　2006
　　781.62′957—dc22

　　　　　　　　　　　　　　　　　　　　　　　　　　　　　　　　2006040445

CONTENTS

ILLUSTRATIONS

ACKNOWLEDGMENTS

It is impossible for me to provide a complete list of teachers, students, family, friends, and institutions that provided financial, intellectual, and moral support both before and during the writing of this book. The number is frankly too great, the experiences too numerous and varied for me to properly recall them in their entirety. The compromise with which I have decided to live is to bring to the fore key individuals and organizations that merit special recognition, presented in rough chronological order according to our initial encounter.

This project would not have gotten off the ground without the proper mindset and "heartset" established early on by my first professors of ethnomusicology at the University of Michigan, Judith Becker and William (Bill) Malm. While pursuing my doctoral studies at the University of London, School of Oriental and African Studies, I received grants from the Overseas Research Award Scheme, the William Goodenough Trust, and the Ouseley Memorial Trust. David Hughes and Robert Provine served as members of my thesis committee, providing astute criticism and encouragement that vastly improved parts of this book in their earlier versions. Rajiv Narayan and Roald Maliangkay (who has since helped me in too many ways to count) were welcome comrades-in-arms during these graduate school days.

My initial training in Korean percussion instruments took place at the National Center for Korean Traditional Performing Arts (Kungnip kugagwŏn) in Seoul, specifically under the tutelage of Pak Chongsŏl, Pak Ŭnha, and Ch'oe Pyŏngsam. Fieldwork in various stages was made possible by grants from the Korean Ministry of Culture, the Kungnip kugagwŏn, the Korea Foundation, and the University of London. While I was in Korea, the help and advice of Son Hŭijŏng and Kim Soyŏn (Korea Foundation), as well as the scholars Yi Pohyŏng, Song Pangsong, and Song Hyejin, proved invaluable.

The majority of this text was prepared while I was a postdoctoral research fellow at the University of California, Berkeley. The Center for Korean Studies was my home during this period and served as fertile ground for interaction with a number of American and Korean scholars; Lewis Lancaster, Bonnie Wade, and Yun Chigwan in particular provided a nourishing and broadening intellectual environment. Research and editorial matters were greatly aided by Luc (Toshik) Walhain and by my parents, Etta and I. John Hesselink. And I would be greatly remiss not to mention Jonathan Petty—master-of-all at the Center—who served (and serves) as an inspiration on so many levels.

The manuscript in its final manifestations was guided and nurtured by Philip Bohlman, a mentor and later a colleague, to whom the words "thank you" can hardly express the range and depth of my appreciation and admiration. David Brent at the University of Chicago Press exhibited superhuman patience and understanding during the acquisition process, and my editor, Elizabeth Branch Dyson, will always hold a place in my heart for her tenacity and courage in seeing the value of this research when others would have given up. I also wish to thank an anonymous reviewer whose sensitive and insightful remarks helped me forge the path eventually taken in this book.

Finally, gratitude at the deepest level is humbly offered to my supervisor and friend Keith Howard and to my wife, Serra Hwang, whose support and guidance are largely responsible for the positive facets of this book. Last, but certainly not least, I wish to acknowledge my indebtedness to my drumming mentors, Kim Hyŏngsun and Yi Sangbaek, whose presence not only shaped the entire experience but dwells within me even now. This work is dedicated to them.

AUTHOR'S NOTE

Romanization

Despite the ongoing (2005) debate in Korea surrounding the use of the McCune-Reischauer system of Korean romanization, I have chosen to adopt this system ("Romanization" 1961: 121–28) with the following modifications. The compound *shi* is used throughout the text in place of *si*, resulting in *shi, shinmyŏng,* and *sanshin,* rather than *si, sinmyŏng,* and *sansin.* When a morpheme-final consonant is succeeded by another consonant it is generally changed to the latter, resulting in a doubled consonant: *kut* + *kŏri* = *kukkŏri* (literally, "section of a ritual"), or *hoet* + *pul* = *hoeppul* (torch).

In the interest of consistent recognition of native terms by the foreign reader, I have chosen to separate grammatical particles such as *e, ŭl,* and *kwa* from the preceding word by a hyphen, resulting in the following examples of romanization: *p'ungmulgut-e* (rather than the standard *p'ungmulguse,* which reflects actual pronunciation), *kkot-ŭl (kkoch'ŭl),* and *kut-kwa (kukkwa).* The only exception to this rule is the possessive marker *ŭi,* which is treated as a separate unit (e.g., *Han'guk ŭi* versus *Han'gugŭi*). I have also opted to isolate the term *kut* (ritual or performance) from compounds denoting an activity, such as in *insa kut* (translated as "moving ritual"), but to include it when referring to a rhythmic pattern (*insagut*).

Authors' names are cited by the romanizations used in the original publications; in the bibliography the McCune-Reischauer version is then provided in brackets immediately following (e.g., Lee Byong Won [Yi Pyŏngwŏn]). Chinese terms are romanized according to the pinyin system, Japanese terms according to Hepburn. Foreign terms are italicized throughout, with the exception of proper nouns, titles of pieces, associations, government groups, buildings, and offices.

Pronunciation

The vowels *a, e, i, o,* and *u* in the Korean language are essentially pronounced as their counterparts in Italian or Spanish; consonants are roughly equivalent to English, with an apostrophe (') indicating greater aspiration. The vowel compounds *ae* and *oe* sound as *a* in American English "hat" and *we* of "wet" respectively. *Ŭ* is pronounced as the *ou* of "should," and *ŏ* between the *ou* of American "ought" and *o* of "come." The consonant *r* is always a "flipped" *r* as in Spanish or Italian, and the possessive marker *ŭi* is often pronounced like the Korean *e*. Morpheme-initial or -final consonants *p, t,* and *k* when surrounded by vowels are pronounced *b, d,* and *g* respectively (e.g., *kuk* + *ak* = *kugak*, "national [Korean] music"). The same is true if the adjacent sound is a voiced continuant consonant, such as *l, n,* or *w* (*p'ungmul* + *kut* = *p'ungmulgut*, "drumming and dance").

☯

A Web site providing transcriptions of the performances documented in chapter 5 is found at http://www.music.ubc.ca/index.php?id=5401.

P'ungmul

INTRODUCTION

On Visiting

Dinner preparations by the local villagers had been completed. Area residents, guests, and dancer-musicians gathered around long communal tables to share in the numerous dishes that had been made especially for the occasion. Nearly forty minutes later we were summoned by the village head to congregate outside; the performance was about to begin. Eleven percussionists—clothed in the loose-fitting white cotton dress of the traditional laborer, complemented by striped-sleeved vests and multicolored sashes—formed a large semicircle around the group that had eagerly assembled. The silence of the countryside was then shattered by the deafening sound of gongs and drums, which quickly dissipated into the cool, dark evening air. After a brief musical introduction, the ensemble began to move in single file along a narrow path that wound its way through the as yet unplanted field. The crowd followed in a similar manner, eventually being led to a grassy clearing flanked on one side by a large pile of carefully stacked timber. As the performers took a short interval to readjust their instruments and secure their spinning-tasseled hats, the wood was set ablaze with a roar that startled even the hardiest of villagers. Gongs and drums were again sounded, and for the next two hours those who had convened danced and drank to the accompaniment of rhythms in the light of the bonfire. The outlines of undulating arms and shoulders combined with the faint traces of gyrating tassels to create a fluid blur of motion, heightening

1

the contrast with the peaceful yet unyielding mountain ranges looming behind in the shadows. (Edited field notes from a March 5, 1996, Taeborŭm festival performance, Chinan county, North Chŏlla province)

The above account is taken from one of my initial attempts to describe, in just a few words, the excitement and allure of a rural performance of p'ungmul, or South Korean drumming and dance. The ensemble, consisting of a core set of two gongs (*soe/kkwaenggwari* and *ching*) and two drums (*changgo* and *puk*), distinguishes itself from other indigenous performing arts by its central focus on rhythm. A tradition steeped in music, dance, theater, and pageantry, it was until the Japanese occupation of the early twentieth century the primary mode of musical expression of the majority of the Korean populace. Before this era of imposed subservience—one marked by gradual industrialization and the forced acceptance of foreign cultural influences—p'ungmul was an integral component of village life, serving as musical accompaniment in the often overlapping contexts of labor, ritual, and entertainment.

Like all enduring artistic practices, p'ungmul is an intellectually and aesthetically engaging entity of considerable and flexible sociopolitical consequence. It is as important and intriguing for what it says about what it meant to be Korean in the past as it is for what it currently means to be Korean in a society that has on many levels abandoned its ties with older tradition. P'ungmul survived centuries of political turmoil, foreign conquest, paradigmatic shifts in religion and ideology, and technological developments, borrowing from and shaping such influences in the manner of a broad cultural repository. In the later twentieth century, after decades of war, destruction, and societal indifference that threatened its very existence, it rose again, almost phoenixlike, adapting and reinventing itself for new frameworks of meaning and enjoyment. With the neglect or loss of many of its original social contexts in the countryside, p'ungmul in modified forms moved into urban spaces at home and in diasporic communities abroad, though it never completely lost its foothold in the provinces. It also came to represent one of the few public spaces in modern Korean life where both sexes and the different generations can and do participate.

It is useful to view the current state of p'ungmul activity—that of the years surrounding the turn of the twenty-first century—in two separate yet interconnected ways. The first is to locate it as a place in the collective Korean imaginary, frequently visited by tourist offices and agencies, educational institutes, nationalist scholars, and Korean cultural centers in the United States and Europe. This is the realm or world of mythos, of a timeless and ahistorical p'ungmul that speaks to homogeneous, pan-Korean sensibilities in the form of a national symbol (after Armstrong 2000: xiii–xvi;

Jung 1997: 180–81). Here the concern is with the origins, nature, and/or essence of Korean culture, the ultimate meanings behind vestiges of a rapidly disappearing past. Differences in social context, regional style, and political motivation are blurred or even erased to create a unified front. The resultant image, one that plays up the idea of a healthy, untutored, and happy "peasant" engaged in the joys of labor, resonates with a population that in many ways still views itself as communally supportive and in tune with nature and spiritual forces, immediate lived realities to the contrary (see also Cumings 1997: 21–22).

This oftentimes romanticized picture is projected in two directions: one internally, toward local Koreans, and the other externally, toward foreigners and/or visiting tourists (though there are occasions on which the audiences are one and the same). For the native population, photographs or cartoon images of p'ungmul performers feature prominently on postage stamps, New Year's Day greeting cards, shopping bags and seasonal food displays at farmers' cooperatives (nonghyŏp), brochures for traditional culture festivals (such as the 1996 Kwangju Kimch'i Festival in South Chŏlla province), or fliers advertising traditional music courses offered at the National Center for Korean Traditional Performing Arts (Kungnip kugagwŏn) in the capital Seoul. The renowned painter and calligrapher Kim Kich'ang—whose artwork, in the form of the image on the Korean 10,000 wŏn bill, is seen daily by thousands—chose p'ungmul musicians as the subject of his first painting on indigenous performing art forms in 1957. Titled "Hŭngnakto" (A Scene of Joyful Music [Making]), Kim's rationale for such a choice included re-creating what he saw as the "humble emotions, simple lives, and joyful performances" exhibited in p'ungmul (quoted in Pak Myŏngja 2000: 129–30). Similar reasoning informed the conclusion of a recently published "fairy tale" for children that places p'ungmul musicians and their music at the legendary founding of the Korean peninsula: "By playing together with such joy and in such harmony the people expressed their thanks to the King of heaven and the guardians who gave them these precious treasures [p'ungmul instruments]. Their hope was to bring human beings, the heavens, and the earth together as one [through] that great and harmonious sound" (Kwak Young-kwon, Kim, and Oh 2003: 26).

Similar scenes or icons, in the form of key chains and other tourist trinkets, "Events This Month" pamphlets, and tourist maps of Seoul and the surrounding provinces, greet the weary foreign traveler arriving at Inch'ŏn International Airport. In the capital itself, the city government and the National Tourism Organization provide numerous brochures graced with p'ungmul imagery—everything from theater announcements to the Korean Folk Village flier to the 2002 World Cup cultural events listing. Cartoon tigers sporting p'ungmul hats and instruments illustrate the walls of the crowded Tongdaemun Undongjang subway station, and p'ungmul paintings and instruments are displayed throughout the numerous traditional teahouses (*yetch'atchip*) in the trendy Insadong art district. P'ungmul groups from the provinces in live performance are regular features of the city- and national government–sponsored outdoor venue the Seoul Norimadang, and during the summer of 2004 such drumming and dance featured prominently at the always well-attended Buddhist Lantern Festival. Photographs or performances of p'ungmul intimately linked to the search for Korean origins also appeared in two high-profile academic forums: Kim Joo-young and Park Seung-u's book *On the Road: In Search of Korea's Cultural Roots,* published by the Korea Foundation for foreign scholars and libraries overseas (2002) and the 2004 international conference "The Korean Beat: In Search of the Origins of Korean Culture," held at Keimyung University in Kyŏngsang province to celebrate the institution's fiftieth anniversary. (I was also happy back in 1997 to discover that the packages of Samyang Ramen Noodles exported to my hometown in Michigan depicted cartoon images of p'ungmul performers with their spinning-tasseled hats.)

P'ungmul and its practitioners, however, also occupy specific geographic and temporal places. In this capacity we approach the world of logos, the locus of the regionally situated, concrete, contested, and pragmatic. Out in the provinces, largely away from the gaze of tourists and the media, is where most of the day-to-day teaching, performing, and theorizing of p'ungmul takes place. Here primary- and secondary-school children, community organizations, university drumming clubs (*tongari*), village inhabitants, and government-designated cultural asset teams perform for their respective communities' pleasure and well-being. These people and spaces are visited by groups of native and foreign sociologists and anthropologists conducting field research (including those with a nationalist bent), and by university drumming group students from Seoul and the United States interested in learning a specific area's rhythms and dance formations (Kwŏn Hyeryŏn 2001). These individuals often bring with them a deeper and more nuanced understanding of the regional differences and contexts, including the historical and symbolic complexity of the art form.

At times, of course, the spheres of mythos and logos intersect or even collide, such as during a labor strike when workers from the countryside come to Seoul to protest. Playing p'ungmul instruments on the front lines in order to intensify the group's sense of resolve (and perhaps also to add to the overall effort at intimidation) creates a cognitive dissonance with the sanitized image of the "happy farmer" held by many visitors and foreign dignitaries. (This was particularly true during the 1980s; see, for example,

Abelmann 1996: plate 9.) Where these two worldviews coalesce more peacefully, however, is in their mutual love and respect of the tradition, their sense of pride in a shared national heritage. It is the tremendous wealth of cultural knowledge contained in p'ungmul that drives the continued efforts of its performers, interpreters, and promoters alike to keep it alive, vibrant, and pertinent for future generations.

This book is about my own encounter with rural p'ungmul as practiced, taught, and talked about in a specific province during the closing decade of the twentieth century. My observations are rooted in fieldwork conducted from 1995 through 1996 in and around the southwestern province of North Chŏlla, though considerable theorizing, follow-up trips, and data collection have taken place since that time. In many ways North Chŏlla can be considered atypical as a region—at least with regard to the folk performing arts—owing to the disproportionate number of instrumental, vocal, and theatrical genres that claim this area as their birthplace (including *sanjo* and *p'ansori*). It is also arguably the most active province for grassroots traditional music making, a statement borne out by the fact that it is home not only to the National Center for Korean Folk Traditional Performing Arts (Kungnip minsok kugagwŏn), but also to the only provincially established center for traditional performing arts in all of Korea (Chŏnbuk torip kugagwŏn). P'ungmul is at the core of such activity, with the multiple influences of this area's repertoire, playing style, and past and present master teachers extending throughout the peninsula in greater force than any other.

As many others before me have found, the task of setting down on paper deeply moving yet complex experiences proved a daunting endeavor. This was due to numerous factors, not least of which was the challenge we all face when attempting to render "foreign" realities comprehensible in our own frameworks of understanding without diminishing or obliterating the distinctiveness of that other culture—the "inherent violence in the work of giving a finished literary form to the love that obscures this difference" (Chernoff 1979: 21).[1] But more significantly, I found myself frequently coming back during the subsequent gestation period to the same core set of oral and literary sources secured in the field. Each time I revisited them something new was revealed to me, an experience confounded over time as my views changed in response to developments in my own thought—despite the fact that the "texts" had remained the same.[2]

I later realized that this conflict had brought me to the very heart of the interpretive enterprise. Although valuable research and insights have certainly resulted from such a theoretical approach—one can hardly imagine our discipline without it today—a central hurdle remains that places an undue burden squarely on the shoulders of the individual ethnologist, the lone cultural mediator playing the role of the objective, transcendent interpreter. As numerous critics have pointed out, ethnology is a social enterprise carried out by all-too-human individuals who possess varying degrees of self-awareness and quite diverse personalities.[3] Differences in motivation, sensitivity, intelligence, and sheer energy level affect not only the data collected but the ethnologist's ability to get along with those under study (Bock 1988: 1–3). The image we form of others often comes as much from ourselves as from them; each of us shows himself or herself differently to each person we meet, structuring the questions we ask and filtering what we see and hear, with the result that the observer may contribute as much as the individual(s) observed to the result of the observation (after Jung 1965: 207; Scheper-Hughes 1987: 450). Related to this is the simple yet often overlooked fact that the writing ability of the author may obscure the nature or quality of the fieldwork, especially when we have little or no recourse to original field notes, recordings, or texts (addressed in Cooley 1997: 3–19). This concern, in somewhat modified dress, has appeared on the Western musicological stage as well: "Analytical readings within the growing cultural studies field often tell us as much if not more about the social contexts of their own production *and about their writers* than about the music itself" (DeNora 1995: 127, emphasis added).

Only after years of agonizing over this dilemma did an at least partial solution present itself: Why not provide my core Korean sources in their entirety in the main body of the text? Instead of tucking them away in an appendix or relegating them to a citation in a footnote, I would move them to front and center as essentially "raw" facts or primary data.[4] By quoting from these oral and literary sources at length and largely without editing, the original intent could be brought many steps closer to proper recontextualization. Such a move away from pure evocation or abstraction also grants more open access to these materials to my readers, who can then in turn visit and revisit them with their own unique perspectives and life experiences, creating multiple interpretations. These sources—in the form of chapters of books or dissertations, government documents, and extended interviews—are still explained and contextualized by me in terms of their musical, historical, and/or social significance for a non-Koreanist readership. Importantly, however, they are all properly identified by place, authorship, and date in an attempt to eradicate the ever-problematic and insidious "ethnographic present," with the understanding that my own observations are similarly linked to a specific time, context, and personage (see di Leonardo 1998: 13–14 for a more recent critique of this phenomenon of the "timeless Others").

This choice of narrative strategy was equally motivated by its ethical and moral implications. The struggle itself to be honest, fair, and self-reflective in documenting and elucidating our experiences certainly indicates a proper stance toward the interpretive ethnographic enterprise, yet still implicit in this model is the idea that those with whom we live and study cannot express something of value and understanding *directly* to another (outside) culture. The act of interpretation itself, regardless of the motivation of the researcher, remains an indicator of power relations that are generally skewed in favor of the investigator. It is not a far leap from "interpretation" as a ruse for the literal and/or symbolic silencing of others to the use of silence to exoticize or—much worse—dominate a group of individuals or even an entire segment of society. Quite frankly and simply stated, granting people permission to speak for themselves fulfills a basic obligation due to all humankind. If we are to truly engage in what has been called "studying up," rather than "down" or even "around" (MacClancy 2002: 11), we must allow room for the unfiltered voices of our teachers, mentors, and significant others to be heard. Only then is the full meaning of "visit" realized, reflecting our presence as a guest with an attitude of respect, expectancy, and friendship.

Although the seeds of such a polyphonic or collage-style approach were planted by my previous readings of postmodern thought, to which I owe a considerable intellectual debt (e.g., Tyler 1986: 126; Clifford 1988: 146–47), I nevertheless became unsatisfied with postmodernism's emphasis on disjuncture and lack of common meaning. The entirety of the fieldwork experience was dictated and shaped by my two remarkable drumming mentors: Kim Hyŏngsun of Iri Nongak, an older established artist recognized by the South Korean government as a "human cultural asset"; and Yi Sangbaek of Puan P'ungmulp'ae, a young ideologue active on the fringes of the same cultural asset system. These two men exerted the greatest influence on my development in terms of the music I learned, the books I read, the concerts and competitions I attended, and the people with whom I socialized. Their presence and input—their wisdom, delight, humor, and concerns—are found on nearly every page of this book, a collaborative move that was as intentional, for the reasons stated, as it was a pleasure and honor. And although Kim and Yi operated in distinct and sometimes even competing musical and social circles, despite living in close physical proximity, they remained unified in their respective resolve to teach and communicate the joy and collective spirit of p'ungmul as communal participation. This, too, is my own most profound personal connection with the sound of Korean gongs and drums, one that informs almost all aspects of my scholarly and creative being. It is this aspect of this revered art form in particular that I hope to communicate in the pages that follow.

The purpose of this law is to strive for the cultural progress of the Korean people, as well as to contribute to the development of human culture by preserving cultural properties [assets] and their utilization.

—Chapter 1, Article 1 of the 1962 Cultural Asset Preservation Law; quoted in Yang Jongsung, *Cultural Protection Policy in Korea: Intangible Cultural Properties and Living National Treasures* (2003)

1

Assets and Contexts

A fragile South Korean nation emerged in the 1950s, the result of more than three decades of Japanese occupation (1910–45) and a devastating civil war (1950–53). The country had witnessed perhaps the largest-scale destruction of Korean culture—both material and human—the peninsula had ever known, the land and its people aching from the almost unbearable loss. The blow dealt by the Japanese was uneven and ambivalent in its effects on traditional music making, since official decrees restricting or even banning outright specific performing arts were frequently ignored or overlooked (Robinson 1988: 80–81; Killick 2001: 29–33). Authorities apparently had less trouble with professionalized genres in confined institutional settings, as attested by the existence of organizations such as the Chosŏn chŏngak chŏnsŭpso (Korean "Proper Music" Training Institute), the Chosŏn sŏngak yŏn'guhoe (Korean Vocal Music Association), and the various female entertainer institutes, or *kisaeng kwŏnbŏn* (Song, Bangsong, 2001; Sung, Ki-Ryun 2001). In spite of distrust exhibited toward much of p'ungmul activity, owing to its close ties with shamanistic ritual (a prejudice held over from previous Neo-Confucian rule), it nevertheless survived in pockets through the efforts of such native folklorists as Song Sŏkha, who promoted p'ungmul performance contests in Seoul, or the American advisor Ely Haimowitz, who beginning in 1946 coordinated an annual "farmers' music" festival (see Yang, Jongsung 2003: 24; Armstrong 2003: 77).

The Korean War was more balanced in the scope of its devastation, bringing desolation to nearly all forms of musical practice regardless of historical or social-class background. Yet afterward the real threat posed to folk performing arts was a modernizing and urbanizing general population that rapidly came to view folk and/or traditional culture as "backward" and "superstitious" and that increasingly embraced anything foreign (Park, Chan E. 2001: 121–25; Hesselink 2002). Officials and academics perceived the situation as dire enough for the South Korean government to promulgate the Cultural Asset Preservation Law (*Munhwajae pohobŏp*) in 1962 in an attempt both to investigate Korea's cultural roots and to preserve and promote its heritage (Howard 1990: 241–54; Munhwajae kwalliguk 1995; Maliangkay 1999; Yang, Jongsung 2003). Ironically modeled on the parallel system established earlier by the Japanese, this document focused on both "tangible" cultural assets, such as historical sites, natural monuments, and folklore materials, and "intangible" cultural assets (*muhyŏng munhwajae*), a category that subsumed traditional performing arts and crafts and the experts who transmitted or performed them. Largely unspoken in this legislation was the emphasis on the folk performing arts: eight of the first ten music and/or dance genres designated originated in the countryside (see Munhwajae yŏn'guhoe 1999 for a sample listing of such assets).

Potential assets were and are researched by a Cultural Asset Committee (Munhwajae wiwŏn) made up of members from various academic disciplines, who are required to travel to the particular site and write up a "report of investigation" (*chosa pogosŏ*). The account is then reviewed by the committee in conjunction with the minister of culture, who together are given the power to accept or reject the motion for designation. The stated goal of this process is to locate the standard or "original" form of an art (*wŏnhyŏng*), though unofficially the item should reflect well on a sense of Korean identity and be relatively easy to promote. The previously ubiquitous influence of p'ungmul among the populace made it an early and obvious choice for consideration as a cultural asset, and it was so designated in 1966. Officially known as Important Intangible Cultural Asset no. 11, it was initially recognized under the title Nongak Shibich'a (Twelve Sections or Movements of "Farmers' Music"), with two lead *soe* (small gong) players from South Kyŏngsang province being designated individual "holders" (*poyuja*) of the tradition (Pak Hŏnbong and Yu Kiryong 1965: 364–67). The name was revamped in the mid-1980s to simply Nongak ("farmers' music") to accommodate regional variations (Korea is divided into provinces, which are further divided into counties).

Five p'ungmul groups are currently recognized as Asset no. 11, listed in order of their date of designation: Chinju Samch'ŏnp'o Nongak, from South Kyŏngsang province (1966); P'yŏngt'aek Nongak, from Kyŏnggi province (1985); Iri Nongak, from North Chŏlla province (1985); Kangnŭng Nongak, from Kangwŏn province (1985); and Imshil P'ilbong Nongak, from North Chŏlla province (1988). Each group is considered the representative model of a particular regional style distinguished by contrasts in rhythmic patterns, costuming, instrumentation, and performance philosophy, as seen in map 1.1: P'yŏngt'aek for *uttari* ("upper leg [or bridge]" = A); Iri for *Honam udo* (Chŏlla province "right side [or way]" = B); Imshil P'ilbong for *Honam chwado* (Chŏlla province "left side [or way]" = C); Chinju Samch'ŏnp'o for *yŏngnam* ("south ridge" = D); and Kangnŭng for *yŏngdong* ("east ridge" = E). North Chŏlla is noteworthy in that it is the only province that claims two distinct approaches to p'ungmul, and in that its designations are determined according to geomantic principles (looking south from the "center," or the capital, Seoul, *udo* [right] means "west," and *chwado* [left] means "east"). Until only recently p'ungmul was primarily a male performance art, but North Chŏlla also distinguished itself by introducing in 1958 the first all-female drumming organizations (Kwon, Do Hee 2003: 185; an early photo of such a performance in the provincial capital of Chŏnju is found in Ch'oe Sangsu 1988: 302).[1]

This chapter will begin with an examination of the pivotal field report written in the early 1980s that led to p'ungmul's eventual name change as a cultural asset and its subsequent expansion in scope. The discussion will then move to a treatment of the historical and social factors that contributed to my two principal drumming mentors' decisions to take up a life of p'ungmul—as revealed in personal interviews—including their respective relationships to the cultural asset system. Though the 1962 law and its after-effects have fueled tremendous criticism of its policies and procedures, the fact remains that without such legislation p'ungmul most likely would have never returned with such force and vigor, an observation I heard time and time again from performers of all walks and regional loyalties.

THE 1982 FIELD REPORT ON TRADITIONAL MUSIC
IN NORTH CHŎLLA PROVINCE

In 1982 a field report was compiled by a team of researchers from the affiliated Cultural Asset Research Institute (Munhwajae yŏn'guso) under the title "Research on the Actual State of Traditional Music in North Chŏlla Province" (Yi Hogwan et al. 1982). Though technically not a "report of

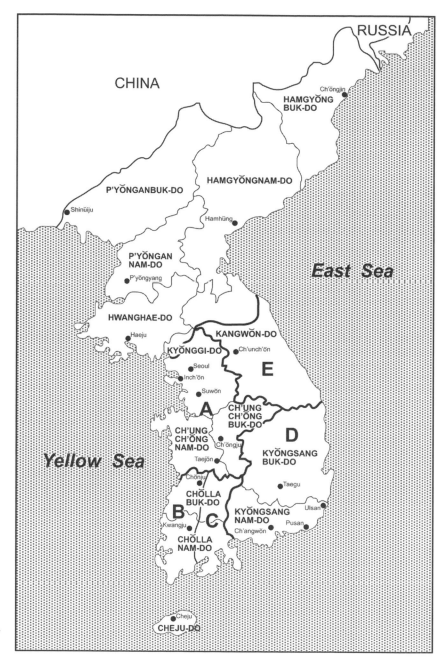

Map 1.1. The five regions of p'ungmul activity as recognized by
the Cultural Asset Preservation Law

Table 1.1. P'ungmul entries in "Research on the Actual State of
Traditional Music in North Chŏlla Province" (1982)

Region	P'ungmul (*nongak*) entry
1. Chŏnju city	1a. Yi Sambok Hojŏk
2. Iri city	**2a. Iri Nongak Group**
	2b. Kim Panghyŏn Nongak
	2c. Kim Mundal Nongak
3. Chinan county	**3a. Kim Pongnyŏl Nongak**
	3b. Chang Kiltong Nongak
4. Muju county	**4a. Osan Village Nongak**
	4b. Sajŏn Village Multŭrŏgagi Nongak
5. Changsu county	*
6. Imshil county	*
7. Namwŏn county	**7a. Koeyang Village Nongak**
	7b. Yu Myŏngch'ŏl Nongak
8. Chŏngŭp county	**8a. T'aein Tapkyo Nongak**
	8b. Yi Myŏngshik Nongak
	8c. Kim Yongŏp Nongak
9. Koch'ang county	**9a. Kim Sanggu Nongak**
10. Puan county	10a. Pak Namsŏk Nongak
	10b. Yi Tongwŏn Nongak
11. Okku county	**11a. Pokkyo Village Nongak**
	11b. Kim Kapsun Nongak
12. Iksan county	**12a. Kŭmma Kisebae**
	12b. Wanggung Subcounty Nongak
	12c. Hamyŏl Town Nongak

Note: An asterisk (*) indicates occurrence of the genre without a specific name association. Sections translated in the text are in boldface type.

investigation"—this document was not written expressly for the purposes of designating a particular tradition or individual—it nevertheless exposed the richness and variety of traditional music genres active in North Chŏlla, a discovery that planted the seeds for the future consideration of a number of organizations as cultural assets. Of particular salience to this chapter are the report's twenty-three entries on p'ungmul, as shown in table 1.1 (the term *nongak* is used in the report; see discussion of terminology below). Taken as a whole, these entries are unique in their range and depth owing to their detailed accounts of specific groups and performers from a cross-section of an entire province (see map 1.2). Until this time (and since), treatments of p'ungmul tended to either deal in generalities (Kwŏn Hŭidŏk 1981, 1995;

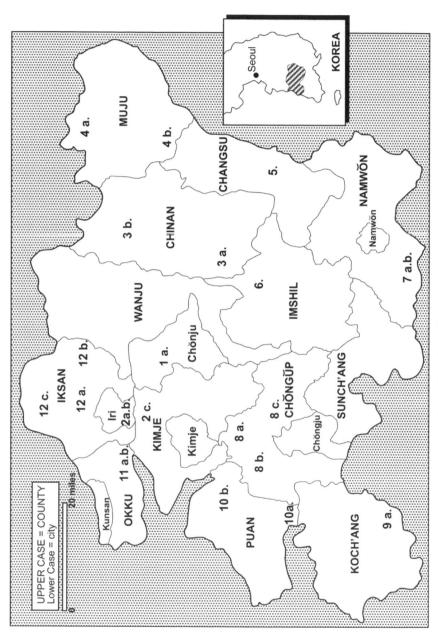

Map 1.2. Regional map of North Chŏlla province with 1982 p'ungmul entries

Kim Uhyŏn 1984; Ryu Muyŏl 1986; Chŏng Pyŏngho 1994) or to examine individual groups without reference to the surrounding regions (No Poksun 1994; Pak Yongjae 1992).[2]

The ethnomusicologist Keith Howard once wrote: "To understand . . . terms in [their] local context, and to appreciate the semantic implications of other, regional terms, is to begin to understand Korean folk music" (1990: 27). My use of the word *p'ungmul* up to this point has masked the existence of a constellation of related terminology surrounding this artistic practice. *Nongak,* the term used by the initial cultural asset report and name designation, is a combination of two Sino-Korean lexigraphs meaning literally "farming music" or "farmers' music" and was the term that dominated academia until the 1980s. Since that time, however, it has come to be hotly contested, largely for its perceived historical associations. In the last two decades many performers and academics alike have directly linked the genesis of the term *nongak* to the Japanese occupation, claiming the choice was born from a sinister motivation by the authorities to limit this activity to just "music" by "farmers" in order to disguise or erase its much broader use and meaning among the colonized (Yang Chinsŏng [1980?]: 11; Kim Inu 1993: 113; Chu Kanghyŏn 1996a). Unfortunately, this community is not in agreement as to the historical source of this proposition: a number of camps gravitate to either the 1931 *Chosŏn ŭi yŏnjung haengsa* (Annual Functions of Korea), credited to a Japanese academic by the name of O Ch'ŏng (Yi Sŏngjae 1999: 95), or the 1936 *Purakche* (Village Festivals; Kim Tongwŏn 2003: 52). Keith Howard has made these claims further problematic by pointing to the existence of some discussion of the introduction of the word *nongak* in the 1870s, as well as the 1902 claim by Kim Chŏngho (1984: 169). Both usages date to *before* the occupation—though Howard himself could find it in print only from the later date of 1937 (Howard 1990: 28).

In *nongak*'s stead is the term *p'ungmul,* itself also a composite of two Sino-Korean characters meaning "wind" (*p'ung*) and "object" or "matter" (*mul*). Despite the absence of historical sources establishing its origin and meaning, according to the recollections of many older generation performers (captured in print in the translated report below), it apparently was the preferred generic term for rural drumming and dance in the early and mid-twentieth century. (One interesting theory, which I learned of in an interview with the folk music scholar Yi Pohyŏng, proposes that wind in Chinese legend was believed to stir humans to sing and dance, hence the name "wind objects." Yi also noted the use of the compound *p'ungak* [literally, "wind music"] to refer to dance music and outdoor music as well [1995: personal communication].) Perhaps the best argument for using *p'ungmul* instead of *nongak*—and the one to which I subscribe in this book—is an etymological one: as a value-neutral designation, it avoids the danger of obscuring the depth and variety of social functions and participants intertwined with such music and dance. As the report that follows will show, p'ungmul in all its guises encompasses men and women from various vocational backgrounds, in addition to ritual, confrontational, and entertainment contexts separate and distinct from communal labor and/or farming (though these last two are central to the tradition). Although it is difficult to gauge officially, *nongak* seems to be falling into disuse.[3]

One more related term often found in conjunction with the word *p'ungmul* is *kut,* a concept in general Korean parlance broadly inclusive of any activity involving shamanistic ritual.[4] In the context of drumming and dance, the word or suffix *kut/-gut* takes on the additional meaning of "performance" (noted in Howard 1990: 29), a distinction blurred by the fact that ensembles often perform rituals that in nature often parallel those of shamanism. One can justifiably argue, however, that ritual by definition cannot exist without performance: as the anthropologist Laurel Kendall observed, *kut* is "high entertainment" (1987: ix). For the remainder of my text, therefore, I will take the liberty of translating *kut* as either performance, ritual, or performance-ritual, depending on the specific context.

In addition to the standard use of *p'ungmul, kut,* and/or *p'ungmulgut* to denote general drumming and dance activity in this report, there are as well many context-specific terms (as the quote from Howard alluded to). We see, as examples, the use of *kŏllip* (fund-raising) p'ungmul in Kimje county (see, in this chapter, entry 2c); *chŏngwŏl kŏllip* or *madang palbi* (January fund-raising p'ungmul), *sanshinje* (village ritual p'ungmul), *kimmaegi* (weeding p'ungmul), and *multŭrŏgagi* (carrying water) *nongak* in Muju county (4a and 4b); *tapkyo* (bridge visiting) *nongak* in Chŏngŭp county (8a); *chiwa palki* (literally, "treading on the roof tiles" p'ungmul) in Koch'ang county (9a); *chishim* (farming) *p'ungjang* in Okku county (11a); and *kisebae* (New Year's–greeting flag p'ungmul) and *nonggi ppaekki ssaum* ("steal-the-farming-banner fight" p'ungmul) in Iksan county (12a and 12c). Various activities may also be coupled with the word or suffix *kut/-gut* (ritual and/or performance): *mae* (village cleansing) *kut, mangwŏl* ("moon of hope") *kut,* and *nonmaegi* (rice-paddy weeding) *kut* in Muju county (4a); *pom sulmegi* (spring wine) *kut* and *isa* (moving) *kut* in Namwŏn county (7a and 7b); *ture* (communal labor) *kut* in Chŏngŭp county (8a); *mun* (gate) *kut* in Koch'ang county (9a); and *mun* (gate) *kut, tangsan* (greeting) *kut,* and *saem* (well) *kut* in Iksan county (12b). In nearly all of the villages researched *mae kut* was performed at the end of December, *chŏngwŏl kŏllip* in early January, and *kŏllip* p'ungmul on a need-specific basis. It is interesting to note that the above dates—really the majority of p'ungmul events—continue to correspond with the lunar, and hence agricultural, calendar.

The passages I have chosen to translate in the following sections, shown in bold in table 1.1, represent entries that specifically address social contexts accompanied by the performance of p'ungmul. The numbering is based on table 1.1; gaps represent entries that only documented names of performers. The translations for regional subdivisions used throughout the text include -*to*/-*do* for province, *shi* for city (metropolitan), -*kun*/-*gun* for county, *myŏn* for subcounty, -*ri*/-*li*/-*ni* for village, *ŭp* for town, *purak*/*burak* for hamlet, and -*tong*/-*dong* for district. The term *maŭl* is translated as "village" as well, though it represents a social unit, not a political one (Pak and Gamble 1975: 24).

❦

Entry 2a: Iri Nongak Group

In Iri, p'ungmul was often done on a large scale centered on the village of Saeshil. In recent times, the Saeshil Village Nongak Group has collected together musicians from the city of Iri and the nearby counties of Iksan and Kimje to form the Iri Nongak Group.[5] In 1981 Iri Nongak entered the p'ungmul tournament held in North Chŏlla province and won.[6] Today it is composed of around thirty members, including Kim Mundal (lead small gong [*soe*]), Yi Sunam (second *soe*),[7] Paek Wŏn'gi (lead large gong [*ching*]), Kim Hyŏngsun (lead hourglass drum [*changgo*]),[8] Kim Kaptong (second *changgo*), and Kim Panghyŏn (lead hand-held drum [*sogo*]).

Entry 2c: Kim Mundal Nongak

Kim Mundal (b. 1909) today lives in Kajŏn village, Paekku subcounty, Kimje county, where he was born.[9] Starting at the age of seventeen, Kim studied lead *soe* for three years in Kimje with the lead *soe* player Kim Tosam; when he was thirty-seven, he played second *soe* for eight years under the lead *soe* player Kim Kyŏngch'ŏn (a native of Puan) in Kimje's Paekku Nongak. After Kim Kyŏngch'ŏn's death, Kim Mundal was active as Paekku Nongak's lead *soe* player: he directed the group, took them touring around the various provinces, and engaged in fund-raising [*kŏllip*] as well as participated in p'ungmul tournaments [see figure 1.1].[10] Kim also led female p'ungmul in the 1960s, when such groups were prosperous. He has recently been directing Iri Nongak.

before Kwanch'on subcounty, Imshil county. It is because Kim lives in this small village that it is known for p'ungmul.

According to Kim, in the old days, when p'ungmul was performed in this village, it was called both p'ungmul *ch'inda* [to play p'ungmul] and *kut ch'inda* [to play a *kut*]; purchasing instruments was called p'ungmul *saonda* [to buy p'ungmul] and *kut saonda* [to buy a *kut*]. P'ungmul groups were known as *ch'ibaegun,* and the clothes they wore called both *ch'ebok* and *soeot.*

ENTRY 3B: CHANG KILTONG NONGAK

Simple mountain village p'ungmul existed even in Wŏlp'yŏng village, Chŏngch'ŏn subcounty. It was in this village that Chang Kiltong (b. 1911) spent his early years until the age of twenty-two, touring around as a *mudong.*[13] There was a lead *soe* player by the name of Han Kidong in those days. In this village, the playing of p'ungmul was called by a variety of names, such as *kut hŏnda* [dialect of *handa*, or "to do"], *kut ch'inda* [to play a *kut*], *p'ungmulgut* [p'ungmul + *kut*] *ch'inda* [to play p'ungmulgut], and *p'ungjanggut ch'inda* [to play an "abundant harvest" *kut*]. Instruments were known as p'ungmul and musicians as *ch'ibaegun.* Clothing was called *ch'ibok,* and the hats were *chŏllip.*[14]

ENTRY 4A: OSAN VILLAGE NONGAK

Osan is a large village approximately two kilometers to the east from the center of the town of Muju. At one time, this village was a place where both *p'ungnyu* thrived and a professionally active touring p'ungmul group was based.[15] Today, however, *p'ungnyu* is gone and p'ungmul is disappearing. The only performer left, Kim Taegil (*changgo*), was out when we came to see him, so we were not able to meet.

Mae kut is not played on the last day of the month in the village,[16] though on the evening of January 14,[17] *nodaragi kut* [ritual performance] is played and on the evening of January 15 *mangwŏl kut* [literally, the "moon of hope" ritual] is played. Village ritual p'ungmul is played on January 2, and fund-raising p'ungmul is played beginning January 3 for a period of two to three days.[18] During both the weeding season and sowing period, *nonmaegi kut* [rice paddy–weeding ritual] is performed. P'ungmul is played after the weeding is finished, around July 15 (the resting period, according to the lunar calendar). When villagers go out to weed, return to the village, or go out fund-raising, *sadang nori* [literally, "ancestral shrine play (or entertainment)"] is performed: *mudong* [dancing children] raise flowering trees and dance the fan dance. It was worth seeing.

From long ago, fund-raising troupes in this village were active on a large scale. They also went out to compete in p'ungmul tournaments with groups from Seoul, Hamyang, Taegu, Chŏngŭp, and Kimje. Because of this, many famous performers came out of this area, including Kim Ŭngdo (b. 1863, deceased), also known as Kim Changgo. The lead *soe* player Kim Ponggil was well known and the *pŏkku/sogo* [hand-held drum] performer Kim Ch'ulgil played very well.

Entry 4b: Sajŏn Village Multŭrŏgagi Nongak

Sangch'on village [*maŭl*], Sajŏn village, Ansŏng subcounty,[19] is a remote mountain village where fund-raising p'ungmul [*madang palbi*] is performed on January 3 and weeding [*kimmaegi*] p'ungmul is played during the weeding season. A special folk custom by the name of *multŭrŏgagi* [literally, "carrying water"] *nongak,* however, caught our attention.

According to Kim Yongjin (a man of the village, b. 1920), *multŭrŏgagi nongak* is played in the village on January 14. Around 10:00 P.M. two able-bodied men suspend a large water jug on a bamboo pole. Carrying it on their shoulders between them, they lead the village members to Malgam Valley located halfway up the village mountain as p'ungmul is performed. When they arrive at a spring by the name of Ch'ansaem, villagers continue playing p'ungmul as water is scooped into the jug. The mouth of the jug is then lightly stopped with pine needles to the extent that water will drip out. The jug is then retied to the pole upside-down.

The two men again shoulder the pole from which the jug is suspended, and, as drops of water fall to the ground, they descend to the village as the musicians follow them, playing p'ungmul. The two men return to the village and go to the public well; the musicians stand around the edge of the well and play p'ungmul. The two men then place the bamboo pole with the water jug attached to it on top of the well, covering it. Because the water jug is suspended upside down, the water drips out continuously; it is left this way until all the water has emptied out. The musicians play p'ungmul one more time passionately at the edge of the well, after which they distribute alcohol, drink, enjoy themselves for a while, and finally return to their respective homes in the village, leaving the water jug in place.

Entry 6: Imshil

Imshil county's p'ungmul, like that of Namwŏn and Chŏnju, is considered Chŏlla province "left side" p'ungmul. Years ago in Imshil there lived a famous lead *soe* player by the name of Yi Hwach'un.[20] Today, an expert lead *changgo* player named Shin Kinam lives in Sangam village, Unam subcounty (though he is ill),[21] and a lead *soe* player by the name of Yang Sunyong (b. 1938) in P'ilbong village,[22] Kangjin subcounty.[23] Yang Sunyong performs with and leads the P'ilbong

Nongak Team in P'ilbong and Seoul. In 1980, leading the P'ilbong Nongak Group representing North Chŏlla province, he entered and won the twenty-first National Folk Arts Competition [Chŏn'guk minsok yesul kyŏngyŏn taehoe]. With regard to P'ilbong Nongak, in 1980 our research institute issued a special publication under the title "A Research Report on P'ilbong Nongak" ["P'ilbong nongak chosa pogosŏ"] (see Chŏng Pyŏngho et al. 1980).

ENTRY 7A: KOEYANG VILLAGE NONGAK

P'ungmul has long thrived in Koeyang village, and in 1981 the group's performance of ritual [ŭishik] p'ungmul under the title of samdong kut [literally, "three-child ritual"] in Namwŏn's Ch'unhyang Festival received favorable criticism.

The playing of p'ungmul in Koeyang is called kut ch'inda [to play a kut], and the preparation of instruments referred to as buying p'ungmul. Village-cleansing p'ungmul [mae kut] is not performed, though from January 5 to January 15 fund-raising p'ungmul [ttŭlbalbi, literally, "treading on the earth"] is played. On January 3 greeting p'ungmul is performed,[24] and on January 15 a bonfire made of freshly cut pine branches is lit on the village's broad courtyard as a talmaji kut [first-full-moon welcoming ritual] is played. On March 3 pom sul-megi kut [literally, "make one drunk with spring wine ritual"] is played, and it is occasionally played in April on Buddha's birthday [Ch'op'ail] as well. Sulmegi kut is also played on June 15. In the summer season, during weeding, a communal work group [ture] is formed, with p'ungmul accompanying the labor.

The weeding is accompanied by call-and-response-style singing [tubŏl], and communal labor p'ungmul [ture kut] is played. After the weeding is finished, p'ajŏmnyera [ritual p'ungmul] is played, usually on Buddhist All Souls' Day [Paek-chung], with p'ungmul played and enjoyed. This activity is referred to as sam-dong kut.

In addition, if public funds are needed, a fund-raising ritual is performed to raise money for the various projects, such as for a mortgage, a bridge, or a school. When someone builds a new house and moves in, or is planning to move to a new location, a moving ritual [isa kut] is played.

ENTRY 7B: YU MYŎNGCH'ŎL NONGAK

Yu Myŏngch'ŏl (b. 1943) both lives in and is a native of Sanggwi village, Kŭmji subcounty, Namwŏn county.[25] His father, Yu Hanjun (b. 1901), a famous lead soe player who died at the age of fifty-two, would be around eighty-two years old if he were alive today. From an early age, Yu Myŏngch'ŏl often saw and practiced with his father's p'ungmul group, and at the age of sixteen he became a training soe player [nonggu] under Kang T'aemun, who had been active as second soe under Yu Hanjun. After this, Yu Myŏngch'ŏl trained under Wang P'anok and was eventually promoted to third *soe*. He returned to Kang T'aemun again to serve as his second *soe*. When Yu was eighteen, he played a lot of fund-raising p'ungmul [*madang palbi*] while working as a lead *soe*.

After this time, Yu participated in many folk tournaments, such as the Chŏlla Cultural Festival [Chŏlla munhwaje] and the first National Folk Arts Competition. Chŏlla "left side" p'ungmul (represented by a team from North Chŏlla province) participated in the latter, the principal musicians at that time being Kim Sudong (lead *soe*), Pak Obok (second *soe*), Yu Myŏngch'ŏl (third *soe*), Ch'oe Sanggŭn of Kŭmsan (lead *changgo*), Chŏng Odong (lead hand-held drum [*pŏpko*]), Han P'anok of Changsu (second *pŏpko*), Chu Kihwan of Kŭmsan (third *pŏpko*), and Hong Kwisŏn of Chŏnju (fourth *pŏpko*). Among these musicians, only Yu Myŏngch'ŏl and Hong Kwisŏn are active; the rest are either dead or have lost their skill due to old age.

Entry 8a: T'aein Tapkyo Nongak

In T'aein town, village-cleansing p'ungmul [*mae kut*] is held on the last day of December, with fund-raising p'ungmul [*madang palbi*] performed early in January, though the latter is referred to as *chŏngjung kut*. *Tari palki* [literally, "tread on the bridge"] is performed in grand fashion on January 15. *Tari palki* refers to when each village organizes a p'ungmul group and, together with the village residents, goes out to a bridge. Villagers believed that traveling back and forth a number of times corresponding to one's age would bring about longevity. *Tari palki* was, therefore, eagerly carried out. Even-number-aged people will arrive back at the point from which they start; odd-number-aged villagers, however, will end up on the far side of the bridge, so they must be carried back by others on piggyback, to avoid tabulating the wrong number.[26] P'ungmul group members of each village travel toward the bridge located to the west of the village; "older brother" [senior status] village p'ungmul bands stand in front, with the rest traveling behind in order. Often "younger brother" [junior status] p'ungmul group members try to walk in front, a violation of protocol that leads to fights. In T'aein there were four villages, with village no. 3 being the eldest and village no. 4 the youngest. P'ungmul group members of village no. 4 often insisted on being in the very front, causing fights to break out. When that happened, many people got injured, in extreme cases resulting in murder.

In olden days, every village had a p'ungmul group, and January fund-raising [*chŏngjung kut*], greeting [*tangsanje*], and communal-labor [*ture*] p'ungmul were played without fail. Today, however, p'ungmul has long since disappeared.

Communal-labor p'ungmul [*ture kut*] is also called *ŏhwa kut* because the words "ŏhwa ŏhwa" are sung during it. At the end of weeding accompanied by song [*mandure*], a communal-labor group is assembled for the purposes of large-scale farming, *mandure* is performed for one or two days, and *ŏhwa kut* is played. On the morning of the day on which *ŏhwa kut* is to be played, farm implements are set up at the village shrine [*tangsan*], with forty to eighty people gathering together to make up a labor team. A p'ungmul group is formed, all bow to the village shrine, and a ritual is performed. P'ungmul is played while members go out to the fields, after which the weeding labor team sings weeding songs [*kimmaegi sori*] as the musicians play p'ungmul [*p'ungjanggut*].[27] As the team returns to the village from the fields, p'ungmul [*kut*] is played; p'ungmul continues to be played in the village while various amusements are enjoyed. Members go around to each of the main farming houses playing p'ungmul, drinking alcohol, and engaging in amusements.

Around July 15, after a day has been decided upon, *sulmegi* [literally, "to become drunk with wine"] is performed at the village shrine. Each house collects together some rice and alcohol, an iron pot is hung in the yard by the shrine, a pig or dog is butchered and boiled, and the meal is prepared. At dawn, before all this takes place, the village streets are repaired, water is drawn from the well for cleaning, and the village is made clean and pure. From the morning on, p'ungmul is played in the yard of the shrine, food is distributed and eaten, and amusements are enjoyed.

Entry 8c: Kim Yongŏp Nongak

Kim Yongŏp (b. 1933) was both born and currently lives in Hwahae village, Puk subcounty, Chŏngŭp county. At the age of seventeen, Kim learned the *ching,* the *soe,* and the *sogo* while performing various characters [*chapsaek*] such as *mudong saekshi* [puppeteer], among others, with Chŏngŭp Nongak. He was, however, mainly interested in the *ching* and eventually became a *ching* player. Since around the age of thirty-five until the present, Kim has worked as a *ching* player with many of the great masters of the genre when going to large national tournaments. Primarily, though, he was the lead *ching* of Chŏngŭp Nongak. When performing in county p'ungmul tournaments in Taep'yoro, Puk subcounty, he played either *soe* or *sogo*.

Kim learned the *ching* from Chŏngŭp Nongak's previous lead *ching* player, Chŏn Honggŭn; *sogo* (when he was twenty-five) from the Chŏngŭp resident Kwŏn Chaegi (who today serves as the lead *soe*); and *soe* from Chŏn Chaesŏn.

Kim Yongŏp plays lead *ching* in national p'ungmul tournaments, second *soe* in Chŏngŭp county's p'ungmul group (lead *soe* is played by Kwŏn Chaegi), and lead *soe* in Puk subcounty's p'ungmul group. He has mentally overcome the physical wounds he received during the Korean War by devoting himself to p'ungmul.

Entry 9a: Kim Sanggu Nongak

Kim Sanggu (b. 1912) is both a native of and currently lives in Taesŏng hamlet, Insŏng village, Kosu subcounty, Koch'ang county. When he was seventeen he learned *kukkŏri*[28] and *p'iri shinawi*[29] from the Mujang resident Shin Hyŏndŏk (b. 1873); he did not learn *p'ungnyu*.[30] At the age of twenty he learned the *soe* with Pak Sŏnggŭn, a resident of Chujin, Asan subcounty. Pak Sŏnggŭn (b. 1902) studied with Kang Sŏngok of Pŏpsŏng subcounty, Yŏnggwang county, South Chŏlla province (Pak Sŏnggŭn's senior, he died at the age of seventy).

Kim was a training *soe* player [*nonggu*] at the age of twenty-six, then played third *soe* until the age of thirty, when he became second *soe*. He played lead *soe* at the age of forty. He is a master of the "right side" spinning-tasseled hat dance [*ppŏssangmo norŭm*]. Kim's group performs *chiwa palki* and similar activities from time to time as well. *Chiwa palki* [literally, "tread on the roof tiles"] refers to an activity in which the p'ungmul group forms a line and hunches down: *mudong* [dancing children], according to rank [by skill], walk over their backs holding the hands of two men standing on either side. After crossing, the *mudong* are carried on the men's shoulders to the front of the line, where the whole process is repeated.[31]

When a fund-raising troupe comes to the village, it takes the place of village p'ungmul. A gate ritual [*mun kut*] is then played [see figure 1.2 and plate 1].

Figure 1.2. *Mun kut* (gate ritual), Koch'ang county, Koch'ang Pangjang Nongaktan

After the village and fund-raising troupes play the field trumpet [*ttŏl nabal/tŭl nabal*] three times, *ilch'ae* [literally, "one stroke"] rhythmic pattern—*ŭng*—*tchak, ŭng*—*tchak* (onomatopoeia for drum strokes)—is played as members step three times forward, three times back. After playing *p'ungnyugut* rhythmic pattern (also known as *t'almŏrigut*), the lead *soe* divides the p'ungmul group into two sides and plays "open-the-gate ritual" [*munyŏri kut*] pattern, *tchaen chae*—*chaeng*——, *tchaen chae*—*chaeng*——. The lead *soe* and large-gunman character [*taep'osu*] play in the center, after which the lead *soe* directs the group into a single line, then back into two sections, then finally back into one line. The lead *soe*, distancing himself from the group, is followed by the gunman [*taep'osu*], characters [*chapsaek*], *pŏkku, changgo, ching*, and *kkwaenggwari* [*soe*], in order. *P'ungnyugut* rhythmic pattern is played as the group enters through the gate.

ENTRY 10: PUAN

Years ago in Puan there lived a famous lead *soe* player by the name of Kim Pau who led a group of prominent musicians. The group's fund-raising troupe was famous; today, however, only Pak Namsŏk remains, and even he is in no condition to perform due to illness. Yi Tongwŏn, an expert lead *changgo* player living in the town of Puan, is still in good health and able to perform p'ungmul [*nongak*].

Puan has no set p'ungmul group. Occasionally there are performances of p'ungmul, though it tends to be in the form of village p'ungmul; performances of entertainment p'ungmul are not possible.[32]

ENTRY 10B: YI TONGWŎN NONGAK

Yi Tongwŏn was born in Kyodong, Sŏngnae subcounty, Koch'ang county.[33] In 1947, at the age of twenty-five, he moved to Puan, and today he lives in Sŏoe village, Puan town.[34]

At the age of nineteen, Yi learned the *changgo* from the *changgo* expert Kim Hongjip, a native of Koch'ang county, who himself had learned the *changgo* from Kim Hakchu and established a reputation for himself as an expert of lead *changgo*, particularly for his solo *changgo* dances *kujŏng nori* and *kaein nori* [literally, "individual play"]. While studying with Kim Hongjip, Yi spent seven or eight years serving as third *changgo* in the p'ungmul group of the famous lead *soe* Kim Pau. Kim Hongjip played lead *changgo* for Kim Pau's ensemble. At the age of twenty-seven Yi played *changgo* under the lead *changgo* player Yi Pongmun in the p'ungmul group of Kim Kwangnak, a lead *soe* player from Chŏngŭp. At twenty-nine Yi played *changgo* under the expert lead *changgo* player Ch'oe Maktong in the p'ungmul groups of Pak Sŏnggŭn (lead *soe* from Koch'ang) and Shin Tuok (lead *soe* from Koch'ang).

Later, Yi played the *changgo* with Yi Chŏngbŏm, Kim Pyŏngsŏp,[35] and Chŏn Sasŏp[36] in Chŏng Isŏp's Chŏngŭp p'ungmul group. When the national p'ungmul tournament was held at Tŏksu Palace, Yi joined Pak Namsŏk's p'ungmul group, performing on the *changgo* under the lead *changgo* player Kim Pyŏngsŏp. In addition, Yi performed in many p'ungmul tournaments, including the National Folk Arts Competition.[37]

ENTRY 11A: POKKYO VILLAGE NONGAK

The performance of p'ungmul in Pokkyo village, Taeya subcounty, Okku county, was called *kut ch'inda* [play a *kut*] or *p'ungjang ch'inda* [play *p'ungjang*]; group members were referred to as p'ungmul *chaebi*.[38] In this village, their main repertoire consisted of village-cleansing p'ungmul [*mae kut*], supplication p'ungmul [*kosa kut*], "energy [or spirit]-regulating" p'ungmul [*ki maji kut*], farming p'ungmul [*chishim p'ungjang*], and the like. P'ungmul of the village was mainly played within the village; it was not professional fund-raising p'ungmul.

ENTRY 12: IKSAN

In p'ungmul [*nongak*] of the Iksan region, the villages around Iri participate and perform with the Iri Nongak Group. In the Kŭmma region, *kisebae nori* [see entry 12a] has been restored and has appeared in the National Folk Arts Competition. In addition, in recent times in Shinhŭng village, Wanggung subcounty, village p'ungmul has been restored under the name of the Shinhŭng Nongak Group, appearing in the subcounty folk tournament. Within Hamyŏl town, there is a Hamyŏl P'ungmul Cooperative [*kye*].[39]

ENTRY 12A: KŬMMA KISEBAE

Kisebae [New Year's flag greeting] was restored in Iksan county, Kŭmma region. It was not only performed a number of times at the Folk Culture Festival, but also at the eighteenth National Folk Arts Competition, giving the group a widespread reputation. The *kisebae* of Iksan was handed down from generation to generation until about forty-five years ago [1937]; since then, this kind of transmission ended completely. Ten years ago [1972], however, the assistant principal of Iksan Municipal High School, Song Sanggyu, together with local landowners, convinced the people of the area to restore the tradition.

Kŭmma's *kisebae nori* is done on January 14. Communal-labor troupe members from twelve neighboring villages centered on Sangdae village [*maŭl*], Tonggodo village, Kŭmma subcounty, give their New Year's greeting to each other while carrying farming flags [*nonggi*] and playing p'ungmul [*p'ungjang*].

In early January, village members from each of the twelve villages fund-raise and collect money. On January 14, each village goes out to its respective village shrine and, while holding up the farming flag and playing p'ungmul, perform greeting p'ungmul [*tangsanje*, also called *ki chesa*, or "flag ritual"].

Sangdae village, the most senior amongst the twelve villages, erects a large farming flag at the village shrine; p'ungmul musicians carry a smaller farming flag, or *sodonggi*. As *oemach'i chilgut* rhythmic pattern is played, the group begins by visiting the youngest village, Taejŏng, to greet its flag, led by a *mudong ch'onggak taebang* [or *such'onggak mŏsŭm*, literally, "young bachelor servant"].

After the musicians in each village perform greeting p'ungmul [*tangsanje*], they erect their farming flag by a large well and continue to play p'ungmul. This goes on until the small-farming-flag troupe from Sangdae comes, at which point both the individual village being visited by Sangdae and the Sangdae group play a greeting ritual [*maji kut*] for each other. After both groups circle the well, led by the small-farming-flag troupe, the junior village carrying their farming flag moves on to the next village. In this manner, eleven village groups end up arriving at the second-most-senior village of Oktong. Here they are treated to liquor and play one more time. Afterward, all twelve village groups arrive at Sangdae's village shrine and play again in front of Sangdae's farming flag. As the *ch'onggak taebang* cries out "greet us" [*sebae tŭrira*], every village's communal labor troupe withdraws except for the second-most-senior troupe of Oktong. Oktong's troupe, holding their farming flag in front of them, move toward Sangdae's flag. After setting their flag in front of Sangdae's, the *ch'onggak taebang* of Oktong cries out *pongshimiyo* [literally, "the innocent (or naive) have arrived"]. Oktong's flag is lowered, in the gesture of a bow, after which Sangdae's farming flag is made to salute in return by having its wooden pole shaken. The *ch'onggak taebang* cries out *chaebaeyo* [literally, "second bow"] and bows, to which the other group shouts *matchŏrio* [literally, "mutual bowing"] in response, and both flags "bow" to each other. The New Year's greeting is then repeated in a similar fashion between Oktong and the third-most-senior village. Then, as soon as the most junior village (Taejŏng) has completed the New Year greeting, various amusements such as the *kkonnabi ch'um* [flower dance], *mudong* [dancing child] dance, *ki ssŭlgi* [flag sweep], *son nori* [literally, "hand play"], *ŏkkae nori* [literally, "shoulder play"], *ima nori* [literally, "forehead play"], and *ttalgi ch'igi* [literally, "to remove the strawberries"] immediately take place. All villages are treated to alcohol and a meal from Sangdae, after which the villagers engage in more amusements before parting [see figure 1.3].

Figure 1.3. *Kisebae* (New Year's flag greeting), Iksan county, Iksan Munhwawŏn Nongak

Today greeting p'ungmul [*tangje*] does not take place on January 14—it is performed at the Kŭmma subcounty Mahan festival. Since it is difficult to gather the twelve villages together, only around six villages now participate.

Entry 12b: Wanggung Subcounty Nongak

Villagers from places such as Kŭmgang, Yongnam, and Nŭngjŏul engaged in *kisebae*. Wanggung's *kisebae* tradition had ended even earlier than Kŭmma's. According to Song Sanggyu, on July 7 neighboring village groups would gather in Kŭmgang village and perform *kisebae* (there was no small-farming-flag tradition).

There is no one left who is able to perform *kisebae* in Wanggung subcounty. P'ungmul had also been discontinued until the Shinhŭng village landowner Yi Tonghŭi (along with others), bemoaning the fact that traditional culture was disappearing, organized the Shinhŭng Nongak Group. The group has been performing in subcounty cultural festivals; however, it is not a professional p'ungmul group. Villagers who want to play together gather and organize a group consisting of one farming flag, one signal flag, a lead *soe* (Yi Tonghŭi), a second *soe*, one *ching*, three *changgo*, one barrel drum [*puk*], and five *sogo* players.

In Kwangam village, Wanggung subcounty, a village-cleansing ritual is held at the end of December, fund-raising is done early in January, a spring wine

Figure 1.4. *Tangsan kut* (greeting p'ungmul), Chŏnju city, Imshil P'ilbong
Nongak with Iksan Kisebae

ritual is held in the spring, communal labor is done in the summer season, and a summer wine ritual is held around July 15. When someone has recently moved, a moving ritual [*isa kut*] is played.

On the evening of the last day of the year, preparations begin with erecting the farming banner and flag at the village shrine. Around 7 : 00 P.M., the village musicians and a ritual specialist [*cheju*] arrive, bringing the ritual table [*chesang*] and playing p'ungmul. The ritual table is set up, and the ritual specialist offers up a prayer. After the ritual paper is burned [*soji*], the musicians play a well ritual at the well, a fund-raising ritual on each street, and a bridge ritual at the large bridge. If there is any time left over, p'ungmul is played at the house that offered the feast.

The village-cleansing ritual is held beginning on January 3 for a period of three to four days. Beginning at the village shrine [*tangsan*], greeting p'ungmul [*tangsan kut*] is played, followed by a *saem kut* [well ritual] at the large well. The group then stops at each home, playing *mun kut* [gate ritual], *urŭm kut* [weeping (?) ritual], *madang kut* [yard ritual], *chowang kut* [kitchen-god ritual], *ch'ŏryung kut* [storage area ritual], and *magugan kut* [stable or barn ritual] in order [see figure 1.4 and plate 2, figure 1.5 and plate 3, and figure 1.6].

Communal-labor p'ungmul is played during the final weeding of the rice paddy, though occasionally it is played starting with the second sowing. The spring wine ritual is held around May 15, when the rice plant nursery is

Figure 1.5. *Tangsan kut* (greeting p'ungmul), front *tangsan namu* (spirit tree), Koch'ang county, Koch'ang Pangjang Nongaktan

Figure 1.6. *Saem kut* (well ritual), Koch'ang county, Koch'ang Pangjang Nongaktan

completed; the summer wine ritual takes place around July 7 or 15, after the weeding is completed. Before the ritual, early in the morning, villagers gather and clean around the large well and streets. Food that has been prepared is shared and eaten, after which p'ungmul is played and all enjoy themselves for the remainder of the day.

ENTRY 12C: HAMYŎL TOWN NONGAK

In olden times in Hamyŏl, there was a performance [kut] by the name of nonggi ppaekki ["steal the farming flag"] nori performed by members of communal-labor troupes from villages around Hamyŏl. Nonggi ppaekki ssaum ["steal-the-farming-flag fight"], like Kŭmma's and Okku Taeya's New Year's flag greeting [kisebae], originally began as a farming-flag greeting among communal labor troupe members of neighboring villages. At some point, however, the other villages began to fight for their rank or position, and the tradition eventually deteriorated into a fight for the stealing of the farming flag.

Hamyŏl's nonggi ppaekki ssaum nori disappeared long ago. P'ungmul had disappeared as well, though fifteen years ago a Hamyŏl p'ungmul cooperative was formed. The group both entered and won first place in Kŭmma subcounty's Mahan Folk Festival. Im Chongt'aek, a lead soe player living in Sangjo village [maŭl] is a village p'ungmul soe player, not a professional one. In olden times, village cleansing, fund-raising, communal labor, and various other p'ungmul were played; today, however, it has all disappeared. Cooperative members who perform fund-raising p'ungmul in early January and make appearances in county folk tournaments are all that remain.

INTERVIEW WITH DRUMMING MENTOR KIM HYŎNGSUN

Personal histories of Korean musicians have tended to be told in an impersonal, third-person voice, with little evidence of direct input from the performers themselves (e.g., Pak Hwang 1974; Chang Sahun 1989; Yi Kyuwŏn and Chŏng Pŏmt'ae 1997).[40] The following interview, like others in this book, is an attempt to remedy this state of affairs by returning the right of the individual to speak for herself or himself, revealing the multifaceted and contested past of musicians living in a modern society.

Kim Hyŏngsun was born in 1933 in Shin'gi village, Chusan subcounty, Puan county. Kim is a changgo player-dancer who hails from a long and impressive lineage (see figure 1.7),[41] and his p'ungmul group was designated Important Intangible Cultural Asset no. 11 by the Korean government in

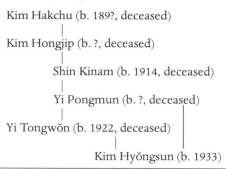

Figure 1.7. Kim Hyŏngsun's teaching lineage

Kim Hakchu (b. 189?, deceased)

Kim Hongjip (b. ?, deceased)

Shin Kinam (b. 1914, deceased)

Yi Pongmun (b. ?, deceased)

Yi Tongwŏn (b. 1922, deceased)

Kim Hyŏngsun (b. 1933)

1985 for the "right side" (*udo*) performance style, Kim himself receiving the individual title of "holder" (*poyuja*) the same year. Although the interview that follows highlights a life of prejudice and hardship, as of 2005 Kim is enjoying a status few in his profession can claim, reflected in his numerous titles and positions: human cultural asset (*in'gan munhwajae*), president of the Iri Nongak Preservation Society, director of Iri Nongak Further Education, chairman of the P'ungmul (*Nongak*) Branch of the North Chŏlla Province Traditional Music Association, director of the Iri chapter of the Yech'ong Traditional Music Association, lecturer at Chŏnbuk University, and faculty member of the North Chŏlla Provincially Established Center for Korean Traditional Performing Arts (located in the capital city of Chŏnju; see plate 4 and figure 1.8).

The interview was conducted on December 16, 1995, in Kim Hyŏngsun's private office in Iri (now the city of Iksan). The session is as illuminating for the themes it touches upon as it is for the fanciful storytelling that binds it together. Kim's recounting of hardship and struggle in his early years is essentially consistent with prevailing stereotypes of folk musicians of his generation. With the exception of the premature death of his father, Kim's suffering during the Japanese occupation, his awareness of p'ungmul's relatively low status among the wealthier villagers, and the nearly nonexistent financial rewards for participating in drumming and dance festivities or functions, leading to near starvation, in all likelihood mirrored the experiences of those born during roughly the same period throughout the immediate area.

Kim's Iri Nongak is a prime example of a touring p'ungmul troupe with nationally oriented aspirations. Almost from the moment of its inception his group was traveling about the peninsula, playing at markets and local competitions. His inspiration was most likely drawn from the example set by his own mentor, the esteemed lead *changgo* player Yi Tongwŏn, who

Figure 1.8. Kim Hyŏngsun in performance attire, Iri city

performed extensively with both Puan and Chŏngŭp Nongak, the two most prominent p'ungmul groups of the region (see entry 10b above). It is interesting if not somewhat surprising that Kim makes no mention of village p'ungmul events, such as end-of-year cleansing rituals or early January fundraising, though he does mention hearing the terms *p'ungmul* and *kut* when growing up. His direct association of the introduction of the term *nongak* with the collection of money from performing is noteworthy as well, though there are no extant historical records that would shed any further light on this observation.

The turning point in Kim's life was undoubtedly his designation as a national intangible cultural asset. This recognition brought not only respect to his group and immediate family, but also long-overdue financial remuneration for years spent in almost total poverty. He took an almost childlike pride in this honor, though I am certain that outsiders at times have credited this stance to an overinflated ego. In the interview Kim mentioned his designation three times, none of them in direct response to a question about his status as a cultural asset. In his perhaps somewhat extreme enthusiasm, however, he overstates a few key facts. When he claims, for example, that everyone knew his name—that he was called "Kim Hyŏngsun of Iri"—he was exaggerating the importance of his role *at the time* within the Iri Nongak organization. The 1982 cultural asset report translated above only mentions his name once (entry 2a), then moves on to a detailed discussion of the group's rhythmic patterns (not translated in this chapter) and an individual entry on their *soe* player at the time, Kim Mundal (entry 2c). The first-place awards he speaks of came only three years (1983) and five years (1985) after the commencement of the Cultural Asset Committee's research. And when he claims that it was his *personal* ability to recruit as well as his upright moral character that was largely responsible for his group's designation, I can only say that that is a partial picture at best. The original cultural asset reports filed on p'ungmul in 1965 and Chŏlla province p'ungmul in 1967 listed knowledge of an old or dying tradition and the authenticity of a characteristic regional style as the two prime factors in being recognized as an important intangible cultural asset (Pak Hŏnbong and Yu Kiryong 1965: 337–38; Hong Hyŏnshik, Kim Ch'ŏnhŭng, and Pak Hŏnbong 1967: 105–6).

All this notwithstanding, the interview adds personal touches of strength, humor, and pathos to Kim's character that are lacking in more formal government reports and academic studies. That afternoon I spent with him talking, eating, and relaxing, away from the hurried atmosphere of the lesson hall, is one of my most cherished memories from all of my fieldwork experiences.

Where were you born, and what type of environment were you raised in?

I was born in Puan, about forty-two kilometers or 120 *li* from here[42]—Puan county is my hometown. I was born in Puan and my father was, in a word, a wealthy farmer. He farmed a lot of land. Father did farming. You know, I was an only child. It was only me. My father—maybe because, strangely enough, it was meant for me to be this way, but my father at that time had quite a bit of money and was called a rich man in the village.

So, since I was an only child, he really wanted to raise me well. Of course every parent has this wish. My father thought he would raise me to be respectable. However, ever since I was little, whenever I came back from school I would only play p'ungmul [*nongak*]. You know, now you call it *nongak* or this or that, but when I was little there was no word *nongak*. The word has changed. We called it p'ungmul or *kut ch'inda* [to play p'ungmul or a *kut*]. The word *nongak* is relatively recent. The word came in around the time of emancipation from the Japanese [mid-1940s].

In our country, each province has its own indigenous and characteristic kinds of play or entertainment [*nori*]. Each area will bring out its own specific characteristics. For example, they play p'ungmul and also *Hahoe pyŏlshin'gut* or *Miryang paekchung nori*[43]—like these, each province will do their own special form of entertainment. But among these, p'ungmul is almost exclusively tied to Chŏlla province [*Honam*]. *P'ansori* [narrative song accompanied by drum] and p'ungmul are what people in Chŏlla province do.

When the government was designating p'ungmul groups as cultural assets throughout the country, a committee of specialists did seven years of research, supported by the cultural research division. You know, there is a book published—it had all the research. Not only p'ungmul, but everything they researched.[44] When I was nominated, they did five years of research. Each year I was researched two or three times. They were looking at me, more or less, as: "Is this person really playing p'ungmul for its own sake, or is it just for profit or fame?"

Anyway, the research took five years. Now that I think back on it, I think they wanted to see my ability. If they were going to come tomorrow for the research, they would call today and tell me to get ready since they were coming down from Seoul. I think they were observing how I prepared as well. I had to recruit nearly fifty people. If you are not capable of recruiting like that, you probably won't get nominated. Because I had my own group from the time I was very young, if I called everybody up in the evening, everyone would be ready the next day. And I think that's how I was recognized, that I had that ability.

When was your earliest exposure to p'ungmul?

When I was growing up, after coming back from school, I should have studied in my room like a normal student, but grabbing a dustpan and some kind of stick I would go out and play p'ungmul. I'd make these kinds of instruments and gather all the kids from the village to play with. Because we were well off, I would buy them cookies and things. They would follow me around. In other words, I was the captain. I would take these kids up to the village mountain and put everything together to form a performance of p'ungmul [*kut*]. It was like dustpans and things—they weren't real instruments. Even at night, if I heard a performance going on somewhere, I would gather the kids together, and since there was no light in the village and it was pitch dark, we'd make torches with straw and

I had to go see what was going on. I don't know why. Now I'm designated for p'ungmul—people say, "He must have been like that since he was little in order to be such a good performer today," but if I hadn't made it and was living poorly they would say, "Ever since he was little he was crazy, never straightened himself out, that's why he's suffering now."

My father had a younger brother. My father had me only, only one child, and my uncle had two boys. And those two boys sang popular songs [*kayo*] very well. Wherever we cousins went, we would take the stage. And my uncle's boys also played the *changgo* and other percussion instruments very well. So the three of us would play. I think the three of us would play because we had musicality [*ŭmaksŏng itta*]. My father and my uncle never touched instruments—my father was absolutely against my doing p'ungmul. The world was a different place then. They talked about aristocrats [*yangban*] and commoners [*sangnom*]—my father and uncle were part of the wealthy class and were the ones who were treated well.[45] And those who performed p'ungmul, they were the ones living as the lowest class of humans, like servants. Therefore, my father was completely against it and I had to do it without his knowing. Whenever there was a performance in our village, they would call me, and I would go quickly and come back.

How old were you when you started studying seriously?

I think I was fourteen. From the time I was fourteen years old I played p'ungmul for real—whenever I sat down I would be playing with something (hands, sticks, etc.). Korea became independent from Japan when I was fourteen [1946]. From then on I started to play what you call p'ungmul. During the occupation, the Japanese took all kinds of things, even musical instruments, for their war efforts in other parts of the world. They took spoons and anything made out of metal, and completely demolished things like instruments. Small gongs [*soe*/*kkwaenggwari*], large gongs [*ching*], anything made of metal they took away. Because they took the spoons that households used for eating rice, we would eat rice with wooden spoons.[46]

During the occupation—I experienced the occupation for fourteen years, up to the fourth grade of primary school—I studied the Japanese language. That's why I speak a little Japanese and can also understand a bit of it.[47] During that time, my father suddenly got ill. He was a very healthy man, but he passed away within a few hours of the sickness. He left a lot of inheritance, but I was alone. That was when I was sixteen. I grew up lonely. I had money, but as a human I was lonely. I didn't have anyone.

I lived like that until I turned nineteen, when I decided to move from Puan to Iri. Iri is a city—it was also a city then, but there were houses far away from each other, and this area was an area where not many people passed by; people probably could have gotten free land out here. I realized after I moved to Iri that I had to do something to eat and survive. Until then I had lived off my father's leftover money, but it soon disappeared. It seemed that I was going to starve to death unless I did something. I cried a lot of blood tears.

Did you study with anyone before you turned nineteen?

Before I was nineteen—now he has passed away, but there was a man named Yi Tongwŏn who played p'ungmul very well. In Korea, the word *nongak* was first used to refer to a group of people who collected money from performing. That kind of group performance began for the very first time in Chŏngŭp—Chŏngŭp Nongak. Do you remember? You've been there. At that time, the first leader of the group was Yi Pongmun. And also, the first person to do tightrope was Kim Yŏngch'ŏl—one of his underlings [*hubae*] still does it. His name is Kim Taegyun. He's probably the only person still doing it these days.

So these people formed a group and performed p'ungmul for the first time in Chŏngŭp. Yi Tongwŏn, he was in that group—he played the *changgo*. As I watched players in that Chŏngŭp group, to my eyes, though he was third or fourth *changgo,* he seemed the best. To my eyes, the form [*mosŭp*] of his playing was the best. Therefore, I followed him around— I followed him around and around.

When I was living in Puan, the distance from my house to his house was twenty *li* [eight kilometers]. There were no cars or bicycles then— you had to walk everywhere. After breakfast, I would go to his house. I would help him with whatever he did, helping him work and learning from him when he took breaks to rest. So we became close—I became as close as a family member. Even now we're like family. His son has a dentist's office in Puan—he calls me "younger uncle" [*chagŭn abŏji*]. We lived together like family, but because I moved to Iri, I realized I had to do something to survive. I had to find a job. Then I only had one daughter— just the three of us.

After paying bribes, I got a job with the railroad—I was twenty then. Once I joined the railroad, I realized even that required me to go in the morning and leave at night. Now the federal workers employed by the railroad, education department, or post office are doing OK—the world has changed. Back then I couldn't even buy a large bag of rice with my monthly salary. It was equivalent to about 100,000 wŏn these days [US$98 in 2005]. Now the world has become much better, yes, much better. People would work the whole month—some could afford to buy a large bag of rice, others couldn't. It was like that then. Nowadays whatever you do, even if you're a nanny, you can live well.

So after I moved to Iri, I got a job I could hardly stand, but whenever I heard the sound of a p'ungmul performance, I'd go crazy, because I couldn't go out. In order to live I had to be there—in the middle of playing—so around half a month later I quit. I quit and stayed home. But there was nothing to eat at home! Even though I could have gone back to Puan, the situation didn't allow it. Even without money or food I still had pride. I was the rich man's son when my father was alive. Those people who used to be poor were now comfortable, so I couldn't say anything.

I lived like that for a while. I don't know how I made it. The days I didn't have money we skipped meals. After I came to Iri I skipped meals and nearly starved. While that was going on, I put about four posters up around Iri. The advertisement said: "Whoever has an interest in p'ungmul [nongak] should come to this place." I put them on electricity poles. Then it was a new place for me—I didn't know where anything was. It didn't feel like home at all. Now I've lived here about forty years—it's become my hometown. Then there was no one I knew, that's why I was so lonely. No one to rely on and no one to have fun with, so that's why I put those posters up.

After about ten days, two people came looking for me. We greeted each other. They were ten to fifteen years older than I was, so we introduced ourselves and I heard their stories—it seemed that they also enjoyed p'ungmul. This art makes people connect faster, so you become compassionate toward each other much faster and people become close. The three of us would then meet, talk, and play. They didn't have much to do either; after sleeping at their own homes, they would come to my house. I was so happy to see them, and it was so much fun. They brought people one by one, up to about seventeen people, so we decided to start a cooperative that would meet once or twice a month and play. Verbally we agreed to meet two or three times, but we met every day. In a place called Songak district there was a wild mountain—we'd play every night there (now that I think of it, they didn't really know how to play). It was nothing.

After our independence from the Japanese, there was a thing called nanjang. Whenever they wanted to develop a city, for example, attract a lot of people, they would open a wrestling [ssirŭm] area called a nanjang. The strongest men under heaven would wrestle there. The prize for winning was a bull. They would wrestle and the government would give permission for gambling. Within the *nanjang* boundary they could do any kind of gambling and the police couldn't touch them. Yes, they gave permission for gambling—and that is *nanjang*.[48] In Korea all the scoundrels would gather there—if there was a *nanjang* in Iri, then everyone in Korea would gather here. And in a place like that, there has to be music—there has to be p'ungmul. Back then we traveled around playing everywhere. There was nowhere I hadn't been. Then I was young and my *changgo* rhythmic patterns [*karak*] were weak [*yak hada*].

What about Yi Tongwŏn?

Now the real story begins. I started a p'ungmul cooperative after I came to Iri, and every now and then when I had the opportunity to perform I would invite Yi Tongwŏn. Whenever I invited him, I would learn from him. Whenever we went different places—he's much older than I am, my teacher—but because I was the group leader then, he was always careful around me. He would always do what I told him to do, and he called me "younger brother" [*tongsaeng*]. We were that close. He passed away a few years ago.

So I continued leading the group until 1959, and when I turned twenty-seven we decided to call it a p'ungmul [*nongak*] group. From then on it became the Iri Nongak Group. I should say that people hadn't really heard of the word *nongak*. Anyway, I formed this group and played everywhere.

During this time, President Park came into power—he came into power through a coup d'état.[49] While he was president, he would hold competitions in different places in order to revitalize p'ungmul. At that time there was no place I hadn't been with my group. Wherever there was a performance [*kut*], they would know Kim Hyŏngsun's group. We were that active. I deserted my family, you know—everyone called me crazy. On top of that, I wasted all my money. I spent my time like that. Because my group was so active, they wouldn't perhaps know my face, but they would know my name. They called me "Kim Hyŏngsun of Iri." That was the life during those days.

And finally in the 1980s, at the national level, they decided to do a report of investigation on folk music. I was telling you earlier, they researched folk music all over the country—p'ungmul, *minyo* [folksong], *p'ansori*, whatever. Members of the committee decided to come research North Chŏlla province. They came to our provincial office. They asked, "Who should we research for p'ungmul?" The government people told them about Kim Hyŏngsun—that's how it all started. But even before I was designated a cultural asset, I had participated in so many events and competitions. There wasn't any place I hadn't been. I had already received two first-place awards before the designation.[50] So whoever was interested in p'ungmul even a little, they knew who Kim Hyŏngsun was—all over the country. In our world, we are all connected.

So in the 1980s they started the research. I really suffered during that time, as did my family. Without my family's help I couldn't have done it. As I told you earlier, I moved my home to Iri and suffered because of a lack of money, and I couldn't eat. During that period, however, by chance I ended up working at a brewery. I got in through a neighbor as a contact, I think. I don't drink these days—I worked there thirty years, making alcohol with my own hands, but I still didn't drink. It wasn't because I was poor, but because of my constitution. The reason why I worked there for thirty years was because each workday ended after two hours. I could do the day's work early in the morning, and during the day I would run around and play. That's why I put up with that kind of life for so long. I never skipped a day—even on [lunar] January [Chŏngwŏl], August harvest moon festival [Ch'usŏk], and similar holidays I wouldn't rest. Even on my birthday I wouldn't rest. I was a person who would do some amount of work everyday—I would never just play p'ungmul.

You made money then through the brewery, not p'ungmul?

Of course! I made money through the brewery. I would spend all the money I made there on p'ungmul. From p'ungmul I wouldn't make a penny—it was a real disaster. It was the brewery where I earned money and saved to buy a rice field, a house, anything I needed. But during that research, I ended up selling my rice field. They researched our group five years, which involved recruiting fifty to sixty people each time the committee members visited. I had to feed everyone, give them fare for transportation, and put them up in lodging—everything ate up money. So I owed, borrowed, and borrowed, and the debt became too much, so I had to sell my rice field.

I sold my land during the research. Even with the research—because these [committee] members were traveling all over the country—there was no guarantee that I would be designated. How could they guarantee it? So these committee members watched me for five years to see what kind of person I was. Actually, they told me to my face, "This person was born to play p'ungmul." I heard those kinds of comments about myself.

A person with a weak will would have given up during those five years, because the research drained money endlessly. Each time cost a few million wŏn [1 million wŏn ≅ $985 in 2005]. But you couldn't stop in the middle—you had to do it till the end. My family pushed me to pursue it until it was completed. They told me if you have to sell more land, go ahead and do it. A man shouldn't give up in the middle. Yes, my family helped me through it all the way to the end.

And fortunately it happened. This is the only "right side" group designated in Korea—this is the one and I was the one. So after the designation, we built this hall, and this is the best p'ungmul center in Korea. That's why so many students come—even today two teams are coming down.[51]

How would you rate your upbringing, compared to other performers of your level around you?

Korean traditional musicians, not only those in p'ungmul, but if you look at teachers at our local center (excluding the very young teachers), the older ones have suffered an incredible amount. They experienced all kinds of hardship, sometimes nearly starving to death. They often would study up in the mountains by themselves. They probably heard themselves being called "crazy ones" [*mich'in nom*], but they've made it where they are today because of it. As you know, at the local center there are fourteen teachers—among them there are five young ones who graduated from universities. The rest of the fourteen are older, and of those, five are regionally designated intangible cultural assets.[52] And then there are two who are not cultural assets but are the best in their respective fields, having received first-place awards. They are assistant instructors [*chogyo*] under cultural assets, so one day these people will become full cultural assets. I am the only national intangible cultural asset.

INTERVIEW WITH DRUMMING MENTOR YI SANGBAEK

The following interview with Yi Sangbaek was conducted on December 15, 1995, at my home at the time in the North Chŏlla provincial capital city of Chŏnju. Born in 1966, Yi claimed an impressive lineage back to the "left side" (*chwado*) p'ungmul tradition (see figure 1.9). Although he was predominantly a *soe* player, serving as lead *soe* both of his university's p'ungmul team in Wanju county and of a newly formed community group in his home county of Puan, Yi was an accomplished *changgo* player as well. His

Figure 1.9. Yi Sangbaek's teaching lineage

Chŏn P'ani (*soe;* b. ?, deceased)

|

Yi Hwach'un (*soe;* b. ?, deceased)

|

Pak Haksam (*soe;* b. 1887, deceased)

|

Song Chuho (*soe;* b. 1900, deceased)

|

Yang Sunyong (*soe;* b. 1938, died 1995)

| |

Yang Chinsŏng (*soe;* b. 1964) Yang Chinhwan (*changgo;* b. 1965)

| |

Yi Sangbaek (*soe* and *changgo;* b. 1966)

account is told in a markedly more contemporary setting, though certain particulars suggest a background very much akin to that of Kim Hyŏngsun: he was born in Puan county, his parents were farmers, and his father died at an early age (see figure 1.10).

From his opening sentences, we begin to sense the pride Yi felt about being from "the real countryside," versus larger semirural population centers around the province. Yi continued to work his portion of the family farm—rice fields set in a plain at the base of the Puan mountain range—even while attending college, a duty requiring a sizable investment in travel time considering the distance between Wanju and his home county (see map 1.2). His childhood memories of Puan, an area that at the time resembled the "typical Korean countryside," are marked by performances of village p'ungmul, particularly fund-raising activities in early January. In fact, he credits his ability to play at the level he currently maintains to this early village upbringing, particularly "compared to city people." His later attachment to and deep connection with the cultural asset troupe in Imshil county and its "original village flavor," as well as the practical and philosophical paths he has chosen to follow throughout his career (documented in this book), are all colored by these early influences.

In obvious contrast to Kim Hyŏngsun, however, is the manner in which Yi was introduced to p'ungmul performance. He did not show the childhood interest exhibited so dramatically by Kim, but rather was slowly drawn into it through his college p'ungmul club, a trend that will be shown in chapter 4 to be the norm for a significant number of performers of his generation. With the exception of the death of his father, Yi suffered little hardship or social stigma associated with his interest in p'ungmul. He was even able to

Figure 1.10. Yi Sangbaek (with Pak Hyŏngnae), P'ilbong village

begin a lucrative semiprofessional career before his graduation from college (further addressed in chapter 4).

Where were you born, and what type of environment were you raised in?

I was born at no. 340, Shin'gi village, Hasŏ subcounty, Puan county, North Chŏlla province. It's in the countryside, the real countryside [*shigol*]. My parents were always farmers. They grew up in a farming village—they were both born in my hometown. Mom was born a little bit away, but father was born there in my present home and was always a farmer. I went to elementary and middle school near my hometown. High school was in Puan, the administrative center for the county.

When was your earliest exposure to p'ungmul?

The very first time I heard p'ungmul was when I was very young. Even when I was in elementary and middle school the countryside was very typical Korean countryside. Nothing about the village was citylike—no modernization or industrialization. No one had a special profession except for farming. Now there are a lot of other jobs, but then everybody was a farmer.

So I probably heard it a lot when I was young. But then I was too young and not interested in that kind of thing at all. I became more concretely interested in p'ungmul and got to know it in more depth through the p'ungmul circle [*tongari*] at the university, as I told you earlier. It was because I hung out with them. It looked great seeing the circle drink together—whenever they drank they would bang on the small gong [*kkwaenggwari/soe*]. It really looked good to me then. It wasn't that I wanted to play, it's just it seemed really interesting and they looked great all hanging out together. But then one day by chance some friends asked me, "Hey, why don't you try banging it?" So that became the start of my *soe* playing career.

At first I didn't think I would do this. Rather, when I hit it I thought, *Ya, chaemi inne* ["Wow, that's great [or fun]"]. After that, I started to play every day. And without knowing it myself, one day I realized I was really into it. The learning method was like this at first: In the very beginning, I learned from people who had started before me. After a while, however, I started to visit cultural asset teachers in Imshil and Namwŏn counties. I learned from them.

In the beginning, I studied with my circle friends for about four months, and then we started going to winter and summer training sessions at the cultural asset training centers [*chŏnsugwan*].[53] The very first time was probably in Namwŏn in the winter, probably after about four or five months. I started with the *soe* and moved to the *changgo* later.

What pressures and/or incentives were there to study p'ungmul?

There weren't any particular difficulties back then. If there were any, it would have been that because we play outdoors on the campus, some professors didn't like our making so much noise. Also, I don't know whether it was a difficulty, but there were some misunderstandings. In the 1980s people considered p'ungmul people to be "demo people," or demonstrators. People thought demonstrators and p'ungmul had some kind of tie or close relationship. Professors looked at us with the preconceived notion that we must be troublemakers and that we were "reds" [left wing or communist]. There were a few of those types of incidents. In my case, I never really experienced any of this. It was true, though, I had friends who were harmed by this prejudice. Imm, p'ungmul and demonstrations. Of course there are some people, but not everybody—there were a few. I wouldn't say there were difficulties, really, but there were those kinds of problems.[54]

Good things—the reason I first got drawn into p'ungmul was because of my father's passing away. My father died in the winter, and I started to play the *soe* the next spring. I really liked being absorbed in one thing. When I was really sad, playing made the sadness disappear from my heart. I was attracted to that aspect of it. Because the *soe* sounds so loud, I couldn't hear anything else. Only the *k'waaaa* [onomatopoeia] of the *soe hwimori* rhythmic pattern echoed in my head. I loved that moment—while I was playing all my sad thoughts and small thoughts disappeared. I wonder if I was drawn into the *soe* so deeply because of that. Those were good things.

How did you choose Imshil county?

It wasn't that I chose those places. When I first joined the p'ungmul group, they were already playing that style of rhythmic patterns [*karak*], so in a way I didn't have a choice. It was more like I was just following what they were doing. That's how I went and studied. In the "left side" style there are two human cultural assets, Yang Sunyong and Pak Hyŏngnae. But they both passed away this year.[55] If I think back, when I first went to Namwŏn, actually the teachers didn't really teach us. It was the master artists [*isuja*] or trainees [*chŏnsusaeng*] under those teachers who taught us. Yang Chinhwan and Yang Chinsŏng are both sons of old grandfather lead *soe* player Yang Sunyong. They are both graduates of my school [Usŏk University]. Yang Chinsŏng played the *soe,* Yang Chinhwan played the *changgo.* Those two taught at Namwŏn. Actually, in the case of the *changgo,* Pak Hyŏngnae is in Imshil P'ilbong, and one could study with him there. They were separated like that [Pak and grandfather Yang]. Even though they play the same rhythmic patterns, the schools are separated between Imshil and Namwŏn.[56]

Probably, in the case of the *soe,* I first met Yang Chinsŏng before going to Namwŏn. I had a chance to hear a tape of his performance. Of course, that wasn't a real "left side" performance. It claimed to be, but it was actually in a modified *samul nori* form.[57] At that time I thought, "That's really great." The *soe* was of course great because of its sound. In the case of the *changgo,* though, it wasn't Yang Chinhwan [brother of Yang Chinsŏng]—it was a fellow from the traditional music department at the university. I once saw him at school accidentally. His way of playing *changgo* was very good. Anyway, I can't say it was Pak Hyŏngnae and Yang Sunyong who taught me, but rather it was Yang Chinsŏng or those teachers' disciples [*cheja*].

I see, Pak and Yang played in the same group but now run their own institutes.

Yes. It was originally Imshil P'ilbong village's P'ilbonggut, but for some reason Yang Sunyong left the village. He went to Namwŏn and was active independently there. So, in reality, there are many more students in Namwŏn studying Imshil P'ilbong P'ungmulgut. There is a training institute in Imshil, but there is one in Namwŏn as well. Imshil P'ilbong rhythmic patterns—there's not really that much to learn, even if there is a human cultural asset. There is nothing all that special. The reason we still went to Imshil, however, was because we wanted to get accustomed to the original village flavor [*mat*] that had been passed down, though there's not that much special in terms of technique.

In the case of the Iri Nongak teacher Kim Hyŏngsun, he plays the *changgo* really well, and also his movement is very special, very unique.[58] With Imshil's Pak Hyŏngnae, there isn't much of all of that. In the case of Yang Sunyong, his spinning-tasseled hat [*pup'o*]—in "left side" style, there is something similar to the *pup'o*, but I can't remember the name— he was excellent at that. He had that particular skill, and also the sound of his *soe* was extremely difficult to imitate. What should I say . . . it was a full sound—in Korean we say *p'ujida* [abundant or generous]. It continues smoothly, at the same time having the feeling it may stop at any moment. And at the same time it is also very powerful. I guess I can verbally express it that way. "Left side" flavor, I think, is very short and articulated [*ttak ttak ttŏrŏjida*]. But even if it's short and articulated, it must flow smoothly, very smoothly [*maekkŭn maekkŭn hage*]. With Yang Sunyong, it was difficult to imitate his style.

As I recall, p'ungmul was still going on in my village until I was about in middle school. For example, *madang palbi* [fund-raising p'ungmul], *chishin palki* [literally, "tread on the god(s) of the earth"]—I can remember those performances or rituals. Those guys went around the village collecting rice. At that time, they collected more rice than money from people's homes. It was usually January full-moon day that they would do that kind of activity. In my memory, it was clear up until about middle school. But now as I look at it, it's all gone. So in some way, the reason I can do p'ungmul the way I do now could have been because of this influence. Because of my childhood, of course, it's a bit more natural. At first, I myself was wondering why my friends in college were playing, but then compared to city people I am in a much better environment for this.

What is the history of p'ungmul?

Honestly, if you look at p'ungmul's origins, as I said earlier, people feel it lies in military music, communal labor teams, and also ritual ceremonies. And of course, there's the guess that p'ungmul is from Buddhism, and also that it came from China.[59] I think since these are all only guesses,

I can't really say what's what. Scholars in a position much higher than my own have been constantly researching the subject, but we are still only left with educated guesses. Of course someone like me, who has only been studying a few years, cannot comment on the topic. But if I have to tell you what I think, I feel Korea has been greatly influenced by China. Even before the Three Kingdoms period [*Samguk shidae*], influence from China was great. Also, if you look at the Korean civil war, one million Chinese soldiers came down. Leading their army in the front line was a p'ungmul troupe playing the *soe* with a *kkwaeng, kkwaeng, kkwaeng* sound. There was that kind of incident. American soldiers wondered what all the commotion was about—I heard they were at first very surprised and shocked.[60]

I'd like to add some supplementary material on this: If you look at our "left side" style, there is a section called *chaenŭnggi*. Within this is *kunyong nori* [military play], and there is also a character called *taep'osu* [hunter]. If you look at all these assumptions and guesses, you can look at it like it came from military origins. In many situations one can surely say it originated in the army. Before farming—well, the reason I think this way is that before farming, what tribes needed most was a group to protect themselves. I think that was the case even before the hunting period. I think the military existed even before farming. Eating, living, and the invasion of other tribes all started before farming did. If I look at our human history, I think the military did p'ungmul to lift people's spirits. If you look at primitive peoples [*wŏnshi in*], you can often see them banging on things. That kind of activity naturally evolved into a military style. And this gradually came down through time, again reshaped or re-metamorphosized by farmers. They independently developed p'ungmul into something closer to what we see today. If I think of all the various influences, the military story seems the most convincing.

[In Mahan,] as was the custom, rituals were performed to honor the spirits at the time of seeding in May and the completion of harvesting in October. Those assembled sang, danced, and drank day and night without rest. Scores of those dancing formed circles, stamping on the earth and moving their hands and feet in a similar manner.

—Chen Shou, *Sanguo zhi* (History of the Three Kingdoms), *Dongyi zhuan* (Account of the Eastern Barbarians); author's translation based on modern edition

2

Historical Traces

The third-century text *Sanguo zhi* (History of the Three Kingdoms), penned by a Chinese scribe, is generally considered the earliest reliable record of ancient Korean music making (Song Pangsong 1993: 796–98). The account is cited widely in standard music history textbooks, for it offers tantalizing glimpses into the social and religious customs of the fledgling Korean nation. It shows, for instance, the early existence of the intimate relationship between music, dance, ritual, the agricultural cycle, and the consumption of alcohol (!), a composite that sums up very nicely festival activity as currently practiced today. It is interesting to note as well that the region the text describes, Mahan, encompassed an area centered in modern-day North Chŏlla province, lending further weight to the region's distinguished reputation for the arts (Lee, Kibaek 1984: 24–25, 37).

In recent years this source has been taken up by a number of p'ungmul scholars and performers looking for a means of grounding the tradition in historical fact (e.g., Kwŏn Hŭidŏk 1995: 43; Yi Sangjin 2002: 27–34). This strategy is problematic, however, since the text makes no mention whatsoever of any kind of percussion instrument, despite the otherwise remarkably similar social circumstances, seasonal markers, and types of ground formation and choreography documented (see Hwang, Mi-yon 2004). Korea's own early chroniclers did hold drums in special

49

esteem, as the *Samguk sagi* (Historical Record of the Three Kingdoms) records in a passage describing events that supposedly occurred during the first century: "From ancient times, Nangnang [northwest Korea] had a mysterious drum which sounded automatically to the accompaniment of a trumpet when rebels arose from within and enemies attacked from without, and at the sound of the alarm the King would order out his army to fight his enemies."[1] But to locate p'ungmul in its current form and practice at such an early point in time creates an intersection of mythos and logos that is tenuous at best, even if many of its practitioners "know" in their very being that it has always existed.

P'ungmul is not devoid of historical substance or traces, however. In sidestepping conventional sources and frameworks of understanding—elite texts are generally silent on any activity occurring outside the environs of the court—I have chosen, rather, to view p'ungmul as a form of (unofficial) record of the populace's encounters with waves of foreign cultural, political, and religious influences, as well as with its own elite culture. Although it is tempting to suggest, for example, that Buddhist remnants in the art form were absorbed during the Koryŏ dynasty (918–1259), when such religious practices were officially adopted, such a view is nevertheless overly simplistic and reductionist, for Buddhism, shamanism, and Neo-Confucianism have and continue to rise, subside, and subtly interact in fluid waves. P'ungmul's historical depth and significance, therefore, is best gauged by the richness, variety, and level of integration of its samplings—by its very hybrid nature as a broad cultural repository—not by any vestiges in print.

In this chapter I will explore the historical roots of p'ungmul by examining the material objects associated with it, focusing on its instrumentation, costuming and other particulars, and ground formations. Each entry addresses both the contemporary setting and related historical considerations.

INSTRUMENTATION

Here I will focus primarily on the instruments used by p'ungmul ensembles in modern-day, entertainment-oriented performances (*p'an kut*), with the exception of the *nabal* (long trumpet), which is generally reserved for fundraising and/or ritual activity. The reason for this choice is mainly pragmatic: Entertainment-based performances born of the *p'an*—the communal village meeting spaces of yesteryear—have come to define almost all current p'ungmul activity (discussed at greater length in chapter 5). Taking into account that any classification scheme reflects the particular classifier's "ideas and beliefs that are held about the social, musical, and other functions of instruments and ensembles at a particular point in time" (Kartomi 1990: xvi), I have included at the beginning of each entry both the traditional Korean system known as *p'arŭm*, based on the Chinese concept of the "Eight Sounds,"[2] and the more standardized Hornbostel and Sachs system.[3] A comparison of instrumentation across related genres as well as ensemble terminology is provided in tables 2.1 and 2.2 at the end of this section.

THE *CHANGGO*

The *changgo*, literally "stick drum," is a double-headed, hourglass-shaped drum; in North Chŏlla province it is just as often called the *changgu* (leather or hide; H.S. 211.242).[4] The drum's use in Korean traditional music is nearly ubiquitous: it is found in almost every genre of vocal and instrumental music from the court to the countryside. A lone image of a *changgo* is frequently sufficient to evoke the entirety of the tradition (as seen, for example, on the opening page of the Web site for the Association for Korean Music Research: www.akmr.org, accessed July 27, 2005).

The body of the p'ungmul *changgo* is generally made of wood and is hollow, though instruments have also been made of ceramic, baked clay (such as that used for roof tiles),[5] and gourds (Chŏng Pyŏngho 1994: 59). The wood version is composed of two bowls joined by a more or less cylindrical waist, with the side struck by the mallet (*kungt'ong*) being slightly larger than that struck by the stick (*ch'aet'ong*). The bowls may be carved separately and then attached, but more commonly the entire body is carved from a single piece of wood and spun on a lathe. In the past, pine was favored (Yang Chinsŏng [1980?]: 22), though today poplar, willow, walnut, and paulownia (*odong namu*) wood are used, the latter being considered the highest quality (see Howard 1988: 123). One often sees the *changgo* painted or lacquered a red or deep maroon color, sometimes with painted designs, but many of the p'ungmul performers I observed or played with chose a natural finish (see plate 5). An exception to this rule was the rather distinctive drum used by my mentor Yi Sangbaek and made in Chŏngŭp county: it was lacquered a deep brown color and then inlaid with dragons in mother-of-pearl (see figure 2.1). *Changgo* are often classified as small, medium, or large, but this depends more on individual perception than on established measurements. Bodies range roughly from 52 to 60 cm in length and from 27 to 30 cm in diameter at the end of each bowl. P'ungmul *changgo* are typically considered lighter than their court and urban folk genre counterparts.

The two circular drumheads covering each bowl are generally made by stretching an animal skin over a metal rim (*t'e*), then sewing them in place; today skins are generally bought pre-made in this fashion. The *Akhak*

Figure 2.1. Yi Sangbaek's *changgo*

kwebŏm (Guide to the Study of Music) of 1493 states that the *changgo* used horsehide (Chang Sahun 1986: 660; 7.4*a*),[6] and deerskin is used on the related *kalgo* drum, but today cowhide and the more resilient dogskin or sheepskin are preferred. In early 1996, a local instrument maker donated a pair of cloth heads he had made to my mentor Kim Hyŏngsun to see whether or not the sound and playing action were comparable to that of natural skin.[7] Kim was duly impressed, to the extent that he only played on the cloth alternatives at the center in Chŏnju. Keith Howard has witnessed the somewhat unusual use of plastic sacking as well (1988: 126).

Once made, the heads are laced together by a series of eight metal hooks (*kuch'ŏl* or *kkaksoe*), with the diameter of each head exceeding the diameter of the bowl by 6–8 cm to create an overlap. Tension is regulated by adjustable leather or plastic thongs (*pujŏn*) placed on adjacent cords. The head covering the larger bowl, or *kungp'yŏn/kungch'aep'yŏn*, is made of thicker skin and is lower in pitch; the opposite head, or *ch'aep'yŏn*, is thinner, so the sound is higher. The researcher Chŏng Pyŏngho has claimed that the *ch'aep'yŏn* produces a female sound (*amsori*), the *kungp'yŏn*, a male sound (*sussori;* 1994: 58), though this would seem to be inconsistent with the ordering of the *soe* (small gongs) as presented at the end of its entry later in this chapter. A past (female) teacher of mine—somewhat tongue-in-cheek—felt that the mallet itself represented the male, not any particular drum head, because the mallet travels to both heads, like a wandering man; the stick plays on only one side, representing the trapped female at home (Pak Ŭnha 1994: personal communication). The Chŏnju music scholar No Poksun wrote of the practice in urbanized p'ungmul (*samul nori*) of using both a female and a male dogskin on a single *changgo* (1994: 101), but this is the only reference I know of that makes such an assertion.

Many of my teachers and friends had seen or heard of p'ungmul performers playing with only a stick and their bare hand, as is still done in a number of folksong and shamanistic genres, but today it seems to be common practice to play the *changgo* with a stick and a mallet.[8] The mallet, or *kungch'ae/kunggulch'ae,* is generally held in the left hand and plays predominantly on the lower-pitched head (*kungp'yŏn*). The shaft of the mallet is taken from the root of a bamboo tree that has been boiled and straightened, then cut to proper size. A round tip, usually made of birch or a similar hard wood, is then attached at the striking end. I have seen tips made of plastic, some which resemble jade, but these now seem to be reserved for mallets used by young students and/or beginners. The hand grip at the opposite end is made by wrapping leather over cloth, then gluing and/or tying it to the shaft to make it secure.[9] The stick, or *yŏlch'ae/karakch'ae,* is generally held in the right hand. It is cut from the stalk of the bamboo tree and is shaved and smoothed out on one side (the playing side), according to personal taste. Six sticks made for me during fieldwork were 41.5 cm, 42 cm (Kim), 42 cm, 42 cm (Yi), 43 cm, and 43.5 cm in length; five mallets made were 28.5 cm (Kim), 28.5 cm, 28.5 cm, 29.5 cm, and 30.5 cm (Yi) in length. *Changgo* sticks and mallets are often made and then signed and exchanged between close friends.

It is unclear when and how the *changgo* made its way from the court and aristocracy to the commoner class, for it is generally believed that the drum was a very early foreign import to Korea's elite (true of many p'ungmul instruments). Tomb paintings from the later Koguryŏ period (37 BCE–668 CE) are traditionally believed to be the earliest historical records of the existence of the *changgo* in Korea—here referred to as a *yogo,* or "waisted drum" (No Poksun 1994: 100)—and carvings of an hourglass drum are found on a bronze *sarira* (Sanskrit) case (reliquary) from 628 CE (Pratt 1987: 149–50, plates 86 and 87a), though both of these remnants depict drums considerably smaller than those used today. The first literary reference to the word *changgo* is credited to the year 1076 in chapter 80 of the *Koryŏsa* (History of Koryŏ), in which the term *changgo ŏpsa* ("one who plays [or teaches] the *changgo*") is used (Chŏng Chaehwan 1971: 413). Chapter 70 of the same document records the gift of 20 *changgo* from Sung China in 1114 (Song, Bang-song 1980: 146), though it should be noted that the *Koryŏsa* was written in 1451, some time after the events it chronicled. A pottery body of an hourglass-shaped drum was excavated from the Koryŏ period (Pratt 1987: 103, plate 18), and 10th-century reliefs depict a smaller hourglass drum laid on the knees, accompanied by a pair of cymbals (Yi Hyegu 1973: 32). Line drawings of the *changgo* appear in the 1454 *Sejong shillok* (Annals of Sejong; 132.15a)[10] and the 1493 *Akhak kwebŏm* (Chang Sahun 1986: 660; 7.3b). The use of two earthenware jars strapped to a wooden frame, called the *chil* (jar) *changgu*, which is found in Miryang, South Kyŏngsang province, however, suggests the possibility of indigenous origins.

The Puk

The *puk*, also known by the names *taebuk* (large *puk*) and the more general *ko* (drum), is a shallow, double-headed, barrel-shaped drum (leather or hide; H.S. 211.228.8). The body (*t'ong*) of the *puk* is made of pine, paulownia, or poplar and is either carved from a single block or constructed with interlocking slats. Skins of a cow, dog, or deer are then stretched over both openings and laced together with rope or leather thongs (*chul*). Tension is maintained by optional wooden chucks (*sswaegi*) wedged between the thongs and the body of the instrument. The stick used to strike the *puk* (*puk ch'ae*) is made of trifoliate orange (*t'aengja namu*) or a similar hard wood (No Poksun 1994: 33) and is carved in the shape of a long cylinder, or of a barbell with two

Figure 2.2. *Puk* (barrel-shaped drum) with various *puk ch'ae* (*puk* sticks)

Figure 2.3. *Puk* player wearing *kokkal* hat, Chŏnju city, Hwach'ŏn Nongaktan

bulbous ends. Larger *puk* average 40–45 cm in width and 21–25 cm in depth; the stick is 31–35 cm in length (see figure 2.2).

The *puk* is generally suspended from the performer's shoulder by a long cord (*kkŭn*) of cotton cloth and is struck with a stick held in the right hand (see figure 2.3). A well-known tradition of playing the *puk* with sticks in both hands, called *ssangbuk* (double *puk*), however, is associated with the island of Chindo, located off the southern tip of South Chŏlla province. Although in theory the *puk* holds the same place of importance as the other three core percussion instruments (*changgo, soe,* and *ching*), it is in practice often omitted in North Chŏlla province p'ungmul performances, particularly those of the "right side" (*udo*) style.

The esteemed "left side" (*chwado*) p'ungmul performer Yang Chinsŏng considered the *puk* to be the oldest existing percussion instrument of Korea. He hypothesized that the move from pre-communal society in the distant past toward one characterized by tribal units brought about a change in the societal fabric, specifically the struggle for power within and without these newly formed groups. These threats, as well as those imposed by nature itself, required the development of some form of communication.[11] Various experiments were conducted, from which emerged the shape of what we would now recognize as an early form of the *puk*. The strength and depth of the sound must have been imbued with some magical power as well: oral history passed down from the period of the Three Han states (1st–3rd centuries CE) tells of a ritual in which a *puk* and bells were tied to a pole and placed on holy ground (*sodo*). The spirit pole was believed to cause the spirits to descend (Yang Chinsŏng [1980?]: 23).[12]

Barrel drums depicted in the 1493 *Akhak kwebŏm* differ considerably with regard to shape and size (Chang Sahun 1986: 640–41; 8.9*b* and 8.12*a*), but the *yonggo* (dragon drum) used in military processional music (*taech'wit'a*) and similar in construction to the *p'ansori* (narrative song accompanied by drum) *puk*, with heads nailed to the body of the instrument, may possess a closer relationship to that used in p'ungmul (see Yi Hyegu 1986: 44 for a picture of the *yonggo*). The *puk* was used within the military to signal advances (Chang Sahun 1995: 122).

THE *SOE*

The *soe*, literally "iron" or "metal," is a small, hand-held lipped flat gong (metal; H.S. 111.241.1). In North Chŏlla province I often heard the instrument referred to additionally as *kkwaenggwari* or *kkaengmaegi*, but other onomatopoeic names such as *kkwaengma, kkaengma, kkwaengmae, kkaengmae,* and *kkwaengmaegi* are used as well in other regions of the Korean peninsula (Howard 1988: 38–39).[13] The *soe*, like its larger counterpart the *ching*, is made of brass (*nossoe*). *Soe* are produced by one of two prescribed methods: pouring the heated metal into a mold (*chumul*), or forging by hand (*pangja*), which requires considerably more time and is reflected in the end price (see figure 2.4). Two holes are then drilled out from the lip (*tulle*) and a cord of straw or rope is threaded through the openings to serve as a handle. *Soe* range from 20 to 23 cm in diameter and from 3.5 to 5 cm at the inward-sloping lip.

The mallet that strikes the *soe*, the *soe/kkwaenggwari ch'ae*, is made of bamboo root or wax tree wood (Yang Chinsŏng [1980?]: 21) cut to 20–30 cm in length.[14] Today the end of the mallet that strikes the front surface of the *soe* (*pangmaengi*) is commonly made of birch, trifoliate orange, or a similar hardwood, though in the past there were instances of four brass coins (*yŏpchŏn*) being layered on top of each other, then sewed together with thread (No Poksun 1994: 96). Rubber ends have begun to be sold in instrument shops,

Figure 2.4. *Soe* (small gong)—molded on left, forged on right—with various
soe ch'ae (*soe* mallets)

though they are commonly advertised as practice aids, since the resulting sound is considerably softer and more subdued. A decorative ornament made of leather (*kkossusul*) is then often attached to the tip of the striking end. The handle is generally covered with leather,[15] then adorned at its base with a series of colored streamers that enhance the mallet's role as a dance prop when used by the (lead) *soe* player during certain specifically designated dance portions of the p'ungmul performance.

Soe are commonly divided into male and female, the former generally associated with a higher and sharper-toned pitch, the latter with a lower and more subdued one. The lead *soe* player (*sangsoe*) tends to play a male *soe*, accompanied by the second *soe* player (*pusoe*) on the female *soe* (Chang Sahun 1995: 123; Chŏng Pyŏngho 1994: 57; No Poksun 1994: 96). Yi Sangbaek demonstrated the *soe*'s versatility as a nonmusical object as well, using it as a bottle opener, an ashtray, and a container from which to drink *soju* (a crude form of Korean hard liquor) after long performances (not necessarily in this order). The *Akhak kwebŏm* lists the *soe* as *sogŭm* (literally, "small metal") and describes it in connection with dance at the Sacrifice to Royal Ancestors (*Chongmyo*), as well as its use at the beginning of the ritual performance (Provine 1984c: 443). A line drawing of the instrument in this treatise depicts the *soe* (*sogŭm*) hung from a curved rod or pole (Chang Sahun 1986: 641; 8.9*b*).

The Ching

The *ching* is a large, hand-held lipped flat gong (metal; H.S. 111.241.1). Depending on the genre, it is also called a *chŏng* (gong), *na* (gong), *kŭm* (metal), *taegŭm* (large metal), *kŭmjŏng* (metal gong), or *kŭmna* (metal gong; Chang Sahun 1995: 121).[16] It is described in the *Akhak kwebŏm* in connection with dance at the Sacrifice to Royal Ancestors (Provine 1984b: 355) and is catalogued with the Chinese characters *taegŭm* (Chang Sahun 1986: 641; 8.9b). Within the military, the sound of the *ching* is believed to have been the signal for retreat (Chang Sahun 1995: 122). The *ching* has also been used as recently as the 1950s in village society as a means of sounding an alarm (Knez 1997: 82).

Ching are commonly made of brass, a synthesis primarily of copper and zinc (*nossoe* or *hwangdong*, literally "yellow copper"). A few are made of bronze, a more ancient material made primarily of copper and tin (*ch'ŏngdong*, literally "blue copper"). The gong is formed by pouring the heated metal into a mold or by forging it by hand, the latter a long and arduous process requiring constant pounding and shaping for readjustment by a number of workers (this is reflected in the improved sound quality as well as the higher price).[17] There are two broad categories of *ching* according to the type of finish applied: the *kŏmun maegu* or *hŭk ching*, literally "black *ching*," made by leaving the body of the instrument unpolished, with the exception of a series of concentric circles etched on the front surface (*padak*); and the *paek maegu* or *paek ching*, literally "white *ching*," made by polishing the body of the instrument. Two holes (*kumŏng*) are drilled in the lip (*shiul*) and a cloth or rope cord is strung through to act as a handle. Ching come in three basic sizes: the smaller children's version, called the *sonyŏn* (boy or child) *ching;* the regular p'ungmul *ching*, called the *wŏn* (primary) *ching*, averaging 40 cm in diameter and 8–10 cm in depth; and the larger *tae* (large) *ching*, used, for example, by the military (Yi Yonggu 1995: 25, 27–28, 68, 100; see figures 2.5 and 2.6).[18]

The beater (*ching ch'ae*) is made of wood wrapped at the striking end with cloth, deerskin, or straw; it varies in length between 20 and 31 cm.[19] The *ching* is struck by the beater in its center (*pokp'an*), which produces a good aftertone characterized by three undulations (*p'adong*) of sound, an effect referred to as *samp'aŭm* (three-wave sound) Chŏng Pyŏngho claims that *ching* are also classified as "male" and "female" in respect to their sound, similar to that of the *soe* (1994: 58), but neither a further literature search nor a review of my fieldwork tapes has confirmed this assertion. The renowned *p'ansori* drummer Kim Myŏnghwan believed that the sound of the *ching*, when it fell upon the ear of the unborn child in the womb of a shaman

Figure 2.5. *Ching* (large gong) with *ching ch'ae* (*ching* beater)

Figure 2.6. *Ching* players wearing *kokkal* hats, Seoul, Imshil P'ilbong Nongak

(*mudang*), would cause his or her bone structure to twist, distinguishing the child from "ordinary" children (1992: 71).

Although the matching of players with instruments within the p'ungmul ensemble is not generally gender specific (though see my discussion at the beginning of chapter 5), the heavy *ching* is nonetheless most often played by men, especially in longer village rituals or festivals lasting three or more hours. Yi Sangbaek felt that the *ching* sound held the entire group together and that a performance was musically and spiritually incomplete without it, yet he often joked about how he would assign the *ching* part to university circle members of whom he was not particularly fond, specifically because of its weight and often "boring" line (1995: personal communication). Group members from both Iri Nongak and Yi's troupe in Puan county told me that a (polished) *ching* turned upside down made an ideal container from which to drink rice wine.

THE SOGO

The *sogo* (small drum), also known by the names *pŏpko, pŏpku, pŏkku, sogu*,[20] and *maegubuk,* is a small, double-headed frame drum with a handle (leather or hide; H.S. 211.322.8). The instrument is often called a *p'an* (performance space) *sogo* when accompanying the folksong genre *sŏnsori* (Chang Sahun 1995: 143). The oldest extant historical records make no mention of the *sogo;* the drum listed by the same name in the *Akhak kwebŏm* differs in almost every regard (Chang Sahun 1986: 641; 8.9*b*).

The handle and body of the instrument are made of wood. The body is made by stretching two pieces of cowhide or two dogskins over a frame, then lacing them together with leather thongs; the completed body is then attached to the handle. The surface of the *sogo* is generally left plain, in which case it is called a *paek sogo* (literally, "white *sogo*"); it may also be painted with the *ŭm-yang* (*yin-yang* in Chinese) or *t'aegŭk* symbol, in which case it is called a *t'aegŭk sogo* (No Poksun 1994: 34). I have as well, on occasion, seen *sogo* painted with the three-colored interlocking pattern called the *samt'aegŭk,* literally "the three Great Absolute" (a Korean adaptation; see figure 2.7). The "front" and "back" of the instrument are determined arbitrarily beforehand by each performer, since the two heads do not differ in any significant way in regard to size, thickness, or color. The length of the entire *sogo* is 32–35 cm, the diameter of the drumheads 20–23 cm, and the depth of the body 5–7 cm. The stick that strikes the *sogo,* the *sogo ch'ae,* is also made of wood and ranges in length from 20 to 29 cm.[21]

The *sogo*'s method of construction and manner of playing results in very little sound production. This is perhaps due to its current main

Figure 2.7. *Samt'aegŭk sogo* (frame drum), Seoul, Imshil P'ilbong Nongak

function in p'ungmul ensembles as a dance prop, though historical precedents employing cloth drumheads would suggest alternate uses in village
activities (see Howard 1988: 45 – 46). Today most of a *sogo* player's energies
are concentrated on the manipulation of their spinning-tasseled hats, a topic
brought up again briefly at the end of this chapter in the section on dance
formations.

The *Hojŏk*

The *hojŏk,* literally "barbarian pipe [or flute],"[22] is a double-reed, conical wooden oboe (wood; H.S. 422.112). The instrument is known by the
additional names of *saenap / soenap / swaenap* (from the Chinese *suona*),[23]
t'aep'yŏngso (literally, "great peace pipe [or flute]"), and the onomatopoeic
nallari. The main body of the *hojŏk,* a conical pipe made of bamboo, Chinese
date, citron, jujube, yellow mulberry, yellow willow, or a similar hardwood,
is generally 3 – 4 cm in width, gradually broadening at its base (see Chang
Sahun 1995: 45). Seven anterior finger holes and one posterior thumb hole
producing a range of a twelfth would seem to be the norm, though the
cultural asset report on North Chŏlla province translated in part in chapter 1 tells of a *hojŏk* used by the performer Yi Sambok with nine holes on
top, one in the rear (Yi Hogwan et al. 1982: 11). The metal mouthpiece (*ku*

or *chorong mok*), made of either copper or brass, consists of a ring placed over a short tube to which a reed (*hyŏ* or *sŏ*) is then attached. Traditionally a natural reed was used, though today it is not uncommon to see a player substitute a small section of a plastic drinking straw, often with surprisingly good results. When the performer is playing, the lips are pressed against this ring, the entire reed being concealed inside the player's mouth. The metal bell at the end of the instrument (*p'allang* or *nabal t'ong*) is made of copper, brass, or tin. Modern *hojŏk* average 30–32 cm in length, considerably shorter than the *taep'yŏngso* depicted in the *Akhak kwebŏm* (see figure 2.8).[24]

Chŏng Pyŏngho claims that p'ungmul musicians in the past (now deceased) spoke of male and female aspects of the *hojŏk,* but no direct sources

Figure 2.8. *Hojŏk* (conical wooden oboe) player wearing *p'aeraengi* hat, Iksan county, Iri Nongak

are quoted, nor are any specifics provided (1994: 58). Although the *hojŏk* continues to play a significant role in both amateur and more profession-alized p'ungmul troupes, particularly in the "right side"–style individual group dances (*kaein nori*), its use is increasingly viewed as a luxury since accomplished players are difficult to find. The rhythmic pattern *kukkŏri*— a rhythm generally associated with dance in an entertainment-oriented performance—is almost invariably accompanied by the *hojŏk*.

The use of the Sino-Korean term *t'aep'yŏngso* is believed to have first been recorded in the *T'aejo shillok* (Annals of T'aejo) in a reference dated to the third year of T'aejo's reign (1394; 6.15*b*), though the instrument most likely was introduced to Korea from China at an earlier date: verse written by the government official Chŏng Mongju (1337–1392) describes an identical instrument in some detail (Chang Sahun 1995: 44). A competing theory posits that the *hojŏk* (*t'aep'yŏngso*) came into Korea from China through a military connection, a fairly credible conjecture given the instrument's description in the *Akhak kwebŏm* as one used in military processional music called *taech'wit'a* (see Provine 1984f: 499; Thrasher 1984: 474–75). Today the *hojŏk* is played in three pieces performed at the Royal Ancestral Shrine (*Chongmyo*), in addition to its regular inclusion in modern *taech'wit'a* and p'ungmul ensembles.

THE NABAL

The *nabal*/*nap'al* (literally, "trumpet bugle"), also known by the name *kodong*, is a long, end-blown straight trumpet with a mouthpiece (metal; H.S. 423.121.12). One source claims that it was imported from Ming dynasty China during the reign of Kongmin Wang (1351–1374) as a military instrument (Pongch'ŏn norimadang 1995: 27), though the first record of its inclusion in military processional music (*taech'wit'a*) is 1608, the last year of the reign of Sŏnjo (Yun Myŏngwŏn 1994: 171). A metal trumpet is depicted in the *Akhak kwebŏm*, but its shape as well as its length seems to indicate an unrelated instrument.[25]

Nabal today are made of brass or wood and are constructed of two to three collapsible sections (*t'omak*). An example of a wooden *nabal* from the city of Taegu made in 1978, called by the regional dialect variant *kodingi*, was on display in 1996 at the Onyang Folk Museum, located in South Ch'ungch'ŏng province (see also Chŏng Pyŏngho 1994: 69). All of the works I consulted gave 115 cm as a standard length, with the exception of the 1967 cultural asset report filed on Chŏlla province p'ungmul, which gave a measurement of 130 cm (Hong Hyŏnshik, Kim, and Pak 1967: 186). Today the *nabal* is used

Figure 2.9. *Nabal* (straight trumpet) played by Yi Sangbaek

in military processional music and Buddhist rites, and sparingly by village p'ungmul ensembles to give signals (see chapter 1, section 9a of the p'ungmul cultural asset report, and chapter 3, section 2, third paragraph under the text of Yi Sangbaek). A metal *nabal* was passed around among villagers observing a rural ritual p'ungmul performance I witnessed in Koch'ang county, North Chŏlla province, on March 1, 1996, but no one seemed to know when to play it (see figure 2.9).[26]

These instruments should not be viewed as existing in isolation within the realm of p'ungmul, but rather as shared across a variety of related genres; this is particularly true of the core quartet of percussion instruments (see table 2.1). Considerable variation in terminology exists, however, within the individual ensembles, owing in many ways to p'ungmul's survival as an oral tradition (see table 2.2).

Table 2.1. A comparison of instrumentation across related genres

	Idealized N. Chŏlla shaman ensemble	Idealized shaman ensemble	Military processional band (1901)	Military processional band (19th c.)	Buddhist outdoor band	Kosŏng Ogwangdae Mask Dance	Tonghaean Pyŏlshin'gut shaman group	Iksan Mokpal ŭi Norae Folk Dance Troupe	Unyul Mask Dance Troupe
changgo	1	1				2	1	1	1
puk	1	1	1	*	1	2			1
soe	1	1		*		1	2	1	1
ching	1	1	1	*	1	1	1	1	1
sogo									
hojŏk			4	*	1 or 2	1	1		1
nabal			1	*	1				
para			2	*	1		1		1
p'iri	1	1							
taegŭm	1	1							
haegŭm	1	1							
nagak				*	1				
taegak				*					
chŏmja				*					
Source:	Song Chiyŏng, Son, and Kim 1980: 82	Pak Hŏnbong, Hong, and Yu 1970: 203	Ten-fold screen of royal party, Royal Museum	Paek Yŏngja 1994: 133–37	Lee, Byongwon 1987: 36	Performance, October 27, 1995	Commercial recording, 1993 NICES SCO-041 CSS	Performance, May 10, 1996	Performance, August 24, 1996

Key: *para* (cymbals), *p'iri* (oboe), *taegŭm* (large flute), *haegŭm* (bowed fiddle), *nagak* (conch shell), *taegak* (long trumpet), *chŏmja* (small bell).

Note: An asterisk (*) indicates that no specific number was given.

Table 2.2. P'ungmul performer terminology (instrument names and ranking)

	Idealized p'ungmul band	Idealized p'ungmul band	Idealized p'ungmul band	Iri Nongak	P'ilbong P'ungmulgut
1st *changgo*	*sŏl changgu*	*su changgo*	*su changgo*	*sŏl changgu*	*sŏl changgu*
2nd	*pu changgu*	*pu changgo*	*pu changgo*	*pu changgu*	*pu changgu*
3rd	*sam changgu*			*sam changgu*	*kkŭt changgu*
4th	*kkŭt changgu*			*sa changgu*	
1st *puk*	*su puk*	*su puk*	*puk*	*su puk*	*su puk*
2nd	*pu puk*	*pu puk*			*pu puk*
3rd	*sam puk*				
4th	*sa puk*				
1st *soe*	*sang soe*	*sang soe*	*sang soe*	*sang soe*	*sang soe*
2nd	*pu soe*	*pu soe*	*pu soe*	*pu soe*	*chung soe*
3rd	*sam soe*	*chong soe*	*chong soe*	*sam soe*	*kkŭt soe*
4th				*sa soe*	
1st *ching*	*su ching*	*chŏng*	*ching*	*su ching*	*su ching*
2nd	*pu ching*			*pu ching*	*pu ching*
1st *sogo*	*sang sogo*	*su pŏpko*	*su pŏpko*	*su sogo*	*su pŏkku*
2nd	*pu sogo*	*pu pŏpko*	*pu pŏpko*	*pu sogo*	*pu pŏkku*
3rd	*chong sogo*	*sam pŏpko*	*sam pŏpko*	*sam sogo*	*sam pŏkku*
4th	*kkŭt sogo*	*sa pŏpko*	*sa pŏpko*	*sa sogo*	*sa pŏkku*
hojŏk			*saenap*	*nallari*	
nabal		*nap'al*	*nap'al*	*nabal*	*nap'al*
Source	Chŏng Pyŏngho 1995: 145–46	Pak Hŏnbong and Yu Kiryong 1965: 349–51	Hong Hyŏnshik, Kim, and Pak 1967: 123–24	1995–96 Iri Nongak roster	Chŏng Pyŏngho et al. 1980: 9–12

COSTUMING AND OTHER PARTICULARS

In this section I spotlight the more visually captivating features of a p'ungmul performance, paying special attention to the clothing, hats, flags, and use of characters. These various components are discussed within their respective historical and contemporary settings and are presented in a compositional comparison in table 2.3 at the conclusion of the section on the characters. It is the dramatic visual aspect of p'ungmul that is most often drawn upon for the presentation to the general public of national identity, unified images that disguise a rich complex of sources and influences of which the average viewer is unaware.

CLOTHING

The majority of p'ungmul groups in North Chŏlla province, if not the entire Korean peninsula, begin with the basic dress of the traditional farmer or laborer: white trousers and coat (*paji chŏgori*) made of cotton, hemp, or, more recently, cotton blends or polyester. The sleeves and pant legs are full length and can be gathered at the wrists and ankles with cloth ties, snaps, or elastic. White calf leggings (*haengjŏn*), made of white cotton, ramie, or hemp, are worn by a number of ensembles, though traditionally their use was restricted to the upper classes, particularly for formal social outings and ritual events (Sŏk Chusŏn 1992: 450). In the past, straw sandals (*chipshin*) were worn on the feet, but today white leather dance shoes and athletic shoes are a more common sight. A number of competing theories have been advanced to account for the predominance of white clothing in traditional Korea, but the folklorist Chu Kanghyŏn offers two of the more convincing arguments. He is of the opinion that early exposure to the Mongol empire and the centrality of white in their daily and ritual lives influenced the fledging Korean nation to the south, though he points out that later, during the Koryŏ dynasty (918–1259), the use of color by the court and aristocracy separated them from the lower classes (Chu Kanghyŏn 1996b: 80–97).

Outerwear generally covering the top half of the body is to a large extent determined by instrumentation. Throughout North Chŏlla province, *changgo, puk, ching, sogo,* and *hojŏk* players tend to wear vests (*chokki*) that are buttoned down the front. P'ilbong vests were deep blue in color, those worn in Iri, a lighter blue with a decorative inner red lining (though a solid purple jacket was favored during tours); the only exception to this rule was Iri's *hojŏk* player, who wore a yellow vest. *Soe* players, almost without exception, wear black or dark-colored outer jackets with half-length multi-colored striped sleeves, called *ch'angot* or *kŏt'ot.* This jacket, according to Yi Pohyŏng (1996: personal communication), was modeled on the military commander's uniform (*kugunbok*), a garment that came into widespread use after the eleventh year of the reign of Ch'ŏlchong (1859; see Sŏk Chusŏn 1992: 425–26).[27] The uniform featured a waist-length jacket with a black or deep maroon–colored body, and light red sleeves with an optional medium-width yellow stripe near the shoulder. Its eventual adoption by rural p'ungmul performers makes perfect sense, since all able-bodied men of commoner status during the Chosŏn dynasty were required to perform military service (1392–1910; see Lee, Ki-baek 1984: 185).

One to three colored cloth sashes (*tŭrim* or *tti*), usually yellow, blue, and red, are then tied over the shoulders and/or around the waist. Yi Pohyŏng believed that the sash was borrowed from the Buddhist monk's robe (which is red in color), but that p'ungmul's past roots in shamanism were responsible for the introduction and later use of the bright primary colors (1995: personal communication). There were no hard-and-fast rules for the positioning of the sashes—even within the same ensemble during the same performance there were inconsistencies. The only semi-accurate general rule I can forward is the wearing of the blue sash around the waist, as evidenced in performances by Iri Nongak (October 1995), P'ilbong P'ungmulgut (August 1996), a p'ungmul competition in Chŏngŭp county (October 1995), and the standard North Chŏlla province p'ungmul texts (No Poksun 1994: 41, 81; Yang Chinsŏng [1980?]: 26).

A general comparison of clothing, hats, and props used by the five regional groups designated as national intangible cultural assets is found in Sŏ Okkyu 1988, which can be cross-referenced with detailed measurements of Chŏlla province ensembles made by the Office of Cultural Assets in the late 1960s (Hong Hyŏnshik, Kim, and Pak 1967: 185).

HATS

Five different hats are used in contemporary North Chŏlla province p'ungmul performances, as listed below. The image of any one of these distinctive items of headgear in isolation is often enough to elicit instant recognition of the entire tradition.

The *pup'o sangmo*

The hat proper, called either a *chŏllip* (battle conical hat or felt conical hat, depending on the Sino-Korean characters) or *pŏngt'egi/pŏnggŏji* (felt hat), is generally recognized as headgear worn by the Korean military during the Chosŏn dynasty (1392–1910). This rounded-top hat with a wide brim is made of either wound straw,[28] black felt, or untanned cowhide dyed black and coated with glue made from glutinous rice (Chŏng Pyŏngho 1994: 54). The researcher Paek Yŏngja surmises that a hat described in the *Koryŏsa* (History of Koryŏ) during the reign of U Wang (1374–1388) is the first documented reference to a *chŏllip*. The hat was seen to have been worn by the Chinese, and within seven years of this initial sighting Korean troupes deployed to Manchuria had included it as a part of the standard uniform (1994: 157). There are no direct historical sources that reveal when p'ungmul ensembles began wearing the *chŏllip*.

Any appendage to the top of the *chŏllip* is known by the generic name of *sangmo*. Red tassels made of thread or cloth, called *sak mo* (lance hair) or *sang mo* (elephant hair), were originally hung from the heads of flags and spears; early military hats sporting these red tassels, therefore, carried on the tradition of the name (Han'guk hyangt'osa 1994: 72). The *pup'o sangmo* worn by p'ungmul musicians today, however, is considerably more elaborate in construction. A small knob or joint (*chinja/chingja* or *chŏpchoshi*) made of brass or wood is affixed to the top of the *chŏllip*; a short segment of wound wire or thread (*chŏkcha*), sometimes ornamented with wooden or plastic beads, is then looped over the knob. An optional piece of thread-wound wire (*mulch'e/mulch'ae* or *ch'ŏlsa*) is then attached to the *chŏkcha*, adding stiffness to the *sangmo*, the inclusion of which distinguishes the "right side" *pup'o sangmo* from that of the "left side." This difference is reflected in their respective names—the "right side" is called a *ppŏssangmo* (from the verb *ppŏt ppŏt hada*, meaning "hard or stiff"), the "left side," a *pudŭlsangmo* (from the verb *pudŭrŏpta*, meaning "soft"). Before the hat is worn, the performer first wraps his or her head with a black cloth or headpiece (*ch'ŏngmok sugŏn*), then ties a thin white strip of cloth (*taemang kkŭn*) around the skull to secure it (if a cloth flower is attached at the front of this strip, then it is called a *kkot sugŏn*). The *chŏllip* is kept in place with an inner head strap (*sok kkŭn*) and an outer head strap (*hullyŏng/hullyŏn kkŭn*) attached at its base (see plates 6 and 7 and figure 2.10).

The hat is completed with a tuft of white feathers (*pup'o*) sewn to the end of the *sangmo*. Feathers were originally taken from the breast of a crane, though today those of the (American) turkey, white heron (Han'guk hyangt'osa 1994: 71), or Australian ostrich (Yi Hosun 1996: personal communication) are favored, if not more readily available. Yi Pohyŏng claims that *pup'o* were originally made of paper, and that today only the Chŏlla provinces feature *pup'o* made of feathers (1995: personal communication), but this is surely true only of professional troupes. Most student and amateur groups I worked and played with could not afford *pup'o sangmo* with bird feathers—hats with paper or plastic streamers were used in their stead. The professional troupes in Iri and P'ilbong reserved the wearing of the *pup'o sangmo* for the *soe* players.

The *kokkal*

The *kokkal*, in its unadorned form a white triangular paper hat, is today primarily associated with Buddhist monks. There are numerous origin theories surrounding the *kokkal*, though most of these center on an ancient conical headpiece worn by 4th-century BCE Chinese. Hats of a similar shape were worn by women in the Shilla period (57 BCE–935 CE), and later by certain ministers and minor government officials in the early fifteenth century. There is also an assumption that the name *kokkal* came from the material traditionally used to make the headpiece (*songnak*) worn by Buddhist nuns modeled on the ancient Chinese predecessor mentioned above (*kok*, meaning "bent" or "crooked," and *kal*, meaning "arrowroot"; Son Kyŏngja 1986: 608).

Today *kokkal* are made of heavy white strawboard (*mabunji*), or by layering three to four sheets of traditional paper[29] over a hemp cloth shell. P'ungmul *kokkal* are distinguished by the paper flowers sewn to the top of the triangular hat. Flowers are commonly cut in the shape of a smoke flower, peony, or crape myrtle blossom and are left white or dyed one or more different colors (see figures 2.11 and 2.12). Iri and P'ilbong hats featured five paper flowers, one for each direction (north, south, east, west, and center),

Figure 2.10. *Pudŭlsangmo* ("left side" *pup'o sangmo* hat), Seoul,
Kŭmnŭng Pinnae Nongaktan

Figure 2.11. *Kokkal* hat worn by Kim Hyŏngsun

but this number could easily expand to as many as forty, as seen in Kangwŏn province (see Chŏng Pyŏngho 1994: 55; No Poksun 1994: 41). The base of the hat is secured to the player's head with an optional skullcap and cloth straps, though performers often tie an additional cloth band—sometimes with a flower attached—or towel around the forehead to help keep the *kokkal* from shifting. *Changgo, puk, ching,* and the majority of the *sogo* players in both Iri's and P'ilbong's bands wore *kokkal*, as seen below in table 2.3.

The *ch'ae sangmo*

The *ch'ae sangmo* resembles in many details the "right side" *pup'o sangmo* described above, but there is a significant difference between the two. For both, a black conical hat (*chŏllip*) is adorned with a top knob or joint (*chinja / chingja* or *chŏpchoshi*), a short segment of wound wire and/or round beads (*chŏkcha* or *kusŭl*), and a stiff cord of thread-wound wire (*mulch'e/mulch'ae*). For the *ch'ae sangmo*, however, the feather tuft of the "right side" *pup'o sangmo* is replaced with a long paper ribbon (or a plastic one, on cheaper models) called a *changji* or a *pujŏnji* (see plate 8 and figure 2.13). The standard length of this ribbon is 90 cm (Chŏng Pyŏngho 1994: 54), though the earlier official government report on Chŏlla province p'ungmul gave a length of 180 cm (Hong Hyŏnshik, Kim, and Pak 1967: 184). Yi Pohyŏng believed that this ribbon was adapted from a horsewhip (*ch'aetchik*) and replaced the red tassel used on the older military hats for the purpose of heightening the visual or dramatic aspect of the performance (1995: personal communication). The hat is secured to the head with an inner and outer strap, in a manner similar to the *pup'o sangmo*.

There seemed to be a common misperception in the majority of the Korean writings I encountered that "left side" *changgo* and *sogo* players could

Figure 2.12. *Kokkal* hat, Chŏngŭp county

Figure 2.13. *Ch'ae sangmo* hat, Chŏnju city, Chinan Chwado P'ungmulp'ae

be recognized by their wearing of the *ch'ae sangmo*, an error that may stem in part from this very claim made in the Chŏlla province p'ungmul report cited in the above paragraph (Hong Hyŏnshik, Kim, and Pak 1967: 117). All of P'ilbong's *changgo* players and the majority of their *sogo* players wore *kokkal*, a tradition the human cultural asset Pak Hyŏngnae, P'ilbong's lead *changgo* player, claimed had existed since the founding of the troupe decades earlier.[30] There is visual documentation as well of a P'ilbong ritual p'ungmul performance in 1980 in which *none* of the group members wore *ch'ae sangmo* (Kim Sunam, Im, and Yi 1986: 58).

The *yŏltubal sangmo*

The *yŏltubal sangmo*, literally "twelve-foot-*sangmo*," is a hat featured in professional p'ungmul performances. The hat proper is more rounded than the

Figure 2.14. *Yŏltubal* hat, Seoul, Iri Nongak

chŏllip and does not have a wide brim. In the past it was constructed of woven straw, though today the use of plastic is quite widespread. The top knob or joint and section of thread-wound wire that rotates around this pivot point are nearly identical to those of the *ch'ae* and *pup'o sangmo*. It is the length of the paper streamer,[31] however, that gives this hat its name. Though the number 12 is symbolic of longevity (Yi Pohyŏng 1995: personal communication), one *pal* as a traditional unit of measurement represented the length spanned by the performer's outstretched arms. Today the streamer has been standardized at 14 meters (see figure 2.14).

The *p'aeraengi*

The 1967 cultural asset report on Chŏlla province p'ungmul documented a fifth hat, seldom used today, called the *ŏsuhwa*. This flat-topped, rimmed hat was made of rough, woven bamboo and was worn by mourners and/or the lower classes. Fresh bamboo branches were inserted into its flat top (Hong Hyŏnshik, Kim, and Pak 1967: 183). The hat in an unadorned form, known by the additional name of *p'aeraengi*, was worn by Iri Nongak's *hojŏk* player (see figure 2.8).

FLAGS

Four flags are currently used by the troupes in Iri and P'ilbong, listed as follows.

The *nonggi*

The *nonggi*, literally "farming flag," is known by the additional names of *yongdanggi* (dragon shrine flag), *tŏksŏkki* (straw mat flag), *sŏnanggi* (tutelary deity flag), *nongsanggi* (farming commerce flag), and *turegi* (communal labor flag).[32] The flag is generally considered a remnant of p'ungmul played as accompaniment to communal labor teams (*ture*), confirmed in somewhat obvious fashion by the Chinese characters printed boldly down its front: *nongja* (farming) *ch'ŏn* (heaven) *ha* (below) *ji* (of) *taebon* (foundation), or, loosely translated, "Farming is the foundation of the world" (that is, below heaven; see figure 2.15). Within a traditional village setting, the *nonggi* often served the same function as the shamanistic spirit pole (*shindae*), as outlined by Lee, Po-hyŏng [Yi Pohyŏng] (1981: 70):[33]

1. Village participants, accompanied by music, carry the spirit pole or farming flag to the village shrine (*tangsan*) to receive the descending spirit or god of agriculture (*nongshin*).
2. After the spirit or god has entered the flag pole, the participants, accompanied by music, visit every house in the village or process out to the fields.
3. Carrying the pole or flag, the participants then proceed to a designated area and hold a rite or make supplications to the god of agriculture for a bountiful harvest.
4. At the end of the above activity, all participants engage in music, dance, and folk games in the communal meeting space (*p'an norŭm/p'an kut*).

Iri's farming flag proper measures 205 cm in width and 367 cm in length. The flag is secured by a horizontal wooden beam, tied to a tall bamboo pole in excess of 30 *ch'ŏk*, or 909 cm. The top of the pole is ornamented with pheasant plumes (*kkwŏngjangmok*) or a metal trident (*samdaech'ang*). Below the top ornament a cloth or paper flower is strung, and multicolored cloth streamers are often hung from the crossbeam. Iri's and P'ilbong's farming flags included their group name, cultural asset number, and designation, written in smaller print parallel to the Chinese characters mentioned above.

Figure 2.15. *Nonggi* (farming flag), Seoul, Imshil P'ilbong Nongak

The *yŏnggi*

The *yŏnggi*, generally distinguished by the Chinese character *yŏng* (meaning "to command or order" or "direction") printed in its center, can loosely be translated as "signal flag." Although there has been some discussion of its having shamanistic roots, its origins most likely lie in the military (No Poksun 1994: 38). The latter theory is fairly credible, both historically and in current performance practice: According to the scholar Paek Yŏngja, a flag called *yŏngjagi* (*yŏng* character flag) was used in the military during the Chosŏn dynasty (1392–1910) as a means of indicating orders given and to signal ground formations (*chinbŏp*), and constables stood watch holding these flags, though she does not specify the particular century or when their use was discontinued (1994: 40–41). In ritual p'ungmul, signal flags often lead the troupe around the village, and they are made to stand guard at the village gate or shrine as prayers and supplications are made.

P'ungmul signal flags are triangular (Chŏng Pyŏngho 1994: 40; Hong Hyŏnshik, Kim, and Pak 1967: 182), square (like the flags on display at the Onyang Folk Museum, South Ch'ungch'ŏng province), or rectangular (like those currently used by Iri and P'ilbong). Iri and P'ilbong flags were wider than they were long (Iri's were 50 cm wide and 45 cm high), had a dark border, and had the Chinese character *yŏng* printed in black on a white background.[34] At the top edge of the flag where it meets the pole was a multistranded thread or paper fringe; the pole itself (Iri = 212 cm, P'ilbong = 303 cm) was adorned at its top with a brass trident (*samjich'ang*). The pole can also be replaced by freshly cut saplings, as I witnessed in Koch'ang county during a ritual p'ungmul performance early in 1996 (see plate 9). Signal flags can also be found in red, yellow, or deep blue.

The *yonggi*

There are two main theories regarding the use of the *yonggi*, literally "dragon flag," in contemporary p'ungmul ensembles. The first, advocated by No Poksun (1994: 38), states that early Koreans, as members of a primarily agrarian society, were almost completely dependent on the sky for their ability to farm. Lack of rain presented the single most serious problem, for without water the crops would be damaged and the people's bodies and village would become physically and ritually unclean. For this reason, a special ritual was developed for the appeasing of the god of heaven (*ch'ŏnshin*) as a necessity for the survival and well-being of the community. During the 1st–3rd centuries CE, the figure of the dragon as a symbol of water was imported from Later Han dynasty China. One who acquired a dragon, consequently, had in essence acquired the equivalent of a magic stone or amulet (*yŏŭiju*). The dragon meant access to the heavens and the power to summon the wind, clouds, or lightning at will. Within this context, it is easy to surmise that farmers carrying a flag with the image of a dragon could be believed to achieve essentially the same purpose (see plate 10). Chŏng Pyŏngho, interestingly, includes a picture of a p'ungmul dragon flag used in South Chŏlla province that depicts a man riding on the back of a such a beast (1994: 39).

The competing theory, backed up by more concrete historical evidence, looks to borrowings from Chosŏn dynasty military practices. According to the researcher Paek Yŏngja, flags were divided into two main categories according to their ceremonial use: the *ŭijanggi* (literally, "guardian flag"), meant to show the power of the court, and the *kun'gi* (military flag), used specifically by the military (1994: 29–33). The two principal military flags were the *ch'ŏngnyonggi* (blue dragon flag), used to signal soldiers in the left ranks, and the *hwangnyonggi* (yellow dragon flag), used to mark the head of each battalion as it was assembling.[35] No Poksun claims there were two types of p'ungmul dragon flags in the past, the yellow and the blue, using the same terms as above, but that Iri currently only used the blue (1994: 36). In the *Akhak kwebŏm*, two flags are listed for use in the military dance at the Royal Ancestral Shrine: one the *ch'ŏngnyonggi*, the other the *hwangnyong taegi* (large yellow dragon flag; Chang Sahun 1986: 641; 8.9*b* and 8.10*a*).[36]

Iri's dragon flag proper was a rectangle two meters wide and one meter high, with a black border framing a dragon emblem printed on a white background. The flag was laced to a tall bamboo pole (909 cm), and the end of the pole was ornamented with pheasant plumes and a black thread fringe, similar to that used for the *yŏnggi*. P'ilbong's rectangular flag featured a five-colored dragon on a white background and was 455 cm wide and 152 cm high. The pole was the same length as Iri's and was ornamented in the same fashion, with an optional branch of a freshly cut tree affixed at the top. No Poksun states that in the past the dragon flag was held by three men, due to its size (1994: 36), a claim confirmed in part by the line drawing of the dragon flag in the 1967 cultural asset report on Chŏlla province p'ungmul showing two sets of double lines or wires (*kitchul*) running from the top of the pole to the ground (Hong Hyŏnshik, Kim, and Pak 1967: 181). Today the dragon flag is held by a single male and is displayed by Iri Nongak in a mock flag battle (*kinnori*) at the conclusion of the individual dance segment of the performance (*kaein nori*).

The dragon flag is considered characteristic of Chŏlla province p'ungmul groups (Ch'oe Tŏgwŏn 1990: 298–300; Yi Pohyŏng 1976: 59), though flags with the name *yonggi* will on occasion depict a turtle or a carp.

The Team Flag

Many established p'ungmul groups also carry a long flag with their name and place of origin printed on it vertically. For lack of a specific indigenous term, I will refer to this as a "team flag" (see plate 11).

CHARACTERS

"Characters" is a loose translation of the Korean term *chapsaek,* meaning literally "various colors." Most ensembles today will include anywhere from one to as many as ten different characters whose main role is to add frivolity and humor to the proceedings, heightening the festive atmosphere through crude gestures, dance, and witty and/or lewd remarks. A number of older performers suggested to me that their original performance context—one in which a space was reserved for a full-length, coherent theatrical act— had, for the most part, become extinct (this is addressed at greater length in chapter 4). The immediate connection between the various roles seems hard to ascertain, since the characters are taken from all walks of social and religious life, though I should point out that similar such interactions be- tween the upper and lower classes are a central aspect of Korean mask-dance theater (see, for example, Chŏng Pyŏngho 1995: 305–80). At first glance the roles appear gender specific, though actual practice reveals men dressing as women and vice versa. The principal characters found in the majority of North Chŏlla province troupes are listed below, in no particular order.[37]

Taep'osu (Hunter or Artilleryman)

The basic outfit of the taep'osu consists of white cotton trousers and a coat (paji chŏgŏri) worn under a longer overcoat. In Iri this overcoat was black with a multicolor-striped half sleeve; in P'ilbong it was dyed a dark color with the root of the indigenous kkottoshi plant. A mesh bag (mangt'aegi) is worn on the back, to which a tuft of bird feathers or animal fur is usu- ally attached. An axe as well as an imitation hunting rifle (sanyangch'ong) was strapped over the shoulders or held in the hands by the Iri taep'osu; in P'ilbong this gun was carved out of wood in the form of a shotgun (yŏpch'ong).[38] Iri's taep'osu wore a simple hat made of animal fur, while in P'ilbong a hat made of rabbit hide with an upper bamboo frame adorned with willow branches was favored. The taep'osu is often in charge of keeping group members within their proper ground formations (see figure 2.16).

Chorijung (Buddhist Monk)

The chorijung character wears the gray pants and overcoat (turumagi) of a monk's attire. A long string of prayer beads (yŏmju) is hung around the neck, and a wooden temple block (mokt'ak) and beater are held in the hands. P'ilbong's chorijung wore a knapsack on the back in which extra soe, ching, changgo, and puk sticks were kept. The round, pointed hat made of woven straw, or songnak, is known by the additional term chori, a reference to the bamboo strainer of the same name (hence the character's title, chorijung, literally "bamboo hat monk"). The performer Yang Sunyong believed that the chorijung were rogue monks who had been banished from temples for going against the teachings of the Buddha (quoted in No Poksun 1994: 83; see plate 12).

Figure 2.16. *Taep'osu* (hunter or artilleryman), Seoul, Imshil P'ilbong Nongak

Yangban (Aristocrat)

The general attire of the *yangban* is white trousers and a long white over-coat. A black horsehair hat (*chŏngjagwan*) is worn on the head, a false beard is often tied over the lower face, and a long smoking pipe is held in one hand. Hemp-cord sandals (*mit'uri*) are worn on the feet (see figure 2.17).

Kakshi (Bride)

A short topcoat is worn over a long skirt (*ch'ima*), the colors of which are determined by traditional combinations deemed suitable for a bride (yellow on red, emerald green on red, or white on blue). A white cotton towel is wrapped around the head, and a white cloth or colorful scarf is often held in the hand and waved about as a dance prop (see figure 2.18).

Hwadong (Flower Boy or Child)

The *hwadong* wears a red (P'ilbong) or yellow (Iri) overcoat over the standard white trousers and coat. In Iri, the *hwadong* wears a crude bamboo hat (*p'aeraengi*) with two branches of the indigenous *ŏsari* flower stuck in the top; in P'ilbong, a straw hat characteristic of young married men in olden times (*ch'orip*), with pheasant plumes or *ŏsari* flower branches attached on either side, is worn. *Hwadong* in P'ilbong's troupe wear a colorful scarf around the neck. An additional role of this character is to raise the level of enthusiasm within the performance area (*p'an*). The meaning of the Chinese characters

Figure 2.17. *Yangban* (aristocrat), Iri city, Iri Nongak

that make up the title of this character would seem to suggest a past relationship with the *hwarang,* or "flower boys of Shilla," as discussed in Rutt (1961).

Ch'angbu (Actor)

The costume of the *ch'angbu* is nearly identical to that of the P'ilbong *hwadong* described above, with the exception that a cuffed overcoat dyed blue with the indigo plant (*tchok*) is worn. Because the character was discontinued in Iri sometime during the late 1980s, today *ch'angbu* are associated with the P'ilbong's troupe (see plate 12). This actor is responsible as well for holding the rhythmic patterns together, achieved in part by waving the ends of the scarf. (See Howard 1990: 89 for a discussion of the ritual connotations of the term *ch'angbu,* particularly in the context of North Chŏlla province.)

Mudong (Dancing Child)

The *mudong* are held on the shoulders of young men, who then wave their arms in a prescribed manner. Little boys wear a blue vest over white trousers and a coat, little girls, a blue vest over a white skirt and coat. Hats of paper, often in the shape of a *kokkal,* are worn on the head (see figures 2.19 and 2.20). The tradition of *mudong* has been discontinued in Iri.

Figure 2.18. *Kakshi* (bride, on far left), Seoul, Iri Nongak

Figure 2.19. *Mudong* (dancing child), Seoul, Imshil P'ilbong Nongak

Nonggu (Training *Soe* Player)

This character wears the same attire as the lead *soe* player, but only carries the mallet (see chapter 3, section 1—"Communal Dance as a Gesture of Spirited Labor"—under the reading passage of Yi Sangbaek).

Table 2.3 presents in summary form the group composition of twenty-one p'ungmul ensembles I witnessed in live performances during 1995–96. Unless otherwise indicated, the groups are from North Chŏlla province (the last four groups are from South Chŏlla province [SC], North Kyŏngsang province [NK], and South Kyŏngsang province [SK]). Abbreviations under instrumentation include P (*pup'o sangmo*), K (*kokkal*), C (*ch'ae sangmo*), P' (*p'aeraengi*), and (X) (no hat worn); abbreviations under flags are N (*nonggi*), Yŏ (*yŏnggi*), Yo (*yonggi*), and Te (team flag); and under characters, T (*taep'osu*), C (*chorijung*), Y (*yangban*), K (*kakshi*), H (*hwadong*), C' (*ch'angbu*), M (*mudong*), N (*nonggu*), and the additional characters of (older) woman, beggar, farmer, and *hamjaebi* (see the end of chapter 4, section on *ham chinabi*). This table not only helps to substantiate observations made in this chapter, but also serves as a reference point for establishing standard instrumentation and costuming throughout the region.

Figure 2.20. *Mudong,* Chŏnju city, Sunch'ŏnshi Nongaktan

GROUND FORMATIONS

In p'ungmul performances with the full complement of musicians and
headgear, at least two simultaneous levels of choreography are taking place
at any one time. The first and most obvious aspect is the twirling of the
spinning-tasseled hats, specifically the *sangmo* and the *pup'o*. Fantastic geo-
metric designs are traced in the air at lightning-fast speeds with just a string
of paper or a tuft of feathers. These gestures, generated primarily from the
neck up, are all the more impressive when considering that most of these
performers are concurrently playing complex rhythms on their respective
instruments. The hat movements are all prescribed and named, and their
execution is intelligently appreciated and criticized by knowledgeable performers and audience members alike. The names of these movements are
mostly descriptive, such as "figure eight" or "four plus four" (four spins to

Table 2.3. A compositional comparison of North Chŏlla province p'ungmul troupes

Group	Changgo	Puk	Soe	Ching	Hojŏk	Sogo	Flags	Characters
Iri (Oct. 27, 1995)	7-K		6-P	2-K	1-P'	16-K, 1-C	1-N, 1-Yo	T, C, Y, K
Iri (May 10, 1996)	9-K		5-P	3-K	1-P'	21-K, 1-C	1-N, 1-Yo	
Imshil (Aug. 24, 1996)	7-K	2-K	4-P	4-K	1-K	7-K, 4-C	1-N, 2-Yŏ	T, C, Y, K, 2-H, 2-C', 2-M, 3-N
Iksan Kisebae/ Imshil (Mar. 4, 1996)	10-K	2-K	8-P	2-K		10-K, 6-C	1-N, 2-Yŏ, 1-Yo, 1-Te	
Iksan Kisebae (May 10, 1996)	19-K	8-K	4-P, 8-K	7-K		14-K	7-N, 12-Yŏ, 5-Yo, 1-Te	Y, 2-H (?), 10-M
Chŏnju Noin (July 7, 1996)	2(X)		2(X)	1(X)		3(X)		Y
Chŏnju Shimin (Mar. 4, 1996)	14(X)	1(X)	3(X)	2(X)				
Chŏnju Kŏllipp'ae (Feb. 23, 1996)	2-K		2-K	1-K				T
Iksan Munhwawŏn (May 10, 1996)	22-K	8-K	1-P, 5-K	4-K	1-K	6-K	10-N, 4-Yŏ, 5-Yo, 1-Te	T, C, Y, K, beggar
Iksan Ch'odŭng (May 10, 1996)	7-K	2-K	6-P	2-K		8-K, 6-C	1-N, 2-Yŏ, 1-Te	T, C, Y, K
Chinan Chungp'yŏng (Mar. 5, 1996)	8-P	1-P	4-P	1-P, 1(X)				
Koch'ang Pangjang (Mar. 1, 1996)	6-K	4-K	3-P	3-K	1-K	8-K	4-Yŏ	T, C, Y, K, 2 women
Koch'ang Pangmun (Oct. 26, 1995)	6-K	2-K	4-P	2-K	1-K	3-K	1-N, 2-Yŏ, 1-Te	
Puan (May 1, 1996)	9-K	2-K	6-P	3-K		10-K, 1-C	1-N, 2-Yŏ, 1-Yo, 1-Te	K

(Continued)

Table 2.3. (*Continued*)

Group	Changgo	Puk	Soe	Ching	Hojŏk	Sogo	Flags	Characters
T'aein Myŏn (Oct. 21, 1995)	5-K	3-K	4-K	3-K		14(X)	1-N, 2-Yŏ, 1-Te	T, Y, K
Shin T'aein (Oct. 21, 1995)	7-K	4-K	1-P, 5-K	3-K		7-K	1-N, 2-Yŏ, 1-Te	T, C, Y, K, 3-H, M, woman
Ip'yŏng Myŏn (Oct. 21, 1995)	4-K	2-K	4-P	2-K		7-K	1-N, 2-Yŏ, 2-Yo, 1-Te	T, C, Y, K, *hamjaebi*
Sunch'ŏn [SC] (Oct. 26, 1995)	5-K	4-K	3-P	2-K	1(X)	7-K, 5-C	1-N, 2-Yŏ, 1-Yo, 1-Te	C, Y, K, H (?), M, beggar
Kŭmnŭng [NK] (Oct. 29, 1995)	3-C	8-K	4-P	3-P	1(X)	10-C	1-N, 1-Te	Y
Hwach'ŏn [SK] (Oct. 26, 1995)	6-C	6-K	2-P	3-K		6-C	1-N, 2-Yŏ, 2-Te	
Munjibang [SK] (Oct. 26, 1995)	4-C	6-C	2-P	2-P	1(X)	6-C	1-N, 2-Yŏ, 1-Te	C, 2-Y, K, farmer

Note: Witnessed by the author in live performances.

Key to abbreviations: under instruments: P = *pup'o sangmo*, K = *kokkal*, C = *ch'ae sangmo*, P' = *p'aeraengi*, (X) = no hat worn; under flags: N = *nonggi*, Yŏ = *yŏnggi*, Yo = *yonggi*, Te = team flag; under actors: T = *taep'osu*, C = *chorijung*, Y = *yangban*, K = *kakshi*, H = *hwadong*, C' = *ch'angbu*, M = *mudong*, N = *nonggu*. For *hamjaebi*, see end of chapter 4, section on *ham chinabi*.

the right, four spins to the left), and have been documented by numerous researchers (Sŏng Chaehyŏng 1984: 83–84, 86–87; Yang Chinsŏng [1980?]: 52–53; No Poksun 1994: 72; Pongch'ŏn norimadang 1995: 396).

Entire-ensemble choreography in the form of ground formations (*chinbŏp/ chinp'uri*) within the performance space seldom if ever receives the same attention or scrutiny as the manipulation of the hats. Two master's theses submitted in the 1980s, however, provide us with tantalizing glimpses into the underlying cultural significance of these gestures. The first, by Kim Okhŭi (1985), examined the ground formations of Chŏlla province entertainment-oriented p'ungmul (*p'an kut*) according to four shared compositional elements: the circle form, the spiral form, the straight form, and straight and curved lines (66–68). Depending on the movement, these elements in isolation or combination serve to establish either a group performance aesthetic emphasizing a cooperative spirit, or a confrontational performance aesthetic emphasizing discord for the sake of shaping consciousness (73). Her views begin to provide a tangible analytical tool for musical ways in which group problem resolution is enacted, as discussed by the performer and researcher O Chŏngsŏp in his translated passage in chapter 3.

The second thesis, by Son Pyŏngu (1988), divided a total of seventy-five ground formations into five subcategories (99–101), determined by overall form: formations based on the *soe* rhythmic patterns, formations imitating play or folk entertainment, formations based on direction, formations in the shape of an object, and formations in the shape of a letter or character. These subcategories were then further broken down into five shared compositional elements (107–10), similar to, but more comprehensive than, those of Kim Okhŭi: a circle form, a spiral form, a *t'aegŭk* (*ŭm-yang*) form, a straight line form, and an oppositional form (two parallel lines). The most exciting aspect of Son's work, if the most open to debate, was the underlying religious, military, and recreational or artistic meanings he abstracted from the ground formations, reinterpreted in the context of each of the five shared compositional elements (113–20). A full exposition of his views is beyond the scope of this chapter, though the significance of the circular and straight forms will be addressed later in chapter 6 within the context of communal or egalitarian versus hierarchical underpinnings in a performance of entertainment-oriented p'ungmul.[39]

Below are listed the twelve ground formations deemed characteristic of Chŏlla province in the 1967 cultural asset report on p'ungmul, compared and contrasted with their modern-day counterparts as documented by the Chŏnju researchers No Poksun (1994) and Yi Chŏngno (1998). It should be noted that Iri's and P'ilbong's troupes practice many other variations on these ground formations, but differences often lie in their respective order or manner in which they are approached, not the form itself.

1. *Ilcha chin* ("one"-character formation): Group members form a single line in the shape of the Chinese character for "one."
2. *Ŭlcha chin* (*ŭl*-character formation): A curved or jagged line in the shape of the Chinese character *ŭl* is traced.
3. *Obangjin* (five-direction formation): Directly reflecting geomantic spatial principles of *p'ungsu* (*feng shui* in Chinese), group members either split up and congregate in or move toward one of the five directions (*obang*: north,

south, east, west, and center). Iri Nongak includes the related pattern *sambang chin* (three-direction formation).

4. *Hwan chin* (ring formation): This pattern is only named in the 1967 source (p. 149), not depicted. It most likely resembles that of modern-day *pangul chin* (drop formation) and *toep'uri chin* (reiteration formation), if the formation by the same name in the earlier p'ungmul cultural asset report is accurate (Pak Hŏnbong and Yu 1965: 406).

5. *Ssangbangul chin* (pair-of-drops formation): Group members split into two groups and form spirals (today this motion includes an unwinding as well).

6. *Sabang chin* (four-direction formation): This formation was traditionally included in the theatrical portion (now discontinued) of the *p'an kut* performance (*twikkut*) featuring the interaction between the lead *soe* player (*sangsoe*) and the hunter or gunman character (*taep'osu*).

7. *Kodong/torae chin* (cross-the-sea formation): This pattern is only named in the 1967 report (p. 149); a diagram of this formation is found in Pak Hŏnbong and Yu Kiryong (1965: 402). *Kodong chin* is not included in performances by Iri and P'ilbong.

8. *Mijigi chin* (push [or thrust]-and-fall-back formation): This formation is generally recognized as a remnant of p'ungmul's military past. Iri Nongak includes the related pattern *majubogo sŏnda* (face each other and stand).

9. *Anjŭn chin* (sitting formation): Group members, moving in a crouched position, circle around a pair of signal flags (*yŏnggi*).

10. *K'ongdong chigi* (carrying beans on the back): Group members, standing back to back, hook arms and lift each other in turn off the ground.

11. *Tŭng mach'ugi* (back to back): Group members lean on one another in a crouched position; one person in each pair looks to the left, the other to the right. In Iri, this formation is also known as *yŏpp'um sari* (sidewise coil).

12. *Chiwa palki* (tread on the [roof] tile): One group member at a time, holding the hands of two others, walks over the backs of other members.

Two omissions from the 1967 report require consideration, because they are the two most common formations shared by the majority of North Chŏlla province ensembles I performed with and/or observed. The first is the circle formation (*wŏn chin*), generally traced in a counterclockwise direction; the second is the *t'aegŭk* (or *ŭm-yang*) form (*t'aegŭk chin*). The circle in particular is seen as an indigenous dance form with deep historical roots (Chŏng Pyŏngho 1995: 491; Son Pyŏngu 1988: 113; see also the epigraph to this chapter). The *Akhak kwebŏm* depicts a circle formation (*wŏn chin*) under the heading of native dance as well, though admittedly within the context of the court (Chang Sahun 1986: 683; 5.3*b*). Perhaps the ubiquitousness of these group gestures was justification enough for their exclusion from the researchers' findings.

THE RECORD

A survey of p'ungmul's instrumentation, clothing and other particulars, and ground formations reveals numerous historical traces of Korean social and religious life as it evolved over the centuries. Remnants of pre-communal society exist in the *puk* (barrel drum) and the circle dance formation, while early influences of Chinese philosophy and geomancy are seen in the gendering of the various instruments (*ŭm/yin* and *yang*), symbols on drums (*sogo* frame drum) and flags (*yonggi* dragon flag), ground formations, and various manifestations of the "five-element template" based on *feng shui* (such as the "five-direction" dance formation and the use of five colors on the dragon flag; see further Hesselink and Petty 2004: 272–74). A number of instruments were imperial gifts from the Chinese court (the *changgo* hourglass drum, *hojŏk* conical oboe, and *nabal* straight trumpet), and many of them were linked to imported military uses, including the *puk, hojŏk, nabal,* and *ching* (large gong). Outerwear, headgear (*sangmo*), flags (*yŏnggi* signal flag and *yonggi*), and the *mijigi chin* (thrust-and-fall-back) dance formation all point to additional examples of military culture.

Vestiges of three major East Asian religious practices also find their way onto p'ungmul's stage. The color of the sashes, the special use of the *nonggi* (farming flag) and *yŏnggi* (signal flag), and the character of the *ch'angbu* all suggest shamanistic ritual influences. Elements of Buddhist rites include the *nabal* (straight trumpet) and various gongs, the use of sashes, the distinctive *kokkal* hat, and the obvious use of a monk character. Neo-Confucian ritual is also represented by the adaptation of the small and large gongs and the *hojŏk* (conical oboe). Rural society in less sacred forms is seen in the white garments and *p'aeraengi* hat, the communal labor flag (*nonggi*), the use of the *yonggi* (dragon flag) to ensure rainfall, and the inclusion of a battery of characters demonstrating the populace's love of theater. Hints of aristocratic social outings are present as well, shown in the wearing of *haengjŏn* (leggings) and the use of the *yangban* (aristocrat) character.

P'ungmul's material record confirms its place as a broad cultural repository where the common and the aristocratic, the secular and the sacred, and the past and the present are collapsed into a composite whole. These connections and interactions are further strengthened in chapter 5, where the origins of the various rhythms will be shown to be similarly diverse and multifarious.

When the annual cycle for the cultivation of rice reaches its end, it is time for the crowning glory, the most important task of the farmer: the harvest of the rice. Under the warm sunshine of autumn, it is the last labor of the year. Even so, the flail can be compared to the swift turning of the hat streamers in farmers' dances [p'ungmul], following the rhythm of the revolving streamers attached to the hat. Likewise, it is not too far-fetched to compare the revolving streamer on the hat to the flail. The streamer makes a whizzing sound, and draws an endless series of circles in the air. The flail, too, performs a circular dance. Dance, movement, and sound become one in a kind of trinity. In an instant, labor reappears as what Grosse called in his *Origins of Art* an "original ballad," where art and labor become one.

—Kim Yŏlgyu, excerpt from keynote speech, "Human Nature versus Culture in the Theories of Beat," Keimyung University (2004)

3

By and For "The People"

Late-nineteenth-century Korea witnessed the rise of a
remarkable indigenous religious and social movement.
Known as *tonghak,* or "eastern learning," its genesis can
be pinpointed to the year 1860, when its founder, Ch'oe
Cheu (1824–1864), is said to have received a divine vision
in which he was called upon to bring about an ideal society
in which all men were equal.[1] The appeal of his vision was
most visibly present amongst the populace, who suffered
under not only the social decay and injustice of a Neo-
Confucian bureaucracy but also the escalating threats
of foreign invasion (Kim, Chongsuh 1993: 224–43; Kim,
Yong-Choon 1997: 249–57, 67). The Tonghak Peasants'
Uprising of 1894—begun, interestingly, in North Chŏlla
province—is believed by many to be in the foreground of
the genealogy of a broader people's movement in Korea
(Lee, Namhee 1991: 209–10).[2]

The most important legacy today of the *tonghak* vision is the concept of *minjung,* meaning "people" or "the
masses."[3] The word *minjung* first appeared in the 1890s,
though its reemergence in the early 1970s in somewhat
modified form provided a new social identity for those
who participated in political, social, and cultural movements in opposition to a system perceived as authori-
tarian (Koo 1993: 131–32). A specifically *minjung* movement began shortly thereafter, led by a group composed

primarily of students and progressive intellectuals who sought to embrace and mobilize workers and farmers in an effort to establish a national identity and ethos in the world of ordinary people. "Interestingly, in this quest for national identity, intellectuals turned to Korean shamanism as a spiritual source of nationalist ideology and to shamanistic rituals as a means of raising critical consciousness and comradeship among the participants of the social movement. In this way, history has been re-appropriated, and shamanism is now used to mobilize the spirit of the oppressed" (Koo 1993: 144). *Minjung* has expanded to include religious societies and theology (Hwang Sŏnmyŏng et al. 1983; Yu Pyŏngdŏk 1985; Lee, Sang Taek 1996) as well as a "people's literature" (Yun Chigwan 1990: 11–36; Kim, Yoon-shik 1998: 135–50). Cho Hung-youn has pointed out an additional connection made between shamanistic rituals and the love of play in a significant portion of *minjung* writings (1987: 7–8).[4]

P'ungmul's close association with shamanistic activity in the countryside, as well as its ties to agriculture and "the earth," made it an ideal candidate for *minjung* theorizing and support. Such efforts often sought to provide unifying symbols and models of behavior to help explain the logic—if not, at times, mysteries—underlying the art form's enduring emotional links to the realm of mythos and the prototypical, timeless Korean "peasant." In this chapter I will explore in some detail two representative examples of this literature as chosen for me by my two principal drumming mentors. An official *minjung* movement by that name may no longer exist in early-twenty-first-century Korea, but its influence and inspiration have come to be felt in almost every facet of p'ungmul's existence, whether it be promotion, transmission, or performance outlook.

READING PASSAGE CHOSEN BY KIM HYŎNGSUN

At the end of the interview with Kim Hyŏngsun recorded in chapter 1, I asked whether there were any historical documents or related literature that he referred to as sources of knowledge or inspiration, to which he simply replied: "I *am* the tradition." Upon further consideration and reflection, however, he did feel that there were a select number of studies published about himself and his group, Iri Nongak, that merited a detailed reading. Turning to the shelf behind his desk, he proudly extracted three works: O Chongsŏp, "P'ungmulgut-esŏ ŭi kongdongch'e ŭishik-e kwanhan yŏn'gu" [A Study of Communal Consciousness in *P'ungmulgut*] (1989); Ch'oe T'aeyŏl, "Chŏnbuk chwa-udo nongak mu-e kwanhan yŏn'gu" [A Study of

"Left Side" and "Right Side" Style *Nongak* Dance in North Chŏlla Province] (1984); and No Poksun, *Nongak* (1994).

The first document, by O Chongsŏp, immediately caught my eye, for I recognized O as a *puk* (barrel drum) player and a part-time member of Iri Nongak who lived and taught high school physical education in Seoul. In contrast to the other two works Kim selected, which were written by academics, O's analysis was rooted in long-term, direct participation that offered a native anthropological view of activity surrounding p'ungmul, especially in terms of parameters of participation (Feld 1984: 386–88) and "functions" as outlined by Merriam (1964: 209–27; see also Nettl 1983: 149–50).

The title of O's thesis also piqued my curiosity, since the concept of "communal consciousness" (*kongdongch'e ŭishik*) was an oft-used construction in *minjung* theorizing. A cursory reading revealed, in fact, a text rich with such phrases and terminology, a few that are worth reproducing here for the purpose of providing some additional insight into the explanatory tack and nuances of this movement. Representative examples include "the people" (particularly laborers and farmers), "oppression under the ruling classes" (native or foreign), "community" (*kongdongch'e*), "communal consciousness," "group consciousness [and/or identity]" (*ŭishik*), and any link established between play and ritual (refer again to Kendall 1987: ix).[5] There is also the direct use of the word *minjung* and the phrase *minjung yesul*, or "the people's art."

If O's work had reflected only a romanticized and abstract rehashing of *minjung* ideology, there would have been little of interest or reward in its translation. "A Study of Communal Consciousness in *P'ungmulgut*," however, provides us with an invaluable road map to contemporary p'ungmul thought and activity. It sheds an interpretive light on its success in strengthening a feeling of community or group solidarity across gender and generational lines, a perspective that surfaces regularly throughout the remainder of this book. His analysis of entertainment p'ungmul also reveals its inherently political makeup, a key insight that begins to explain its use in rallies and demonstrations throughout the Korean peninsula (as alluded to in the introduction and addressed further in chapter 6). His thesis suggests that p'ungmul's role in village ritual closely parallels the role folk music played in Europe until well into the twentieth century: "The musical performance was part of that larger dramatic enactment which we call ritual, where the members of the community acted out their relationships and their mutual responsibilities and the identity of the community as a whole was affirmed and celebrated" (Small 1998: 40).

Table 3.1. Table of contents for "A Study of Communal Consciousness in *P'ungmulgut*"

Note: Sections translated in the text are printed in boldface.

Table 3.1 provides the table of contents for O Chŏngsŏp's work; passages from the sections set in boldface type are translated below. I have chosen to render the text in a slightly stiff manner, reflecting O's writing style and construction.

III. RITUAL AND CEREMONIAL ACTIVITY OF *P'UNGMULGUT*

If we divide into rough categories the occasions when p'ungmul was performed by the peasantry, we see their merriment centered around the lunar calendar months of January (Chŏngwŏl), May, July, and October, with farming as the basis of these dates. In the beginning of January, greeting p'ungmul [*tangsan kut*] was performed for the purpose of [providing] village solidarity and as a means of preparation against evil spirits; in May, at the height of farming activity, p'ungmul as labor music was effective in increasing the efficiency of the work. P'ungmul could not be omitted in July, at the conclusion of the rice weeding, when the peasants would temporarily rest and amuse themselves with *homi ssikki*.[6]

In October—the season in which the year's harvest is gathered—p'ungmul is again heard on the threshing ground. As the year comes to a close, p'ungmul is played once more as ritual music within a *tang kut* and as entertainment music within the spirited entertainment ground [*norip'an*].[7]

Greeting p'ungmul in particular as village ritual and ceremonial activity causes one to have an undefiled attitude and state of mind [when] welcoming the New Year. Communal-labor p'ungmul [*ture kut*] strives for a productive, efficient nature through common labor, while entertainment p'ungmul [*p'an kut*] provides an arena in which individual or group problems are resolved.[8]

The current study uses Iri Nongak as a model to examine how the execution of p'ungmul both maintains and solidifies communal consciousness [*kongdongch'e ŭishik*]. This is [accomplished] through an analysis of greeting p'ungmul (ritual and ceremonial activity), communal-labor p'ungmul (productive activity), and entertainment p'ungmul (group theatrical activity).

III.1. The Ritualistic Character of *P'ungmulgut*

If we view p'ungmul as having originated in supplications for success during sowing and the harvesting in the fall, as well as the appeasing of the various evil spirits or gods [*kwishin*] within the farming household, it is therefore an integrated art in the form of supplications exhibiting the character of the farming population's indigenous religious ceremony. Greeting p'ungmul and village-cleansing p'ungmul [*maegwi kut*] employing the farming flag have been handed down from ancient times, the former being understood as supplications to the village guardian spirit.[9] Similarly, because p'ungmul is also called *kut* [shamanistic ritual], we are able to see its differentiation and transmission originating in purely religious ritual. On January Full Moon Day, village residents ascend the village's guardian mountain while playing p'ungmul, to attend to the spirits.[10] After descending, they hold a large performance-ritual, again stopping at each home performing fund-raising p'ungmul [*chisin palki*] to usher in the benevolent spirits [*sŏnshin*]. Fund-raising p'ungmul is enacted in order to pay respects to the house spirits [*kashin*] for the tranquility of the home and to entertain the various evil spirits [*akshin*] so that they will withdraw.

Even within the ritual ground, where purification rituals [*ssigim kut*] and sickness rituals [*pyŏng kut*] originating in the hopes and desires of the individual are performed, p'ungmul is not omitted. The village shrine, the primary religious ground where p'ungmul was conceived, was originally the place where the people [*minjung*] both deliberated over and prayed for the entirety of their problems, as well as where they resolved and carried into effect the fundamental rules of [village] behavior.[11]

There p'ungmul as greeting p'ungmul played the role of ritualistic activity. The sound of the *kkwaenggari* [small gong] being played was the most cheerful [yet] driving sound to Koreans, while on the other hand it provided rhythms [*karak*] that brought about an awareness in the midst of being startled yet reflective.[12] The sound of the small gong played in greeting p'ungmul is broad and clear while at the same time reflective.[13]

The fact that p'ungmul uses the same four percussion instruments [*samul*] used in shamanistic music [*muak*] substantiates the reality that p'ungmul and shamanistic music ultimately came from the same source.[14] Greeting p'ungmul came into existence as an animism system for village communal members, and as such it became the basis of the formation of their feeling of emotional unity.

III.3. A Feeling of Unity within Ritual and Ceremonial Activity

A uniform standard exists both in the selection of the ritual specialist [*chegwan*] and in the observation of various taboos during the period of time when greeting p'ungmul is performed. Specific rules are applied to the structure of the ritual as carried out by the ritual specialist. Taboos such as pregnant women leaving the home, the holding of funeral rites, and outsiders entering the village retain a rather sorcerous character; many of these, such as not looking at a corpse, not going near unclean events, exercising self-restraint in one's sexual urges, or not quarreling with others, function as standards of societal value. Cleanliness inside and outside the home, refraining from ordinarily unclean behavior, the selection of a village elder exhibiting an exemplary home life as ritual specialist, not bargaining when purchasing ritual materials, and the especially clean preparation of the sacrificial offerings all preserve some nature of societal standards. The general function of spiritual lore [*tangshinhwa*] surrounding greeting p'ungmul, like myth, is to establish a model activity with prescribed customs. It shows the power of these standards to impart dignity and gravity to a specific institution.[15]

Greeting p'ungmul as ritual and ceremonial activity [performed] to safeguard the village from various diseases and calamity, as well as to provide supplications for a bountiful harvest, eliminates phobias associated with natural calamities and unexpected incidents while maintaining the religious function of subjugating the mental states of uncertainty induced by everyday life. This makes possible the acquisition of psychological stability and mental and physical purification through ritual. Owing to the solemn and chaste nature of the ritual, village community members—through the cleaning of the ritual specialist's home, the environs of the village shrine, and the village itself   [are able] as a group to strive for a clean or sacred life under a communal consciousness.

Because the ritualistic ceremony requires the tidy preparation of a sacred space, the village well is neatly cleaned up and refuse is removed, after which the well and its surroundings are sprinkled with red soil and marked off by a *kŭmjul* to prevent the comings and goings of outsiders.[16] Ritual offerings are then prepared with newly drawn clean water. This kind of ritualistic ceremony ultimately not only served to purify the village's source of drinking water but became the driving force that shaped, maintained, and developed the customs and sentiments of the lives of the community members.

In this type of greeting p'ungmul, community members acquire a feeling of emotional unity as a communal religious society [*shinang kongdongch'e*] by jointly serving a spirit that in turn [provides] them with protection. This acquisition by means of a joint observance of taboos and ritual structures and the collection of expenses through the process of attending the performance of greeting p'ungmul plays the role of elevating their regional collective consciousness.

V. Group Theatrical Activity of *P'ungmulgut*

V.1. Entertainment *P'ungmulgut* [*p'an kut*] as Group Play

The historical development of group play began with p'ungmul [*p'ungmulgut*] as an expression of the collective responsibility of group communal society [*chiptanjŏk kongdongch'e*]. We may deduce from ancient records such as the *Wiji tongijŏn* that ritual ceremonies of the period, in which there was no separation of religion and state, required communal group ritual [*chiptan cheŭi*] and unified play [*taedong nori*].[17] In primitive communal societies, community members worked together, expressing their joy through common sacrificial rites and unified play. That is to say, it is clear that group activity expressing this joy of labor through singing and dancing or supplications involved festivals of work and play among productive communities.

The form of unified play is roughly divided into religious play and the play of hard work, the former being associated more with greeting p'ungmul [*tangsan kut*], the latter with communal-labor p'ungmul [*ture kut*]. Both, as ritual play [*kut nori*], have an essentially playful character. If we classify and observe p'ungmul as one of the most common forms of unified play, we see its clear differentiation into categories of prayer, hard work, entertainment, and fund-raising, a scheme that starts from a more religious- and labor-oriented form and progresses toward the spiritedness of folk art.

The aim of group play is consistent with the demands of village communal society, namely, to strengthen psychological ties through religion as a medium and to bring about societal unity. Greeting p'ungmul achieves this by the unified apparatus of group play, through the spread of group intoxication, and group belief, with a communal god serving as an intermediary; communal labor p'ungmul accomplishes societal integration directly through the cooperative play of communal labor.

After the devout or serious ritual, the people who have taken part in this group play attack with fervor the governing order through the loose atmosphere of the entertainment ground and the characters' [chapsaek] timely criticism; homi ssikki performed in the midst of communal labor p'ungmul in particular takes charge of the assertive role of peasant society.[18] Even among the ruling class, this activity was tacitly approved as a compromise that allowed the peasants to breathe a little, operating as an apparatus of release from oppression. Mask dances [t'al ch'um] and the actions of the characters in particular served this function; furthermore, enmity or strife within the community culminated in activities such as ki ssaum [flag battle], sŏkchŏn [literally, "rock fight"], chultarigi [tug-of-war], and ch'ajŏn ssaum [literally, "vehicle battle"].[19]

During this period of intense criticism on the entertainment ground, a feeling of united energy among community members is internally validated. Through the performance of p'ungmul, members establish a democratic cooperative system between villages that measures the collective consciousness and depth of relationship between the communities. In ordinary times, it is demonstrated by a cooperative spirit; in times of need, it serves as the fighting spirit behind social insurrection.[20]

Group play, more than just the play or feasting of a village, becomes the scene of the people's art [minjung yesul] in which the people's unconscious cognition of reality acquires concreteness. This type of group play is able, as a festival, to become a superb medium for the criticism of reality; for this reason, the festive nature of group play requires an open structure or framework, obtaining a feeling of emancipation owing to the structure's communal foundation. In other words, in village communal society wholeness is emphasized, while freedom or emancipation is emphasized in the dialectical worldview of work and play.

Entertainment p'ungmul of this kind is the historical path taken by the robust peasantry released from work, confirming their self-esteem and their sense of democratic collective responsibility.

V.3. The Nature of *P'ungmulgut* Group Play

Communal consciousness in village communities comes into being under the assumption that neighborhoods within a single village get along together. For those who live together within a neighborhood, a spirit of cooperation in which one must help others functions in the form of a communal standard of conduct, while at the same time through this need to live and help each other a sense of collective responsibility based on regionalism creates a feeling of unity, of communal relationship. This type of neighborhood spirit, together with a spirit of cooperation—a sense of collective responsibility—is an essential element in the creation of a common purpose, set of rules, and consciousness. Ordinarily, however, it is difficult to jointly guarantee these notions or concepts; even if opportunities are provided, the occasions on which all are able to universally participate are few, though in situations where p'ungmul has been transmitted from generation to generation within the village, these notions are much more noticeable.

Although play exists that is self-sufficient, in that one is able to enjoy oneself alone, play done in the company of many others gives a richer and more joyful satisfaction.[21] If a group splits and its members compete against each other, excitement grows even more, and if spectators encourage or stimulate this desire for contest (victory or defeat), then the character of group play is that in which liveliness and joy [*hŭngyŏum*] are all the more emphasized. In order for this to occur, the play must be able to be watched and jointly participated in by the entire village. A common goal must be established for this type of play to be possible.

In contrast to the unified play of p'ungmul, which guarantees a combined feeling of oneness through song and dance, team play arouses a collective consciousness acquired as a reaction against the clashing and competition against one another of groups from different areas. Communal consciousness is not cultivated for the sole purpose of individual village unity, in which societal group strength is a central focus—rather, it is enhanced as a reaction against those situations in which one group receives a threat from another or receives unjust treatment and suffers defamation, and when there exists a state of discord and confrontation.

Consequently, team play in the form of group competition has the function of solidifying communal consciousness by deliberately producing conspiratorial, antagonistic relationships with other groups. That is to say, through competition with an outside power, team play collects strength for the purpose of common success and an abundant harvest, as well as providing a joint momentum for intensifying group will.

Even in villages where disputes and enmity lie dormant, by the act of team play, of competing with other villages, villagers are united more than ever by a strong sense of communal consciousness, coping with this competition and banding together by means of a collective consciousness. As a result, the winning side solidifies its love of its fellow players in the midst of enjoying the thrill of victory, while the losing side is made all the more keenly aware of the necessity to hold together as a unified group.

From the standpoint of form, p'ungmul that has been transmitted from generation to generation within the village unit as either unified or team play solidifies in a concrete manner both societal integration and collective consciousness, at the same time preserving psychologically a certain ritual mysticism in which supplications are offered for the prosperity of the village and an abundant harvest. As a consequence, these forms of play have the function of providing unity and communal collective responsibility, as well as being a psychological driving force behind the members' ability to devote themselves with conviction to productive action. Team play in a special way firmly emphasizes communal consciousness by deliberately creating conspiratorial, antagonistic relationships with neighboring groups while intensifying the spirit of unified play; it has the additional pretext of mystical experience in which supplications are made for an abundant harvest.

We must, therefore, while elevating collective consciousness and a feeling of regional unity by establishing our own play culture, rejecting cultural infiltration and cleansing external remnants of imperialism and commercialism, resuscitate p'ungmul as village communal folk entertainment [minsok nori] in the form of a festival for the purpose of raising the standard of the quality of our current existence, which is directly connected to productive action.

READING PASSAGE CHOSEN BY YI SANGBAEK

At the end of his interview in chapter 1, I asked Yi Sangbaek whether there were any written sources he consulted for clarification or inspiration. He replied that his primary means of gathering information on p'ungmul activity was through direct observation, either of a live performance or from an electronically mediated source (television or video). I noticed, however, that two books in particular that I had seen on his office bookshelf continued to surface among his student groups at the university and in his hometown: Chu Kanghyŏn, Kut ŭi sahoesa [A Social History of Shaman Ritual] (1995); and Minjok kut hoe [Folk Ritual Society], Minjok-kwa kut: Minjokkut ŭi saeroun yŏllim-ŭl wihayŏ [Folk and Ritual: Toward a New Understanding of Folk Ritual] (1993). I asked Yi whether these publications would be of any interest to a foreign audience; he told me that he would spend the weekend looking them over and get back to me.

Yi returned the next week to tell me that there were three passages in one of the essays in Minjok-kwa kut that he thought would be extremely valuable if translated and presented to English readers. The essay was written by Kim Inu and is titled "P'ungmulgut and Communal Spirit" (P'ungmulgut-kwa kongdongch'ejŏk shinmyŏng).[22] The three passages fell under the subheading "Primary Features of P'ungmulgut" and were socioanalytical studies of the central role of dance, the use of "oral verse" in the transmission of tradition, and rhythmic patterns as both the development and functioning

Table 3.2. Outline of *"P'ungmulgut* and Communal Spirit"

---

1. Introduction
2. The Current State of *P'ungmulgut*
3. Primary Features of *P'ungmulgut*
    a. The Communal, Philosophical Nature of Our Existence
    b. Communal Dance as a Gesture of Spirited Labor
    c. Oral Verse: A Shared Aesthetic Sense of Practical Wisdom
    d. Rhythmic Patterns: Life's Rhythm as Tension and Release
    e. The Communal Blessing Ritual of Well-wishing and Supplication
    f.   The "Back Ritual" [*twikkut*]: The Establishment of Unity through Play
    g. Ground Formations: The Everyday Practice of Discipline
    h. The Growth and Transformation of [*P'ungmulgut's*] Function of Humanization
    i.   The Primary Feature of Our [Korean] Culture
4. Fund-raising [*madang palbi*] *P'ungmulgut:* Examples of *P'ungmulgut's* Revival
5. *P'ungmulgut's* Revival and Return to Popularity
6. Conclusion

Note: Sections translated in the text are printed in boldface.

of a "spiritual flow" (see table 3.2; translated passages are shown in bold-face type).

I should begin by providing some background details on the volume of which the passages translated above are a part. Publication was carried out under the auspices of the Folk Ritual Society (Minjok kut hoe), a loose association of performers, actors, producers, and academics bound together by their common goal of supporting and actively promoting *minjung* and, by extension, nationalist ideals. The group's statement of purpose is printed on the last page of the book: "The Folk Ritual Society was established for the purpose of contributing to an independent *minjung* culture as well as the creation of culture healthy to today's common masses by the [act of] ritual [*kut*]—the essence of *minjung* culture—in which the *minjung's* structure, beliefs, play, democratic assembly, and method of struggle are united as a whole." This intellectual and philosophical persuasion is reflected in the titles of the essays (see table 3.3) and in the biographies of the contributing authors: Paek Kiwan, vice president of the Democratic Unification Minjung Movement Alliance, chief of the Research Institute on the Issue of Unification, and advisor to the Folk Ritual Society; Chu Kanghyŏn, folklorist, playwright, and member of the steering committee of the Folk Ritual Society; Kim Inu, previous representative of the *p'ungmulgut* group Chŏnnoktugol (literally, "mung bean village"); Pak Inbae, cultural critic, member of the executive committee of the Minjung Cultural Movement Alliance, and

Table 3.3. Table of contents for *Folk and Ritual*

Preface: Folk and Ritual	Paek Kiwan
Part I	
A Study of Village Communal Society and Its "Village Ritual" and "Communal Work Ritual"	Chu Kanghyŏn
P'ungmulgut and Communal Spirit	Kim Inu
Communal Culture and a Democratic Spirit	Pak Inbae
Questioning the Practice of Cheju Island's Ritual Movement	Mun Mubyŏng
Part II	
An Account of the West Coast "Unification Ritual"	Chu Kanghyŏn
The Poetry of Ritual: "If I Die, Bury Me in the Paper Mulberry Field"	Mun Mubyŏng
The Grand Celebration of Life's Liberation: The Buddhist Holiday of Uranbunjae	Yi Inmuk, Chin Ch'ŏlsŭng

consultant to the Folk Ritual Society; Mun Mubyŏng, folklorist, stage director of the group Madang Kut (literally, "yard [or ground] ritual"), previous representative of the group Sunorŭm, and consultant to the Folk Ritual Society; Yi Inmuk, Buddhist monk, previous departmental head of Minburyŏn (folk Buddhist society), and individual cultural asset "holder" (*poyuja*) for Buddhist chant; and Chin Ch'ŏlsŭng, stage director of Madang Kut and member of the steering committee of the Folk Ritual Society.

The first passage of Kim Inu's text was especially close to Yi Sangbaek's heart because of its focus on the importance of dance. Though the issue of movement in general was a passion for both Yi and Kim Hyŏngsun, this particular account was attractive to Yi for its attention to nonstylized, nonprofessional performances of p'ungmul, which Yi saw as a direct contrast to what he perceived as slicker renditions of the "right side" counterparts in the neighboring regions of Iri and Chŏngŭp. He often spoke of simplicity of gesture and the creation of a spiritual energy achieved only in the presence of others engaged in a common act, views directly expressed by Kim at the end of this passage. This portion of the essay can be viewed as a thinly veiled attack on the related modern, urbanized genre of p'ungmul known as *samul nori,* with its emphasis on rhythmic patterns and technique divorced from the act of dance (here referring to the seated version; see Hesselink 2001: 54–75, 2004). It is noteworthy as well that the opening language is couched within the context of the Japanese occupation and refers to scholars sympathetic to their cause—another allusion to the supposedly degrading influence of the Japanese and the creation of the word *nongak*.

The next passage makes its points through the telling of two folk tales. After a brief excursion through *minjung*-laden vocabulary—"the people," "stars of the people" (*minjung sŭt'a-tŭl*), "common spirit," and "communal consciousness"—we are entertained with the story of a perhaps mythical young lead *soe* (small gong) player. Through its narrative we are provided with the first cultural-historical explanation in print of the genesis of oral verse, today a valuable teaching tool used in conjunction with oral mnemonics throughout semirural North Chŏlla province as well as in more cosmopolitan settings such as Seoul.[23] Yi always stressed the necessity of first verbalizing the rhythmic patterns, a habit he carried without fail into the wide variety of teaching environments in which he was often engaged. The *samch'ae* rhythmic pattern example *ttang-to ttang-to nae ttang ida, Chosŏn ttang-to nae ttang ida* is perhaps the most widespread and well known of the entire oral verse repertoire—both Yi and Iri Nongak's lead *soe* player, Pak Yongt'aek, employed it as part of their regular teaching regimen (Pak is interviewed in chapter 6).

The second story concerns a farmer and his rice paddies. The account is effective, if somewhat quaint, in its effort to humanize and empower the "uneducated" and "ignorant" farmers as the masses possessing both wisdom and independence, distinguished from the so-called educated classes by the attention the former pay to practical details. *Minjung* inspirations aside, the story speaks in a language directly understood by Yi, a college graduate who nonetheless made regular visits to his natal home in Puan county to tend to the family's fields.[24] It foregrounds as a source of knowledge the common activity of labor, not an esoteric or highly technical written document. This distinction had been made previously in Kim's discussion of oral verse: the aesthetic sense of the laborer considered not only the beautiful, but also the various facets of daily life and work surrounded by nature. This embeddedness of work in the total fabric of nonindustrial segments of society suggests a number of cross-cultural resonances (Herskovits 1965; Applebaum 1984).

The opening of the section of Kim's text presented here as the third reading passage—the strongest of the sections translated from this chapter, in my opinion—both echoes and reinforces previously stated material. He reminds us that other studied traditions often conceptualize music in a more holistic way, linking it to other performing arts (such as dance) and the social context surrounding its production (versus, for example, a surface analysis of the rhythmic patterns). His description of a properly balanced percussion sound through onomatopoeia is an additional marker of a verbal and aural orientation, which creates a synesthetic metaphor in which one can almost taste the rhythmic pattern. Emphasis is placed as well on the inclusion of the audience response.

The concept of tension and release is essential to the inner workings of any musical or dance tradition. Kim demonstrates convincingly its presence not only in the rhythmic patterns themselves, but within the larger movement and overall performance, providing micro- to macro-level vantage points. His coupling of tension and release to *placement* in a performance—a structural or functional analysis versus a purely musicological one—moved beyond verbal abstraction to inform the core of Yi's teaching and performance strategy before my departure from Korea in 1996 (intimations of these leanings appear in his interview in chapter 6). What distinguishes Kim from other music analysts, both native and foreign, is the eloquence with which he further links tension and release to the daily labor cycle of the farmer through narrative *and* musicological means, establishing another point of intersection between music and culture. His idea of time as being determined by work and seasonal cycles also provides a common meeting ground for social scientists in related disciplines (in the West, for example, see Friedmann 1960). This culminates in the graphic provided at the conclusion of Kim's endnote f, as well as the pattern-by-pattern breakdown of an entire performance provided in Kim's endnote g. The ultimate goal, then, is not that of beautiful performance, as it is in an aesthetic perhaps more typical of the Western concert hall, but rather the generation of energy and a common spirit through the joint activity of all the participants. This interpretation not only furthered my own understanding of p'ungmul, but also served to shape the way in which I now present it to others in a performance class setting, particularly with regard to pacing and the use of structural climaxes.

The overall success of Kim Inu's text—within the environs of North Chŏlla province—lies in its pedagogical use of storytelling, linking theory and analysis to concrete examples and images familiar to an audience still living in predominantly nonurban areas. It provides the cultural outsider a glimpse into the inner workings of a slowly disappearing society; the foreign researcher, an alternative way of coming to grips with ground-level or native thinking and scholarship. It speaks as well to the larger issues of preservation and revitalization brought about by outside threats and loss of tradition, concerns that underpin discourse throughout this entire chapter. Tellingly, this very same text may attract percussion enthusiasts dwelling in larger metropolitan areas by its references to a way of life now missed (and perhaps romanticized) in their own daily experiences.

Footnotes in Kim's original text have been changed to lowercase letters in brackets and are provided as endnotes at the conclusion of the third reading passage (below, p. 115).

❧

3B. COMMUNAL DANCE AS A GESTURE OF SPIRITED LABOR

Of all the views of p'ungmul [*p'ungmulgut*], the view that hinders one the most in coming to an understanding is to see p'ungmul purely as rhythmic patterns [*karak*]. To speak of p'ungmul only as a genre of music in terms of "high musicality" or "internationally superb among percussion musics" is to rend its essence to threads. We are left, consequently, with p'ungmul being classified as "music" [*ŭmak*],[25] as well as generally being referred to as *nongak*, a word intentionally made up by folklorists and imperialists during the Japanese occupation. Furthermore, beginners attempting to learn and internalize a p'ungmul that emphasizes only the rhythmic patterns are learning a dead or meaningless p'ungmul. This is not said in order to emphasize the point that the rhythms are unimportant; rather, if asked to state the most important factor in the revival of p'ungmul's spirit [*shinmyŏng*],[26] it would be dance, not rhythm. It is to emphasize the fact that p'ungmul is communal dance [*taedong ch'um*], always involving a large number of people.

"P'ungmul is played with your heel!" are words spoken by many a famous lead *soe* player [*sangsoe*]. No matter how well the rhythmic patterns are produced, it is dance that produces them—if this gesture of labor [dance] is unable to create enthusiasm, the p'ungmul is considered dead or *malttukkut* [literally, "post [or stake] performance"], and regarded as lacking power or ability. Though rhythm provides an impulsive stimulus, it is unable to generate a people's enthusiasm for participating in the entertainment space [*p'an*]; ritual [*kut*] as only rhythm becomes dead ritual.

There is a character called the *nonggu* who follows the lead *soe* player around at his side wearing the same attire; it is this *nonggu* who will one day succeed the lead *soe*. The *nonggu*, however, goes about carrying only the mallet, not the instrument itself. Often it may seem as though the second *soe* player [*pusoe*], who is always right next to the lead *soe*, will succeed him. The second *soe* player, however, is always second *soe*, until his death. The most important aspect of a lead *soe*'s temperament is not his ability to play rhythmic patterns, but his ability to lead. The secret of this leadership is no doubt the power to lead musicians and others [observers] into the entertainment space and make them perform well; this strength in concrete form is the dance, whether it is the *kunmori* [general ground formations of the entire group], the *pup'o norŭm* [a dance featuring the head or upper part of the body], or the *pal norŭm* [a dance emphasizing the feet or lower part of the body]. The candidate for lead *soe*, therefore, does not learn the rhythmic patterns first but must follow the lead *soe* player about, becoming proficient at the dance. In the case of the *nonggu* it is the dance, rather than the rhythmic patterns, that lies at the heart of p'ungmul, crystallizing a spirited performance. A performance that consists merely of musicians playing rhythmic patterns is in its early stage, coarse or unrefined; in order to perfect the performance, even the audience must join in. The common bond between the performers and the audience is their shared gesture of labor, namely the dance.

If you step away from a performance of p'ungmul that is going very well, just for a moment, and look back, you see that everyone is floating about in a spiritual state or state of oneness. When the gestures match well, moving up and down in a simple and unreserved way, a group flow full of life takes form. The simple *porittae ch'um,* danced by individuals, when done as a group and well coordinated certainly creates a spiritual state of ecstasy [*muajigyŏng*].[27] When done individually and spontaneously it is only the *porittae ch'um,* but when done as a group it creates in its place a certain precision or elaborateness, producing an ideal spiritual energy. This type of performance is a successful p'ungmul performance, and if the dance is not jointly owned by all, this spirit is not created. The secret of this dance becomes the *porittae ch'um.* It is not stylized, professional dance; it is a gesture of natural labor that emerges from the process of one's own productive activity, one's daily life. Only this type of dance—one with which all are familiar, established through a shared gesture of labor—can generate true enthusiasm in a performance of p'ungmul.[a]

3c. Oral Verse: A Shared Aesthetic Sense of Practical Wisdom

In former times, p'ungmul [*p'ungmulgut*] performers were popular among the masses [*taejung-tŭl*]. Touring fund-raising troupes in particular, with their well-produced performances, were greatly loved by the masses. As stars of the people [*minjung sŭt'a-tŭl*] they were warmly received by all, receiving recognition for their skill at the level of *ttŭnsoe*.[28] Unlike the manufactured stars of present-day commercial mass culture, these p'ungmul stars were at the heart of the masses, possessing a common understanding through a shared existence. Those who received this recognition, therefore, were like magicians, conjuring up their spirit or essence from an authentic communal consciousness [*kongdongch'ejŏk konggam ŭishik*].

There was once a young lead *soe* player in a certain area who was said to have been a good performer and received recognition as such from the masses;

he was also unmarried, a rare condition among lead *soe* players. One day, the p'ungmul troupe to which this lead *soe* player belonged left to go fund-raising among the various neighborhoods and villages. This lead *soe* player was particularly popular among young women, being a bachelor; ultimately he became attracted to a woman in one of the villages, and he fell in love and spent the evening with her.

Signals for a p'ungmul troupe are played by the *nabal* [straight trumpet], one blast signaling for the troupe to be on alert—p'ungmul is about to begin. The musicians, who had already split up among the various homes and slept after the performance had finished the previous evening, were to stop any other activity and be on the alert. Two blasts on the *nabal* are the signal for putting on the uniform and inspecting the instruments, a command to "Put on your clothes and finish all the preparations!" When the *nabal* is sounded three times, all are to gather in one place.

The young lead *soe* player, however, having stayed up most of the night having a good time, did not hear the first and second round of blasts from the *nabal*. When the third round sounded he barely managed to gather up and put on his uniform, then dashed hurriedly to the meeting place (the performance had just started). At the height of the performance, however, he realized that he had come without putting on his spinning-tasseled hat [*sangmo*]. Because p'ungmul requires handling the instruments with both hands, one's ability in dance must be displayed through the feet and the movement of the head. The lead *soe* player's hat dance [*pup'o norŭm*] in particular is a skill truly produced from "the heel" and is eagerly awaited by all. Soon the time for performing the *pup'ojil* drew near;[29] as he was not able to perform this section,[b] he thought of an oral verse that would go well with the rhythmic pattern they were now playing,[30] saying to his fellow performers:

> *Pŏnggŏji pŏnggŏji hwaettaekkŭt-e kŏm pŏnggŏji*
> *Pŏnggŏji pŏnggŏji multongu-e nae pŏnggŏji*

> [Hat, hat, black hat on the end of the clothes rack,
> Hat, hat, my hat on top of the water jar.][c]

The gist of this verse is: "My hat is on the end of the clothes rack where I hung my clothes last night, girl, so pretend you're going to fetch water, but actually hide the hat inside the water jar and bring it to me." The hat dance was, therefore, performed safely, and it is for this reason that the verse, with the same meaning, continues to be maintained in the p'ungmul rhythmic patterns of certain areas.

This was a rather amusing example, but as the story above illustrates, oral verse is real-life rhythmic patterns [*changdan*] created out of everyday routine,[31] intimately connected to tangible expressions of life's joy and sorrows. This verse is still handed down in the environment around us as specialized wisdom for the transmission of p'ungmul. Let's look at a few more examples:

Pyŏl ttase pyŏl ttase hanŭl chapko pyŏl ttase
[Let's pick stars, let's pick stars,
holding the sky, let's pick stars.]

K'ongkkŏkcha k'ongkkŏkcha turŏngnŏmŏ k'ongkkŏkcha
[Let's pick beans, let's pick beans,
going over to the next ridge, let's pick beans.]

Chulgi chulgi sanjulgi koltchak koltchak muljulgi
[Range, range, mountain range,
valley, valley, stream of water.]

Chwin chwin mun yŏsu pok tŭrŏgangkke mun yŏsu
[Head of the house, head of the house, open the door,
luck is entering in, open the door.]

Ttang-to ttang-to nae ttang ida Chosŏn ttang-to nae ttang ida
[Land, land, my land,
Korea (Chosŏn) is my land.]

Odongdongdong kashinaya panggu tongdong kkijimara pungŏsaekki nollanda
[*Odongdongdong* [farting onomatopoeia], girl,
do not fart, you will startle the young carp.]

Verse such as this is how p'ungmul is transmitted. Oral verse conveys in an excellent manner not only the rhythmic pattern's intonation, length, and accents, but its feeling as well. Rhythmic patterns are usually conveyed by oral mnemonics [*kuŭm*, literally, "mouth sounds"],[32] such as *kaenji kaenji, kaeng—mae kaekkaeng ŭng—mae kaekkaeng*, or *nirigaeng turigaeng turŭp'aeng kkaeng*. Even beginners, when they hear these types of oral mnemonics, are able to clearly understand in an instant the rhythmic pattern's feeling and pacing [*hanbae*].[33] In addition to rhythmic patterns that are transmitted by oral mnemonics are a number of important rhythmic patterns handed down from long ago in the form of oral verse (as shown above) and considered quite poetic, even by today's standards. *Ttang-to ttang-to nae ttang ida, Chosŏn ttang-to nae ttang ida* is most often used for *samch'ae* [literally, "three strokes"] rhythmic pattern,[34] with *pyŏl ttase, pyŏl ttase hanŭl chapko pyŏl ttase* being used for *ich'ae* [literally, "two strokes"] rhythmic pattern.[35] Even today these verses can be heard all over the country. If one must label oral verse, as described above, it would be as a phrase from life's poetry, distinct from verse that is separated from the larger sphere of living written by (so-called) professional poets, such as, "Simone, let's go to the forest where the leaves have fallen."[36] The aesthetic sense of the people [*minjung*] did not rid itself completely of everyday life, nor did it magnify only that considered "beautiful." It did not, at its core, run contrary to communal life [*kongdongch'ejŏk saenghwal*], but rather embraced the lifestyle itself. It was a popular aesthetic sense born not of the rough or crude laborer but of a healthy lifestyle in which one is directly in charge of one's own production, coupled to an affinity for nature and work.

There are many *taraengi* [regional dialect for *tarangi,* or a small strip of rice paddy] in rice fields of remote mountain regions. One rainy day the master of the house, carrying an umbrella, went out to the fields to water them, only to realize one *taraengi* had disappeared. As he continued counting he discovered that a few more *taraengi* were hidden beneath the ridge of his umbrella (called *usan taraengi* [literally, "umbrella *taraengi*"]); through this discovery he realized there were many such *taraengi*.

Having many *taraengi* requires a lot of hard work cutting the grass along the ridge of the paddies. If you postpone cutting the grass, on the pretext of being busy with this and that, you will likely receive a fair amount of teasing by those who pass by. You will be called crude, unable to properly cut the grass along the paddy ridge, and receive severe criticism for your labor skill or ability. Cutting the grass is not, needless to say, done so as to look good for others. If the grass is not cut along the ridge of the paddy, it is difficult to move about to water the field. More than anything, because the wind is not able to circulate well, there is a good possibility of disease spreading among the crops; the grass must, therefore, be cut. It is done not just for these practical reasons—if the grass along the ridge becomes thick, not only the owner himself but other villagers walking by would feel concerned. It would leave them with a rough or unsettled feeling, anxious and ill at ease. This unsettling feeling is unbearable to people who have been raised with farming and its lifestyle—they will have to say something to the owner of the paddy. Therefore, after the grass has been cut over a period of a couple of afternoons, all feel refreshed, as if they have eaten well, saying, "Ah, that's great." Actually, when the grass has been cut, both the paddies and the crops have a beautiful and serene look to them. And when the grass is cut, it must be done stylishly and tidily—if it is uneven, like an unfinished haircut, the owner will without a doubt be criticized for his lack of ability. Linked in this way to a communal lifestyle, a well-cut ridge is one example of the people's aesthetic sense, a sense inseparable from everyday life experience.

Though they may have been ignorant farmers, uneducated and unable to notate their music (with pitches such as *chung, im, mu, hwang,* and *t'ae*),[37] they overcame this lack of formal education with an independence derived from an ability to both accurately and directly solve concrete, real-life situations. The people possessed a wisdom for living that superbly systematized life in all its entirety, brought up as they were naturally with an aesthetic sense inseparable from this life, as seen in the oral verse of p'ungmul.

3D. RHYTHMIC PATTERNS [*KARAK*]: LIFE'S RHYTHM AS TENSION AND RELEASE

Many folklorists focus on p'ungmul primarily as a collection of rhythmic patterns, referring to it as "farmers' music" [*nongak*] possessing a high degree of musicality. Rhythmic patterns are, of course, an important compositional element of p'ungmul and therefore cannot be disregarded as a primary musical factor. Emphasizing only its musicality from the viewpoint of Western genres, however, kills p'ungmul's original features. We are left, as a consequence, with the current situation, in which the original vision we ought to have has become extremely confined or limited.

The composition of p'ungmul's instruments is, for the most part, considered a gift of nature. When the percussion instruments *soe, ching, changgu* [*changgo*], and *puk* and the lone wind instrument *nallari* [*hojŏk*] are well matched, the feet and body are made to move spontaneously, bringing forth cries of *chajirŏjida* [it's exquisite], *p'ujida* [it's abundant], and *shinmyŏng-ŭl kŭlgŏnaeda* [it lifts (or stirs) one's spirit]. As the *soe's* sound, *chagal chagal chagal* [onomatopoeia], comes to a boil, the weighty *ching* sound of the *ching* shelters it both abundantly and moistly. In addition, as the sound rings out of the *changgo's* leather being struck, *k'ongbak k'ongbak,* the *puk* adds depth with its *k'uung k'ung* [onomatopoeia]. The omission of even one of these elements creates a feeling of emptiness in the back of one's head, to the extent that a group's spirit will hardly be stirred; because the makeup of the ensemble has been organized for this very purpose (to assemble group spirit or create oneness), a passive or calm experience is never possible.

The full effect is not complete, however, only with these instruments (as given by nature). In a successful p'ungmul performance, there is a sound more important than the instruments' sound, one that doubles the spiritual energy, namely, the sound of people [the audience]. The irregular sound, coming from all around, of people unable to control themselves serves to heighten the general level of enthusiasm. These sounds, in the form of simple shouting, *ch'uimsae,*[38] clapping, or the heavy breathing of those actively participating, become another unbroken stream of rhythmic patterns, a flow of enthusiastic sound acting as an additional instrument. Furthermore, these sounds are necessary in order for the established instruments (*soe, ching, changgu, puk, nallari*) to play the rhythmic pattern with true *ki;*[39] only when the rhythmic pattern of human sounds is present does the spiritual flavor become complete. Without the participation of this flow of people, a performance becomes unsatisfying and forced.

The character not only of p'ungmul but of all our music shares a similar composition, expressed by the concepts of "produce" [*naego*], "heat up" [*tara*], "tie up" or "tense" [*maekko*], and "unbind" or "release" [*p'unda*].[40] A sound is considered complete when these conditions have been met, based on the underlying principal of tension and release. That is to say, the interplay of tension [*kinjang*] and release [*iwan*] is the life of a sound.[41] Although "producing" (playing with it little by little, skillfully) and "heating up" (drawing out the energy that has just been produced and making it hot) a sound are of course important in the creation of tension, they are both equally needed for release.

The problem lies with how to accomplish this flow of tension and release. One of the most intricately organized rhythmic patterns of the p'ungmul repertoire is *och'ae chilgut* [literally, "five-stroke road ritual"].[42] It is extremely difficult, for it alternates irregularly between duple- and triple-subdivision beats [composite meter], referred to as a "limping beat" [*chŏllŭmgŏrinŭn pakcha*]. *Och'ae chilgut* has been highly praised for its "musicality" as rhythmic music, to the extent that even world-famous musicians are said to be astonished. Although it is unknown where the basis of this musicality originated, the soul of *och'ae chilgut* is thought to lie in the rhythm of labor. It would be a mistake not to consider the flow of tension and release in *och'ae chilgut* as having come out of the rhythm of labor; however, since this rhythm differs from that of present-day labor, we are still truly left with an unsolved mystery. Famous lead *soe* players, as well as *soe* players at the village level, will invariably tell you: "*Oemach'i hŭtchilgut*[d] is not the true *chilgut*. *Chilgut* is only proper and abundant when *chŏpchilgut* [i.e., *och'ae chilgut*] is played."[43] Only when *och'ae chilgut* is played properly and connected closely to the body of the ritual does everyone feel peace of mind.

To say that people are familiar with their bodies is to say that they are familiar with their life rhythm; there is, therefore, a rhythm of labor that matches *och'ae chilgut*. Every form of labor clearly has its own rhythm of tension and release, beginning with a gentle coaxing or fondling, increasing little by little in energy or swing until the rush to the finish. This cycle must be completed properly in order for this swing to be established again (the restoration or resuscitation of work energy). Furthermore, there is not only a rhythm of everyday labor but also a seasonal and a year-long rhythm that combine to create this rhythm of labor. This labor rhythm, this tension and release experienced through a lifestyle of working, is life's rhythm, a rhythm that has developed naturally. Therefore, it suffices to say p'ungmul rhythmic patterns that developed directly from familiar body movements came out of the rhythm of labor, this rhythm of life. Rhythmic patterns that reflect life's rhythm of tension and release are more accurately understood by the *soe* players' expression "weave in and out" [*anp'akkyŏkkŭm*], rather than *och'ae chilgut*.

The composition of p'ungmul performers is fairly deliberate. Even the arrangement of the *kkaengmaegi* [*soe*] is well thought out. For example, the *soe* are ranked in order, beginning with the lead *soe* [*sangsoe*], who is followed by the second *soe* [*pusoe*], third *soe* [*chungsoe*], and fourth *soe* [*chongsoe, kkŭssae,* or *maksae*], and alternating between male *soe* [*sukkaengmaegi*] and female *soe* [*amkkaengmaegi*]. The lead *soe* plays on a male *soe,* producing a broad and open sound with an echo similar to that of crying (*ung ung*). The second *soe* plays a female *soe,* its sound coming to a boil (*chagal chagal*), then trailing off abundantly yet delicately. The remaining *soe* players alternate respectively between male and female *soe.* The lead *soe* holds the position of leading the entire group, while the second *soe* is mainly responsible for just playing. The reason for alternating between male and female *soe* is not only to divide up the role of the sound in order to help create tension and release within the performance as a whole, but also to produce a more abundant harmony of tension and release within the rhythmic pattern itself. The composition of the *soe* as well as the rhythmic pattern should weave between male and female. This is the meaning of "weave in and out."

For example, if we look at the often-played *samch'ae* rhythmic pattern, we see an opening phrase[44] of *ttang—to ttang—to nae—ttang ida,* followed by a closing phrase of *Chosŏn—ttang—to nae—ttang ida.* This alternation of female and male, of opening and closing, is considered weaving in and out. *Soe* players never, therefore, play the same rhythmic pattern continuously, but always alternate between female and male in order to give some variation. On the surface, these may seem to be nothing but diverse variations of the rhythmic pattern for the purpose of putting on a good performance, but there are many other meanings behind these patterns. First of all, there has long been a strong tradition of recognizing the importance of the role of call-and-response [*purŭgo taedap hada*] in rhythmic patterns. Secondly, rhythmic patterns that alternate abundantly between female and male produce a single flow of rhythm for the purpose of heightening enthusiasm. Most important, however, is for this enthusiasm lying at the subconscious level to be pricked or stirred, causing it to be drawn out to the surface. The point is that these various experiences from real-life situations of weaving in and out have been put into practice. As shown by the *samch'ae* example above, this function of weaving in and out is better exhibited by the

Plate 1. *Mun kut* (gate ritual), Koch'ang county, Koch'ang Pangjang Nongaktan

Plate 2. *Tangsan kut* (greeting p'ungmul), Chŏnju city, Imshil P'ilbong Nongak with Iksan Kisebae

Plate 3. *Tangsan kut* (greeting p'ungmul), front *tangsan namu* (spirit tree), Koch'ang county, Koch'ang Pangjang Nongaktan

Plate 4. Chǒnbuk torip kugagwǒn (CTK; North Chǒlla Provincially Established Center for Korean Traditional Performing Arts), Chǒnju city

Plate 5. Author's *changgo* (hourglass-shaped drum) with natural finish

Plate 6. *Ppŏssangmo* hat, Iri city, Iri Nongak

Plate 11. Team and farming flags, Chŏngŭp county, Opening Flag Ceremony

Plate 12. *Yangban* (aristocrat), *chorijung* (Buddhist monk), and *ch'angbu* (actor), Seoul, Imshil P'ilbong Nongak

Plate 13. *Hoegap kinyŏm* (60th birthday commemoration), Chŏnju city

Plate 14. Yi Sangbaek giving lesson to farming cooperative employees, Puan county

Plate 15. Iri Nongak performing at the Seoul Norimadang

Plate 16. Iri Nongak's *changgo nori* ("*changgo* play"), Iri city

flow within the length of a single cycle [*han'gŏri*], rather than just the alternation between female and male within a single rhythmic pattern.

If we look at the flow of weaving in and out in *kaenjigaen* rhythmic pattern,[e] we see a basic rhythmic pattern [*kibon karak*] composed of four beats with triple subdivisions:[45]

| *kaen*—|—*ji* | *gaen*—| *kaen*—|—*ji* | *gaen*—|
| *kaen*—|—*ji* | *gaen*—| *kaen*—|—*ji* | *gaen*—|.

After playing *chilgut* or *pan p'ungnyu* that are "producing and heating up" [*naego tanŭn*] rhythmic patterns, one crosses over by intensely playing the above basic form of *kaenjigaen,* followed by the repetition of a new flow of sound:[46]

| *kaeng*—| | *mae*—| *kaen*—|—*ji* | *gaen*—|
| *kaeng*—| | *mae*—| *kaen*—|—*ji* | *gaen*—|.

One finishes by playing

| *kaeng*—| | *mae*—| *kaen*—|—*ji* | *gaen*—|
| *ŭng*—| | *mae*—| *kaen*—|—*ji* | *gaen*—|,

producing yet another variation (*ŭng* refers to a damping of the *soe* with the left hand, resulting in a silent beat).

One's spirit or energy is truly moved when two *soe* players are able to switch spontaneously between the basic rhythmic pattern and the two variants, creating a long rhythmic flow alternating between female and male. It doesn't end there: by weaving even subtler variations of female and male within the same flow, a tightening [*choida*] effect occurs:

| *chae jaeng* | | *gi*—| *kaen*—|—*ji* | *gaen*—|
| *ŭng*—| | *mae*—| *kaen*—|—*ji* | *gaen*—|

or

| *chae jaeng* | | *gi*—| *kaen*—|—*ji* | *gaen*—|
| *ŭng*—|—*ji* | *gae*—| *kaen*—|—*ji* | *gaen*—|

or

| *chae jaeng* | | *gi*—| *chaeng*—| | *chaeng*—|
| *ŭng*—| *jaeng*—|—*gi* | *chaeng* (etc.).

When this weaving in and out is achieved, either by the continuous repetition of a single rhythmic pattern, by a long or short repetition of two rhythmic patterns, by indiscriminately mixing a number of rhythmic patterns, or by a set repeat of two or three rhythmic patterns, the intensity of the energy produced is both loosened and tightened, completing the flow of a single cycle.[f] This flow gradually tightens until all are dripping with sweat, at which point the performance moves to *ich'ae* [a closing rhythmic pattern], the final stage of ecstasy. The achievement of weaving in and out through *ich'ae* rhythmic pattern marks the completion of an entire cycle. The performers then have a period of relaxation, until the time to commence is again ripe.[g] That is to say, the weaving in and out of the rhythmic pattern itself, the tension and release within the flow of a single cycle, and the flow of weaving in and out in an entire performance are all present in a single performance of p'ungmul.

In this manner, the essence of a rhythmic pattern—its primary function—is not the excellent or beautiful performance of the musician, but rather the establishment of an enthusiastic performance in which people's dormant energy or spirit is stirred up through the tireless efforts of all. As this energy spontaneously tightens, ceaselessly weaving in and out, both the undulations and the intensity of the body movements naturally tighten and relax, gradually creating a more unified group spirit. The need for this gesture of labor to adhere closely to the rhythm of life became the standard by which rhythmic pattern variations developed; this connection became the reason for the rhythmic pattern's existence.

Dance performed in the performance space in the form of simple body movements or the farmers' dance (which naturally bears a resemblance to actual labor), the various stages of weaving in and out, and the single cycle of tension and release all point to an intimate relationship between not only labor and the performance of p'ungmul itself, but with the life rhythm of the farmer in its entirety. A good example of this is the labor flow of rice sowing. The act or performance of rice planting is nearly identical to a performance of p'ungmul in its rhythmic flow: early in the morning, starting with the sowing, the farmer begins by slowly warming up his body into a condition suitable for work; this is followed by an intense period of rice transplanting. The farmer then eats a snack, works, rests, works again, and then eats lunch, after which the body is in a perfect condition to operate efficiently, the work taking on a certain fervor until its final completion. In a similar vein, the performance of p'ungmul, alternating between smaller cycles of tension and release, creates a larger flow. In this way, we see the performance of work and the performance of play sharing a common rhythm.

Rhythmic patterns in p'ungmul should not, therefore, be viewed as the development of musicality, but as the development and functioning of a

spiritual flow. The standard for this development has been the tension and release of group spirit, the flow of tension and release reflected in the labor rhythm
of those who produce [farmers], and a life rhythm centered in this rhythm of
labor.

NOTES TO "*P'UNGMULGUT* AND COMMUNAL SPIRIT"

[a] Furthermore, the mastery of p'ungmul requires that the dance be learned
before the rhythmic patterns. The farmers' dance [*porittae ch'um*], learned through
the very act of doing, serves as a general model for anyone, as demonstrated
by some examples [of onomatopoeia]: *chagu˘ttong chagu˘ttong* (the manner in
which the feet move when walking), *omtchil omtchil* (movement of the upper body
and shoulders), and *kkanttak kkanttak* (movement of both arms being lifted).

[b] In p'ungmul, even though the lead *soe* player is the leader, he or she is
not able to stop in the course of playing according to his or her own wishes.
If the group's spiritual flow is cut off in the middle of the performance, the
lead *soe* player and his or her ability will be severely criticized as both ignorant
and rude.

[c] The *sangmo* hat worn by the lead *soe* player, known by the various names
of *pup'o*, *chŏllip*, or *pŏnggŏji*, is made of black wool or yarn with a *pup'o* or single
pudŭl [literally, "cat tail"] attached to the top.

[d] *Chinggil sandon tatton, chinggiri sandon tatton* is the simple form of *chilgut*
(same structure as the *kukkŏri* rhythmic pattern).[47]

[e] The playing of *kaenjigaen* rhythmic pattern, similar in style to *samch'ae*, is
considered the easiest way to arouse enthusiasm in a performance of "left side"
p'ungmul [*kut*], rushing toward a climax until one can hardly breathe. It is a
"heating up and tensing" rhythmic pattern.

[f] *Han'gŏri* [single section] refers to a smaller flow of energy possessing both
tension and release; a *hanp'an* [single performance] is composed of a number of
sections or cycles [*kŏri*] that gradually build; it refers to the larger flow of energy
present in an entire performance of p'ungmul from start to finish. For example,
when one says, "play *chilgut*" or "produce *chilgut*," it does not mean playing just
the rhythmic pattern called *chilgut*, but rather an entire section of *chilgut*. The
sole purpose is the need to create a single smaller cycle of energy called *chilgut*,
unlike the current and rather strange practice of playing only the *chilgut* rhythmic pattern, stopping whenever one pleases.

This flow of energy exists because of an inherent law of p'ungmul: the ability
to collect or compose enthusiasm becomes the standard by which the character
of p'ungmul is judged. The flow within a section of *chilgut* is very precise (as are
all sections of a performance)—and not only the rhythmic pattern called *chilgut*

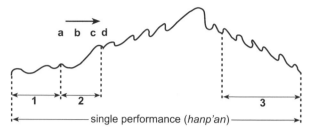

Diagram 1. Representation of *p'ungmul's* spiritual curve. Key: a = produce [*naego*], b = heat up [*tara*], c = tense [*maekko*], d = release [*p'ulta*], 1 = to play with or coax [*ŏrŭgi*], 2 = one cycle [*han'gori*], 3 = group solidification [*p'ajŏmnye*].

and its variations. Looking at the composition of *chilgut* [the entire section], it begins with *chilgut* rhythmic pattern, alternating between the front phrase and the main phrase, followed by a tightening of *chilgut* (in the form of the *kukkŏri* rhythmic pattern, moving toward a *samch'ae* style), a crossing-over [transitional] rhythmic pattern that must be done naturally, *kaenjigaen* rhythmic pattern, the weaving in and out of *kaenjigaen* rhythmic pattern, the tightening of *kaenjigaen* rhythmic pattern, a crossing-over rhythmic pattern, *hwimori* rhythmic pattern (in the style of *ich'ae*), the weaving in and out of *tadŭraegi* rhythmic pattern, a tightening, and a conclusion.[48]

The purpose of this composition is to create spirit or enthusiasm both distinctly and naturally; every cycle has been precisely constructed in this manner for this very purpose, the quality of a section being measured by whether or not it made people play well [both performers and the audience]. The energy of one cycle gathers to create a larger flow of energy (the unified energy of an entire performance); the aim of all p'ungmul, then, can be visualized as a spiritual curve, graphically represented in [diagram 1].

[g] Rhythmic patterns cannot be judged using so-called musicality as a standard. As has been repeatedly emphasized, the reason for a rhythmic pattern's existence is the generation of spirit or oneness as conveyed through life's rhythm. The standard by which this spirit is established is composed of producing, heating up, tensing, and releasing; each rhythmic pattern has its own characteristic role and position for this very purpose. The false and rather absurd view of p'ungmul currently held is based on a narrow concept of musicality grounded in a Western sensibility, resulting in the reorganization and glossing over of p'ungmul rhythmic patterns' original characteristics.

It is desirable to classify these rhythmic patterns according to their characteristic role and position within the overall flow: (1) playing with or coaxing [*ŏrŭnŭn*] rhythmic patterns, (2) producing [*naenŭn*] rhythmic patterns,

(3) producing and heating up [*naego tanŭn*] rhythmic patterns, (4) heating up and tensing [*tara maennŭn*] rhythmic patterns, (5) tensing and releasing [*maekko p'unŭn*] rhythmic patterns, and (6) releasing and again coaxing [*p'urŏ tashi ŏrŭnŭn*] rhythmic patterns. Using *chilgut* [the section] again as an example, the front and main phrases of *chilgut* [the rhythmic pattern] produce sound as coaxing rhythmic patterns, the crossing-over *kaenjigaen* is a heating-up rhythmic pattern, the weaving in and out and tensing of *kaenjigaen* is a heating and stirring-up rhythmic pattern, the crossing-over *hwimori* is a tensing rhythmic pattern, and the weaving in and out until the last breath is a complete tensing rhythmic pattern, the level of tension achieved determining the quality of the following release (at this point the chaotic appearance and the noise of people eating and resting become their own rhythmic pattern). This group of rhythmic patterns is again played in order to produce the next cycle of spirit or oneness.

It becomes, therefore, more desirable to classify rhythmic patterns based on the establishment of this spirit, rather than by the current practice of the number of *ching* strokes (which determines the tempo of a single rhythmic pattern) or by the ambiguous name of a single section of play.[49] Though the system is incomplete, if one classifies the rhythmic patterns from the various sections of the front ritual or performance [*apkut*] of Imshil P'ilbong P'ungmul (Kut)—*moimgut, hullyŏnggut, chilgut, oemach'i ch'ilch'aegut, hohŏgut, p'ungnyugut, panguljin'gut, yŏngsan'gut,* including the rhythmic patterns, group formations, and dances of the entire performance—using the above criteria, we are given the following:

Produce and coax [or play with] with rhythmic patterns: The assembling rhythmic pattern *moimgut;* the shaking-off rhythmic pattern *hullyŏnggut;* the front and main phrases of *chilgut;* the primary phrase of *oemach'i ch'ilch'ae;* the opening and primary phrases of *hohŏgut; p'ungnyu* rhythmic pattern; the shaking-off and coaxing rhythmic pattern *kajin yŏngsan;* and the coaxing rhythmic pattern *panguljin.*

Heat and stir up rhythmic patterns: Kaenjigaen rhythmic pattern of *chilgut* [the section]; *kaenjigaen* rhythmic pattern and the tensing phrase of *oemach'i ch'ilch'aegut; chajin hohŏgut* rhythmic pattern from *hohŏgut* [the section]; *kaenjigaen* and *chajin p'ungnyu* rhythmic patterns from *p'ungnyugut* [the section]; the main phrase of *kajin yŏngsan;* and the main phrase of *chaenŭnggi yŏngsan.*

Tension and release rhythmic patterns: Ich'ae rhythmic pattern of *hullyŏnggut* [the section]; *hwimori* and *tadŭraegi* rhythmic patterns of *chilgut* [the section]; *toen samch'ae, hwimori,* and *tadŭraegi* rhythmic patterns of *oemach'i ch'ilch'aegut* [the section]; the *tchakturŭm* of *hohŏgut* [the section]; *hwimori* rhythmic pattern of *p'ungnyugut* [the section]; the *ssajaebi* of *panguljin'gut;* and *tadŭraegi yŏngsan* rhythmic pattern.

Release rhythmic patterns: The contented sound after the spirit or enthusiasm [*shinmyŏng*] has been exhausted,[50] the last moment of release as *shinmyŏng* still lingers, the praise and evaluation of the ongoing section of performance, and the sounds accompanying eating and drinking all contribute to the rhythmic pattern of human sounds.

The establishment of *shinmyŏng* as conveyed by life's rhythm appears not only in the tension and release of a single cycle but within the structure of an entire performance. Each rhythmic pattern and individual section has its own prescribed role and position in the creation of an overall flow of *shinmyŏng*. Looking at an outline of P'ilbong P'ungmul's front ritual or performance composition as an example, we see the the order, strictly observed, of *moimgut, hullyŏnggut, chilgut, oemach'i ch'ilch'aegut, hohŏgut, p'ungnyugut, panguljin'gut,* and *yŏngsan'gut. Moimgut* and *hullyŏnggut* as opening sections have the role and position of alerting the musicians to the performance's commencement; *chilgut* and *oemach'i ch'ilch'aegut* are producing sections; and *hohŏgut, p'ungnyugut,* and *panguljin'gut* are producing and heating-up sections. The highlight of the "left side" repertoire is *yŏngsan'gut,* which acts as a closing section, depicted by a large spiritual curve within the overall flow of *shinmyŏng;* it serves as a bridge to the following back ritual or performance whose focus is on group playing, rather than the playing of individuals. In performances today, sections of rhythmic patterns possessing these attributes are arranged arbitrarily and in no particular order, resulting in a dead p'ungmul that bears no relation whatsoever to the people's life rhythm or flow of *shinmyŏng.*

☯

THE *MINJUNG* WORLDVIEW

Beginning with the opening epigraph and continuing on through the translated passages, we see a number of common threads that present a remarkably unified theoretical approach to interpreting the place and role of p'ungmul activity. *Minjung's* holistic worldview encompasses and embraces p'ungmul's connection to the realms of labor, ritual, play or entertainment, and art, with special attention being paid to the shamanistic underpinnings of most of this tradition. In both O's and Kim's work we witness the beautiful intersection of mythos and logos where the logical, pragmatic details are masterfully provided to guide us toward an understanding of p'ungmul as a model activity occupying the same symbolic space as myth. The overarching leitmotif here is the participatory nature of the art form, with communal, joint action as the ultimate goal. An egalitarian work and performance ethic serves as counterpoint to this theme.

In the next chapter I will delve into the lesson process and the teaching strategies of my two principal drumming mentors. *Minjung* theory and its emphasis on oral transmission (particularly as elucidated in Kim Inu's text) resurfaces as a player in my teachers' broader narratives of assimilation as they negotiate the space between ideology, cultural asset policy, and the practical challenges of day-to-day instruction.

Kujŏn shimsu. (Transmitted by mouth, taken in by heart.)

—Korean proverb

4

Transmitted by Mouth, Taken In by Heart

The lesson, with the teacher-pupil relationship at its core, has long held the imagination of the anthropological-ethnomusicological community. This is entirely fitting, considering how central this process of transmission is to the continuation of musical tradition, and for what it reveals about broader societal attitudes concerning questions of aptitude and talent (Brinner 1995). Under ideal circumstances this often sacred bond represents a combination of respect, admiration, discipline, and profound personal sacrifice. Issues of pacing, pedagogical style, and personal approaches toward the act of teaching are generally of primary interest, yet of only slightly less importance are the circumstances under which a student meets his or her mentor and how this relationship changes over time. These latter, seemingly "extra" details expose the interactive, fluid, and negotiated realms of the lesson that almost always occur when "outsiders" engage a foreign tradition as participant-observers (Bakan 1999: 279–333; Williams 2001: 121–37). Such contextual information also provides valuable guidance for others in the planning stage of working or studying in the particular cultural arena.

This chapter chronicles the complex assimilation process underpinning the ongoing teaching strategies of my principal drumming mentors. Their stories tell of both subtle shifts and foundational changes taking place within a single lifetime, accounts that are all the more remarkable in light of my mentors' reliance on (and subservience to) the cultural asset system. What has changed in this narrative is that I am now acting, for the first time, as a full participant. There is little question that my presence as a foreign researcher influenced the overall lesson experience, to a greater or lesser extent depending on the teacher. My mentors' ruminations on this topic are reproduced at length in the pages that follow.

Underlying these various historical, personal, and philosophical encounters is the conflict or tension between the oral and the literate. P'ungmul traditionally was taught, conceptualized, and appreciated solely by oral/ aural means, a process expressed and preserved poetically in the opening epigraph of this chapter. Though Kim and Yi keenly appreciated the advantages of a cultural asset policy that brought them name recognition and financial remuneration, they also, conversely, felt constrained and threatened by notation and other forms of official documentation required by their institutional supporters, for reasons that will be outlined below. Both men nevertheless found creative—if not subversive at times—ways to incorporate their roots in orality and aurality, regardless of surface appearances. To this end I have included examples of lessons conducted beyond the formal confines of the studio or practice room.

KIM HYŎNGSUN

From the Beginning

I first saw Kim Hyŏngsun perform with Iri Nongak at the Seoul Norimadang during the summer of 1994.[1] It was the first live performance of p'ungmul I had ever attended, and the memory of it lingered long after that initial experience. As my plans for fieldwork developed over the next year, I decided to contact Kim in the hope of securing institutional sponsorship for my scholarship and visa. My initial idea was to establish a base in North Chŏlla province's capital city of Chŏnju, then to look outward to Iri and the surrounding environs for research data. When a telephone call was made to the North Chŏlla Provincially Established Center for Korean Traditional Performing Arts (Chŏnbuk torip kugagwŏn, hereafter abbreviated as CTK) in Chŏnju, however, the secretary informed me that Kim had a studio in the building next door.[2] Kim apparently spent the majority of his time teaching in Chŏnju, leaving instruction at his home institute in Iri in the hands of teaching assistants. Kim was both interested and pleased during this very first conversation; he accepted me right then as a student and sent a letter of sponsorship within the month. The letter was as cordial as it was brief—he looked forward to meeting me and would give me a two-hour lesson once a week at the CTK and waive the lesson fees. No further instructions were included, regarding either repertoire or length of study, and none would follow before my arrival in Chŏnju the fall of 1995.

Our first meeting was accentuated by mutual misunderstanding. I had naively assumed I would be receiving individual lessons similar in type and content to those I had taken at the National Center for Korean Traditional Performing Arts (Kungnip kugagwŏn) in Seoul the previous two summers. Kim, however, had assumed that as a foreigner I would naturally commute from Seoul once a week, since living in Chŏlla province would be too difficult or inconvenient. Our surprise was reciprocal. That first day I found myself part of a beginner's class numbering nearly fifty, a class, I was told, that met every day. That suited me quite well, I responded, because the small house I had recently rented was only a five-minute walk away. We modified our study plan that very day; this first encounter was to sustain an ongoing inside joke between the two of us, lasting well up until my final departure from Korea.

GENERAL LESSON FORMAT

I was first impressed by the size of the CTK in Chŏnju: fifteen full-time faculty taught an average of nearly 1,100 students (see plate 4). Classes were offered in the vocal genres of *p'ansori* (narrative song accompanied by drum), *minyo* (folksongs), and *shijo* (sung poetry); *kosu* (*p'ansori* accompaniment); the string instruments *kayagŭm* (twelve-string plucked zither), *kŏmun'go* (six-string plucked zither), *haegŭm* (two-string bowed fiddle), and *ajaeng* (eight-string bowed zither); the wind instruments *tanso* (small end-blown bamboo flute) and *taegŭm* (large transverse bamboo flute); dancing; and p'ungmul (*nongak* on the official lists). The p'ungmul course averaged 150 students per term and was the largest single class in the institute. Kim had taught in Chŏnju since 1987, despite having spent a considerable amount of time and energy raising money for a p'ungmul educational institute in his current hometown of Iri (see figure 4.1).[3]

Kim was driven into Chŏnju early each morning by his youngest son (he had nine children), approximately a thirty-five-minute ride, and was picked up in the late afternoon after his teaching responsibilities were completed. Though Kim taught in Chŏnju for various reasons, the one he most often expressed verbally was related to finances: the institute in Iri barely broke even and relied on out-of-province student groups during term breaks to make up the difference. Even though Kim felt very close to his Chŏnju

Figure 4.1. Iri Nongak Educational Institute, Iri city

pupils, a certain degree of bitterness emerges in his description of the more affluent capital city: "Most students come from Chŏnju. They're all big spenders, the people who sign up here for p'ungmul class. They're mostly well-to-do. In our class, a lot of the women are housewives with college degrees, and many of their husbands are college professors, state employees, court clerks, all kinds of professions. So a lot of these housewives have money and social status."

P'ungmul class was primarily a *changgo* class, divided into three levels: beginner (*kich'oban*), intermediate (*yŏn'guban*), and advanced (*chŏnmunban*). Each level met for an hour once a day, five days a week. The "piece" being taught was from the entertainment-oriented portion of the p'ungmul repertoire, the *p'an kut*. The *p'an kut* was traditionally performed after a long day of communal labor or ritual fund-raising to entertain village residents and their guests. Kim, however, limited the use of this term to presentational performances offered by professional traveling troupes.

Classes met as a group, with lessons and practice considered essentially the same activity. Few students ever took their instruments home over the weekend to practice, and the tape recording of lessons was, as a rule, not allowed. Each of the three levels had its own specific content.

Beginner

Because of the intricate rhythms and relatively sophisticated dance steps required at the higher levels, the beginning class was taught from a seated position. The first month of each new term was spent acquainting the incoming students with the basic order of strokes. Each rhythmic pattern was played in turn by Kim or a teaching assistant a few times, after which the entire class joined in. The name of the particular pattern, as well as its historical background and performance context, was seldom if ever given; students who wanted to know more about these subjects usually asked more senior members or Kim himself in private after the class was finished. For the majority of my fieldwork period, rhythmic patterns were presented in roughly chronological order, moving from the first movement (*madang*) through to the fourth (each movement is considered a self-contained unit, with the movements generally progressing internally from a slower to a faster tempo).[4] This was true until July 1996, when Kim changed the lesson order: *och'ae chilgut*, the first main rhythmic pattern and perhaps the most difficult, was now introduced for the first time at the intermediate level. This was perhaps a reflection of the policy practiced at the institute in Iri, where *och'ae chilgut*, as well as the fourth movement, or solo drum dance, was taught at the more advanced levels.

Once all the rhythmic patterns had been learned satisfactorily, the studio became a place where students could go every day to play through the entire piece a number of times in order to gain confidence, as well as to increase playing speed. During this second phase of the beginner's class, students were occasionally allowed to ask direct questions. It was at this point that I noticed a curious habit of Kim's: whenever there was a question or problem with a particular passage, he would revert to what seemed to be a simplified version of the pattern we had learned. A later conversation with him revealed a very important concept, one that will be dealt with in more detail throughout this remaining chapter: the existence of a primary form (*wŏnbak*) of each rhythmic pattern.[5] Kim noted that although professional players were all aware of this form, which varied somewhat depending on the individual, there was nevertheless a more involved style that performers usually played. I will, for lack of an indigenous term, refer to the latter as the "performance form."[6]

Intermediate

Students at the intermediate level were taught how to tie the *changgo* to the body and were led through the basic dance steps. Because there was always some overlap between new members and those who had been in the class for a term, Kim rarely stopped to demonstrate a particular step.

Students were thrown in with little or no preparation, which often accounted for a considerable amount of confusion during the first few weeks,
if not a few bruised knuckles and chipped instruments as people went spinning into each other. Only much later into the course would Kim stop a
practice to single out an individual having trouble and gently reprimand
him or her, though compensation was allowed in the form of playing the
primary, and hence simpler, form of the rhythmic pattern. It was at this
stage that Kim began teaching rhythmic variations (*pyŏnbak*):[7] a number of
patterns had set variations that could theoretically be played at any point
during the playing of the particular pattern. From this emerged a tripartite
model of rhythmic construction: *wŏnbak* (primary form) → performance
form (elaboration on the *wŏnbak*) → *pyŏnbak* (rhythmic variation).

Advanced

The goal of the final, advanced stage of lessons was the smooth integration
of hand and leg movements, with special attention paid to the timing and
placement of the feet. Additional rhythmic variations were taught as well. Iri
Nongak's fourth *soe* player, Yi Hosun, accompanied the advanced class acting
essentially as lead *soe,* leading the group through the elaborate ground formations (*chinbŏp*).[8] Iri Nongak's acting lead *sogo* player-dancer, Cho Myŏngja,
often served as second *soe* under Yi (Cho is interviewed in chapter 6).

Memorization was emphasized at all levels. Kim had reluctantly developed a shorthand notation, but he surrendered it only if he was pressured,
and it was seldom allowed during the actual lesson. Kim offered little explanation as to why he was opposed to the creation and use of notation, but
I believe that in general he thought the written record threatened the nature of his music making and its relationship to the tradition, stymieing the
natural flux and flow inherent in the lesson process and larger performance
contexts (see Small 1998: 115). From the perspective of my background in
Western musical training, I was interested to see that progress was assessed
primarily by the amount of time the student had invested in study, not by
his or her having achieved a certain technical level. A student was allowed
to proceed from the beginning to the intermediate level after six months;
the intermediate class advanced after an additional year and a half, and the
advanced class graduated after three more years—a total of five years of
instruction. When asked how this method differed from that he had undergone as a youth, Kim responded:

> It's *totally* different. When I was learning, we never studied in such a systematic
> [*ch'egyejŏk-ŭro*] way, sitting down with the teacher up in front like they do at

the Chŏnju center. We never studied like that—there was no place for that kind of study. These days anybody can do it, as long as they are able to pay. When we were young and learning, it was far from this type of environment, so far. If you wanted to play *changgo,* you had to walk twenty to thirty *li* [8–12 km] and work with the teacher at whatever he was doing, helping with the tilling of the soil, if that was what he was doing. You would follow him around. And whenever he took a break, even for just a minute, you could sit down and ask him a question about playing. In olden times, even if you had played for thirty or forty years, you often didn't know how to play *och'ae chilgut* rhythmic pattern. These days they learn how to play it first.

Kim made a notable exception in my case, however, allowing me to join the intermediate and advanced classes simultaneously within my first month of study. My previous experience on the *changgo,* coupled to a heightened dedication motivated by time constraints, apparently impressed him enough that he could temporarily break with convention.

Technique

Changgo (Seated)

The student begins by sitting in a cross-legged position behind the drum so that the right head of the instrument bisects the body along an imaginary line.[9] This forces the left arm to extend fully to reach the left head, the proper position when standing and playing. The right foot is then placed at the base of the right drumhead, acting as a brace to stop the drum from sliding to the right from the force of the left-hand stroke.

The stick (*yŏlch'ae*) is held in the right hand with the thumb and second, third, and fourth fingers; the first finger is left in a relaxed position. This represents the "closed" position and is responsible for the basic stroke, *tŏ* (or, alternatively, *tŏk* or *tta*): the stick strikes the right drumhead and is left in contact with the inner rim, the speed of the stroke causing the tip of the stick to rebound sharply off the center of the head. Alternately, the second through fourth fingers can be relaxed, creating an "open" position that is used when striking the drumhead lightly with only the tip of the stick, referred to as *ki*. A closed-position stroke, *tŏ*, preceded by an open-position stroke, *ki,* becomes *kidŏk*. The speed of the *ki* stroke is inversely proportional to the tempo of the rhythmic pattern: the faster the tempo, the more "measured" (even) the *ki* stroke; the slower the tempo, the more closely *ki* resembles a quick grace note.

The mallet (*kunggulch'ae*) is held in the left hand. The handle is grasped lightly between the thumb and first finger at the crotch and left to hang loosely, acting as a pivot point. The first, second, and third fingers are then gently closed over the top of the handle, with the fourth finger placed below it. Loud strokes are produced by a combination of downward arm speed and a quick flexing of the fingers at the point of impact—the hand squeezes to make a fist, then quickly releases to let the tip of the mallet rebound off the head. Softer strokes are produced with only a flexing of the fingers; both loud and softer strokes are referred to as *k'ung*. The mallet can be used to strike the left drumhead or to cross over the body of the instrument to strike the right, though in most cases the latter is a softer stroke (the central concepts of strong [*kang*] and weak [*yak*] did not surface until the interview with Kim recorded in chapter 6). When the left and right hands strike the drum at the "same time," the sound produced is called *tŏng*.[10]

The only words of instruction Kim gave at this stage were to keep the body in an upright but relaxed posture and to avoid excessive movements of the head.

Changgo (Dancing)

The first order of business in learning the dancing was learning how to tie the drum to the body. This is achieved by knotting the end of a long cord of cotton cloth on the drum, then pulling it behind the back and over the player's right shoulder, looping it around hooks on the drum, repulling the cord around the waist, then looping and securing the cord back on the drum with a final knot. The orientation of the right drumhead is similar to that when the player is seated: resting comfortably in the center of the body near the point where the abdomen meets the rib cage.

"Right side"–style p'ungmul dancing is known for its relative complexity and highly synchronized foot movements. The various steps are better illustrated through musical and movement notation (see the Web site provided in the author's note), but the basic step should, in Kim's words, "resemble walking on a tightrope." One foot is placed directly in front of the other when moving forward, so that the toes strike the ground before the rest of the foot; the motion is often accompanied by a gentle rising of the body on the back foot before the toes make contact. The effect is one of lightness and elegance.[11] This movement is coupled with a slight turn to the right of the upper body when the left (back) head is struck with the mallet, and to the left when the right (front) head is struck. This is done to accommodate the path of the mallet as it moves from the back to the front drumhead, as well as for a specific visual effect.

Kim admitted that he himself had developed much of the choreography he taught, which was therefore unique: "Many of the rhythmic patterns

I play these days weren't really played in the past. I should say, rather, that the patterns themselves may have been played by others, but they didn't have the body movement. These movements, especially those of the feet, I created through my own private study and contemplation."

BEYOND THE FORMAL LESSON: SIXTIETH BIRTHDAY COMMEMORATION (*HOEGAP KINYŎM*)

Almost any occasion could be (and frequently was) celebrated by Kim's CTK p'ungmul class, whether it was a birthday, a term graduation, an engagement, or even the first few days of good weather after snow or a heavy rainstorm. An outside observer could have easily gotten the impression that his class existed solely for the giving of parties, with the learning of the rhythmic patterns as a pleasant side benefit. Every few weeks a group composed of Kim Hyŏngsun, some *changgo* and *soe* players from Iri Nongak, and students from all three levels at the center would go out to a large field or park, prepare and consume large amounts of food and alcohol,[12] then play p'ungmul for a few hours. These occasions were always a great chance to meet fellow students one wouldn't usually see during the course of the regular lesson day and were particularly valuable for me as a an introduction to playing with Iri Nongak itself.

One day in May 1996, Kim told me there would be a performance the coming weekend, and that I would be picked up in front of my home by his youngest son. I was told to bring my p'ungmul outfit and a set of drumsticks, and that I would be gone for a few hours. When the van arrived late in the morning of the day appointed, however, I noticed that everyone in the vehicle had dressed up (with women wearing jewelry)—not the sort of attire people wore for our usual class outings. When I asked where we were going, I was told we would be visiting an apartment complex on the edge of town. Only after we arrived did I realize that I had been invited to a sixtieth birthday commemoration. I knew from previous conversations with my in-laws that in olden times the survival of an elder to his or her sixtieth birthday was a truly auspicious event, and even though in modern times many Koreans live past this age, this particular birthday is celebrated in the grandest fashion.

The party was being held for a Mrs. Kim, a close personal friend of Kim Hyŏngsun and many of the members of Iri Nongak. The nursery of the apartment building where she lived had been converted into a small banquet hall, with long lines of tables dominating the interior space. A few tables were placed outside, and a medium-sized area had been cleared in the parking lot for a later performance of p'ungmul. The next five hours were spent in a cycle of eating, drinking, singing, and dancing. A master of ceremonies had been hired to accompany singing and to provide a disco beat on a synthesizer for group dances, but the acknowledged main events of the day were a mini–*p'an kut* performance by a quartet from Iri Nongak and a larger *p'an kut* event in which almost everyone present participated.[13] This latter event was for me the most interesting and noteworthy, for all invited participants were given a chance to play on any one of the four core percussion instruments, something I had never seen in previous performance contexts. I also noticed that the teachers themselves occasionally traded gongs and drums, and that some of them even experimented with rhythmic patterns and variants from other regional traditions, experimentation that went against official cultural asset policy (see plate 13 and figure 4.2).

As the party drew to a close, Kim pulled me aside to explain that this was the true reason for p'ungmul's existence: to bring everyone closer together in a festive setting. He hoped I had gained a greater understanding of how Koreans traditionally celebrated when they gathered and of how p'ungmul could be adapted to any number of different social situations. He especially wanted me to grasp the fluid and changing nature of the tradition, how it might exist free from more official or formal dictates.

Though there was little question that p'ungmul still held a place of importance for many Koreans living out in the provinces, the memory of an

Figure 4.2. *Hoegap kinyŏm*, Chŏnju city

event I had attended only three days earlier sobered my enthusiasm for that day spent at the birthday commemoration. A look at figure 4.3 reveals how even in a city like Chŏnju, far away from the metropolis of Seoul and its attendant Western tastes, there was a marked difference—even a clash—in the social and leisure habits of the Korean populace. The Western reception recounted there reflected a broader trend I witnessed time and time again, namely, a moving away from traditional Korean dining and social practices in more formalized settings toward more Western ones. This was perhaps always true, but I couldn't help but wonder how secure the place of the day's events I had just enjoyed was in the future annals of North Chŏlla province history.

YI SANGBAEK

In the Beginning

I first met Yi Sangbaek on a Wednesday afternoon at the CTK in Chŏnju during a drum lesson with Kim Hyŏngsun. Yi had come with a friend to observe the proceedings to determine whether or not they would officially enroll. I immediately noticed them that day, not because they were new—people were always stopping in to watch or talk to Kim—nor because they were younger than most of the other students (which they were), but rather because of their fearlessness. Yi and his friend began practicing their dance steps from the very first day, weaving in and out of students at will, even standing directly behind Kim as he was demonstrating. Though the general public revered Kim with a certain awe, as if they were in the presence of royalty or even a god, Yi responded to him as more of a curiosity to be pondered or an interesting toy to be figured out.

The next day I was invited to join them as they took a smoke during a break. They asked all the standard Korean questions: What's your name? Where are you from? How old are you? Are you married? Then Yi offered an interesting proposal: How would I like to study p'ungmul (p'ungmulgut was Yi's preferred term) with them back at their university? I had only been in Chŏnju for three weeks and was interested in learning more about the student scene, so I agreed to get together with them that weekend. On Saturday I met Yi and three other members of his student p'ungmul circle (tongari) in Samnye, where their university was located (Samnye is the next small town just north of Chŏnju). After six hours of heavy drinking, talking, and singing at a local noraebang (literally, "song room"—the Korean version of karaoke), Yi unfolded his plan. I was to come once a week, every Wednesday, to spend the morning and early afternoon with

Figure 4.3. A comparison of party receptions attended by the author in May 1996

Event	Violin and piano recital	60th birthday commemoration
Presenting	Chŏnju University violin professor and visiting Australian pianist	Personal friend of Kim Hyŏngsun and Iri Nongak
Location	Bountiful Harvest Bakery [pastry and pizza shop]	Taeu Apartments nursery
Seating	Pairs of tables (6 people per group); high tables with chairs	Six tables together (45 people per group); low tables with cushions
Clothing	Three-piece suits and tuxedos; women in Western-style dresses	Casual, some in sport coats; women in traditional dress (in general)
Languages spoken	Korean, English, German, Italian	Korean
Food	Rolls, cream pastries, strawberries, rolled sushi (made with bread and sandwich meats)	Eggs, clams, pickled cabbage (*kimch'i*), rice, seafood stew, beef barbecue, cucumbers, apples
Drink	Brown tea, black tea, coffee, milkshakes	Brown tea, 7-Up, beer, hard liquor (*soju*), rice wine (*makkŏlli*)
Entertainment	None	Korean *karaoke* (*noraebang*), unaccompanied folksong, dancing
Highlights	1. Speech by local Rotary Club President	1. Yi Hosun (fourth *soe*) placing bottle caps in eyes and playing metal serving tray with spoons in p'ungmul style
	2. Introduction of visiting foreign guests	2. Older woman student in a beggar's outfit and make-up tying a Coke bottle around her waist to resemble a penis, then gyrating at the hips to the beat of a drum machine (see fig. 4.4)

him learning the p'ungmul repertoire. Without knowing specifically what I would be studying, either the music or the instrument, or knowing anything about his past or future goals, I agreed. And so my relationship with Yi began.

Yi later admitted to me that he had never spoken to a foreigner before. His friends were even reluctant to meet me, especially because many of them had demonstrated against the strong American military presence on the peninsula. Yi was fascinated, if not baffled, by the "hairy giant" who had come all the way to Chŏlla province just to study drumming; this was the primary reason he gave for inviting me out to talk that second day. The weekend drinking binge is worth highlighting as well, in that it seems to point to an additional example of an alcoholic "rite of passage," a preliminary testing ground to ascertain my willingness to become part of the group (see note 12). Most of my initial meetings with p'ungmul performers and scholars were accompanied by hearty drinking, with the notable exception

Figure 4.4. "Life of the party," Puan county, Puan Nongaktan

of Kim Hyŏngsun, who had given up alcohol early in life (see his interview again in chapter 1).

PRELIMINARY DEFINITIONS

Yi spent a good portion of our first lesson explaining his situation at school and the background of the music I would be studying. Yi was in his fourth and final year as a broadcast journalism major at Usŏk University. He was president of Ch'adolp'ae (ch'adol, "pebble"; p'ae, "troupe" or "team"), a p'ungmul and t'al ch'um (mask dance) circle boasting the largest membership among the university's fifteen groups. His club played and promoted the "left side" (chwado) style of p'ungmul; the official title of the rhythmic patterns I would be learning was "Honam [Chŏlla province] chwado Imshil [county] P'ilbong [village] kut [p'ungmul]," a repertoire based directly on the group from P'ilbong in North Chŏlla province designated as an intangible cultural asset.

The first order of business was to correct my then "bad habit" of using the term nongak. In olden times, Yi pointed out, this activity was most commonly referred to as p'ungmul or p'ungmulgut and was an integral part of village society. P'ungmul was played everywhere throughout Korea, generally regardless of occupation, as accompaniment to labor, ritual, and entertainment. Under Japanese occupation, however, the practice was limited to just farmers, hence the name nongak (literally, "farmers' music"). Yi felt that by narrowing its scope and degrading it as an activity, the Japanese, as well as Korean scholars sympathetic to them, were able to undermine its strength and role as a collective power behind social insurrection. During the next few months, other circle members would echo this sentiment in often very unsubtle ways.[14]

Yi's knowledge of p'ungmul rhythms was quite extensive, yet he felt it was important for me to first learn the core or standard "piece" of the "left side" repertoire, the p'an kut. He explained that although technically speaking the p'an kut was entertainment oriented, it traditionally came at the end of a long day of fund-raising and supplications for a village's well-being. The latter context was often called madang palbi/madang palki, literally, "treading on the earth [or yard]," and contained most, if not all, of the rhythms used in ritual p'ungmul performances. Yi felt that nowadays ritual events such as madang palbi were difficult to find; even for those living in the countryside, it had become "too noisy" (shikkŭrŏpta). He attributed a large part of this attitude to the Japanese occupation, when much of this practice was banned under the pretext of its negative influence as "superstition" (mishin).

Later, government policy and village restructuring through programs such as the *Saemaŭl undong* (New Community Movement) further disrupted traditional village life.[15]

As lessons progressed, Yi felt it was important for him to point out to me the differences between the "left side" and "right side" style of performance, presentation, and ideology (in the list below the Korean terms *chwado* and *udo,* respectively, will be used to unclutter the text). He strongly believed that both styles had sprung from the same source in the not-so-distant past, but he also thought I should keep them distinct in my own mind, at least in the earlier stages of study. "Left side" defining characteristics were always taught in context in conjunction with the learning of a particular rhythmic pattern, but because comments were often repeated and scattered over the period of a number of months, I have condensed them into one list, in no particular order:

1. *Chwado* ("left side") is best defined musically as "fast and short."
2. There is a common misperception that *udo* ("right side") is complicated and *chwado* is simple. On the contrary, *chwado* is complicated, with many rhythmic patterns and movements; *udo* is relatively simple in this regard.
3. If you play *chwado,* your IQ will improve (said a bit tongue-in-cheek).
4. *Chwado* is more famous for its *p'an kut* and *tanch'e nori* (group play), *udo* for its *kaein nori* (individual play).
5. *Chwado*'s true character or flavor (*mat*) lies in the proper balance of *kang* and *yak* (literally, "strong and weak"), meaning the dynamic shape or internal accents of the drum and gong strokes.
6. *Chwado* sound should be "played plentifully [or abundantly]" (*pujige ch'inda*), to quote P'ilbong's lead *soe* player, Yang Sunyong (now deceased).
7. Musically speaking, *chwado* has many "climaxes" (Yi used the English word), while *udo* is basically level or even (*p'yŏng p'yŏng hada*).
8. The *chwado p'an kut* is distinguished by its use of *hwimori* as a closing rhythmic pattern at the end of each movement; *udo,* by its use of *samch'ae.*
9. One can honestly learn all the basic rhythmic patterns of the *chwado p'an kut* in one week (not this author's opinion), but acquiring the proper feeling, flavor, or character requires a great amount of time and effort.
10. *Udo*-style dancing is highly coordinated, with everyone basically matching their feet and body movements to each other. In *chwado,* players move according to their own feeling, with more emphasis placed on personal expression. According to Yi, "*Chwado* is not great to look at" (*Poginŭn an chot'a*).

11. *Chwado* dance movement is concentrated in the head and upper body (*unnorǔm*); *udo,* in the feet and lower body (*araennorǔm*).

12. The *udo p'an kut* form is basically fixed, while *chwado* has much more flexibility.

13. *Chwado* is more *soe* oriented; *udo* focuses more on the *changgo.*

14. *Chwado* has deeper roots in "original" village music making, as evidenced by the large number of folklore writings dealing with the *chwado* tradition of p'ungmul.[16] *Udo* is more a mixed or *tchamppong* (a seafood dish with various kinds of fish and vegetables mixed together) style, taking one rhythm from here, another from there.[17]

15. *Chwado* is masculine in character; *udo* is feminine.

This list is presented only to demonstrate *perceived* differences in the repertoire and to show the importance that performers from both sides (right/west and left/east) of North Chŏlla province placed on distinguishing what they did as separate from and often superior to the style practiced by their counterparts. I will return to this theme with concluding thoughts in chapter 6 (a more detailed discussion of the left-right dichotomy is provided in Hesselink 1998c: 513–29, 1999).

GENERAL LESSON FORMAT

The first lesson set the precedent, in terms of form, for the majority of the lessons to follow. Yi and I would meet at his p'ungmul circle room at Usŏk University every week for a three- to four-hour individual lesson that included a short break for something to eat. I use the word "individual" loosely: friends and fellow members of the circle would stop by for a while every thirty minutes or so to listen, talk, or even participate by picking up a drum or gong and playing along. Circle members spent a considerable amount of time away from the group practicing on their own, and I was expected to do the same. This reflected one of Yi's practical as well as aesthetic views: although it is important for the entire group to be present for the full enjoyment of p'ungmul, a player is able to find satisfaction playing alone (in other words, personal fulfillment is a worthwhile goal). Yi had no reservations about lessons being tape recorded, though he had never done so with his own teachers. As my lessons advanced, he even began to favor the method of playing a particular rhythmic pattern in its entirety "for the tape recorder," so as to provide a model for me to work from when I was away from his guidance.

Yi decided to begin with the *changgo* and move on to other instruments as time allowed. He felt that mastering the *changgo* gave one such a good core understanding of the rhythmic patterns that learning other instruments would then require little effort, at least in regard to the order of the strokes. This same opinion was expressed almost verbatim by the acting lead *soe* player at the CTK in Chŏnju only a month later (Yi Hosun 1995: personal communication), calling into question the basic assumption of many p'ungmul and folk scholars that the fundamental rhythm lies in the *soe* line (e.g., Yi Pohyŏng 1984; Kim Hyŏnsuk 1987; Chŏng Pyŏngho 1994). Lessons followed a basic order: Yi would begin by giving the name of the movement (*madang*) and the rhythmic patterns (*karak*) it contained, then follow with a brief explanation of their place within the overall performance of the *p'an kut*. He then wrote verbal notation, or oral mnemonics (*kuŭm*), in my notebook and demonstrated them by singing to show the pattern's pacing and the internal structure of strong and weak strokes. Yi made it very clear that every rhythmic pattern contained strong and weak strokes (by extension, "beats"), with strong strokes tending to coincide with the sounding of the *ching*. Learning a rhythmic pattern correctly meant understanding its feeling (*nŭkkim*) or its "flavor" (*mat*); hence, a rhythm played well had *mat* (*mashi itta*), but a rhythm played poorly did not (*mashi ŏpta*).[18]

Yi would then proceed to play the rhythmic pattern as given through oral mnemonics on the *changgo*, stressing that this was the pattern in its simple or primary form, namely, the *wŏnbak*. After he had repeated it a number of times, I was encouraged to join him, and we would continue playing together until he was satisfied I had a feeling for the basic order and flow. I was then instructed to play alone, receiving criticism where necessary, at which point he would accompany me on the *soe* to give a feeling of how the two lines fit together (this process was reversed when learning the *soe*). This last step was continued for fifteen to twenty minutes per pattern, after which I was taught the appropriate rhythmic variations (*pyŏnbak*). (Regarding repetition, Yi said at a later lesson that it was "the only way to really get the feel of a rhythmic pattern.") We then took a break, giving us both the chance to relax and Yi the opportunity to give the background (if any) of the rhythmic pattern and its musical similarities to any other patterns in the "left side" or "right side" repertoire. Questions were allowed and encouraged at any point during the lesson.

After three months of study, I asked Yi how the method of training I was receiving compared to that he had undergone during his early university days. His answer is worth quoting in its entirety:

> In our case, when we went in for training at a cultural asset institute, it usually lasted about fifteen days at the longest. But then again our team was unusual

in that we would go for a ten-day program, but after the other teams left we would stay and practice and receive instruction as long as we wanted. As for our teacher, he wasn't there all day. He would come about an hour a day for instruction, kind of to look after us. The rest of the time we were left alone to practice. Sometimes we practiced with just oral mnemonics, other times by playing.

It was always group lessons. With "left side" style, there is never personal instruction, unless they are teaching their son (or a similar circumstance). It's almost always group lessons. The sons of the human cultural assets were the principal instructors for the practice sessions away from the main teacher. Because the sons are the main disciples, there is little need to foster any more disciples. We will be considered the master's disciples as well, but not directly. Of course, there are direct disciples among some of the local village p'ungmul members.

In playing the *kkwaenggwari* (*soe*), we usually learn by imitation. We just accept it directly, and we try our best to do it exactly. That's the normal case for beginners, because we have to know the style correctly. We have to feel the taste of the rhythmic pattern. Yang Chinsŏng, Yang Sunyong's [lead *soe* of P'ilbong Nongak, now deceased] son, was on a radio show called "Kugak Hanmadang." He said in order to feel "left side"–style p'ungmul correctly, you had to play for ten years. I agree, it takes ten years to understand even a little bit. So I don't really want to say too much.

When asked how he would teach in the future, he responded:

When we say we play "left side"—or "right side"—style p'ungmul, we should attempt to teach it the way it is. I've been teaching you the "left side" style, haven't I? And in this case, I've tried my best to teach you the individual style. Even playing a single pattern, I try to teach people the original pattern. Even with the rhythmic variations, there is a set form. Therefore, I at first always try to teach the original style clearly, and when the person understands a bit about it and plays it at a minimum level of proficiency—when the person can bring out even a little of the proper taste—then I will teach them another form. In your case, it's been a little special. Because you're doing this as research, I am teaching you this and that, a bit of everything. But I will always try to communicate the original style first. For those doing it as a hobby, it doesn't really matter, in my opinion.[19] But if they have any serious interest in playing, I will teach them the original style first. And after that I may move to some creative things.

I honestly think the distinction between "left" and "right" is funny. "Left side" performers become cultural assets and those people can only do that style. And these people, of course, naturally talk about its fine points or how great it is, talking as if it's the best. "Right side" is the same way. For example, Kim Hyŏngsun can't play anything else, he is only allowed to play within the "right side" style. They don't have any choice but to play in the style in which they've been designated a cultural asset. It is the principle that they must do so. This phenomenon, however, harms some people. People like us suffer the consequences. For example, "left side" insists on playing only "left side," and if people like us want to learn "right side" we have to be careful, we have to be secretive about it. The reason is that if we say we're learning the "right side" style, the other people will talk badly about us. But actually, when people like me look at it carefully, the difference in feeling between "right" and "left" isn't all that great—they're really quite similar.

If you look at what they play, "right side" has *och'ae chilgut* rhythmic pattern and our tradition has *och'ae*. Our *och'ae* is technically part of the *ch'aegut* movement, but it doesn't really fit. It's too slow. And if you look at a pattern such as *yangsando* [a "right side"–style pattern], it's played in our *pan p'ungnyu* or *samch'ae* style—it's quite similar. Of course there are differences, but I don't know why they insist on only one way. I think about it a lot. This or that, or both—they could easily popularize it by combining the styles.

Yi's sense of hostility and competition between "right" and "left" was rooted in real-life circumstance. This was true to the extent that even though Yi and I were very open about my studying with Kim Hyŏngsun when we were alone, he nevertheless had to introduce me to almost everyone else we met as a "left side" student performer and researcher. This secrecy extended even to our playing with other groups within the same performance style as well. A close friend of mine at the CTK told me one afternoon that he would be going to his hometown in neighboring Chŏngŭp county over the weekend to play with a local p'ungmul group. He called me later that evening, however, to ensure I would not tell anyone in our class, especially Kim, who might feel that he was splitting his allegiance (Hong Chunp'yo 1996: personal communication). The lingering presence of factionalism was never more evident than at the Thirty-third Annual "Citizens of Puan Day" on May 1, 1996. The festival featured a local p'ungmul competition at 2: 00 P.M., preceded by a qualifying round that morning. Puan county has traditionally been regarded as a "right side" region; of the seventeen bands that registered, only five were "left side" (including a group Yi regularly taught), of which only one was allowed to further compete (four "right side" teams passed this round). Yi later apologized to his group for having let them down by shielding them from local prejudice.

Technique

Changgo (Seated)

The first three months were spent exclusively in learning the *changgo* from a seated position. The manner of sitting and stroke technique are similar enough to that demonstrated by Kim Hyŏngsun so as to not warrant a full repetition here, with the exception of the new sound, *ttak,* created by the stick's (*yŏlch'ae*) striking the part of the drumhead extending beyond the bowl of the instrument (the hand is in a closed position). Though Yi never directly expressed it verbally, he exhibited a general tendency to accent or stress the "downbeat" of each rhythmic phrase, particularly in the mallet (*kunggulch'ae*) hand. In contrast to Kim, who favored little or no movement of the head when playing sitting down, Yi encouraged moving the head in the urbanized *samul nori* style, namely, in the opposite direction to the path of the mallet.[20]

In the previous section on general lesson format, I stated that the primary form (*wŏnbak*) was taught through oral mnemonics and later demonstrated on the instrument itself. What I did not mention, however, was Yi's habit of reverting to what appeared to be a more complex or technically sophisticated pattern when accompanying me on long sections of repeats, a process that seemed to be the reverse of Kim's method of teaching, in which the playing version was taught first and then simplified to the *wŏnbak* if students showed any sign of difficulty. I never brought this up during these earlier stages of lessons, but months later, after I had become comfortable with the *soe* rhythms, Yi announced it was time to return to the *changgo* to learn "technique" (Yi used the English word).

My earlier impressions were confirmed: although in fact performers were familiar with the primary form of each rhythmic pattern, this primary or simple version was seldom if ever played at the advanced or professional level. Yi's "left side" style also encompassed a stage I have referred to as the "performance form." It was at this point that Yi specifically began teaching the *ki* stroke, achieved by striking the drumhead with the tip of the stick with the hand in an open or relaxed position. The *ki* stroke was a defining feature of the performance form. It created a more interesting and sophisticated rhythmic line that challenged the player by keeping the right hand (or the hand holding the stick) more active. What emerges again, then, is a tripartite model of rhythmic structure based primarily on technical proficiency, essentially the same as that transmitted by Kim: *wŏnbak* (primary form) → performance form (elaboration on the *wŏnbak*) → *pyŏnbak* (rhythmic variation).

Soe (Seated)

Soe lessons began after the basic form of the *p'an kut* had been learned on the *changgo*. The lead *soe* player (*sangsoe*), I was told, played a very important role in a successful p'ungmul performance. The lead *soe* was not only responsible for leading the entire group through the proper ground formations within the performance space (*p'an*), but for signaling rhythmic pattern and tempo changes clearly and accurately to other group members. From the very first lesson, Yi stressed the necessity of playing loudly and clearly, for the purely practical reason of balance: three or four *soe* had to be heard above forty to fifty other instrumentalists.[21]

Today the majority of *soe* players tend to hold the instrument in the left hand in one of two prescribed ways. The first and more common method involves suspending the *soe* with the first finger, leaving the three remaining fingers within the body of the *soe* and the thumb protruding to the side. The second method involves suspending the *soe* with the thumb so that the entire hand is hidden within the body of the instrument. Yi demonstrated an older style, more prominent among village p'ungmul players, in which the *soe* is suspended with the second finger and the first finger and thumb are left protruding, but this style was thought to be rapidly diminishing.[22] The mallet (*ch'ae*) for striking the *soe* is held in the right hand with the second, third, and fourth fingers grasping the handle at the base comfortably, creating a pivot point. The first finger and thumb are left in a relaxed position; this method of holding is essential for the playing of rhythmic patterns at higher speeds involving a technique in which the mallet must freely rebound off the surface of the *soe*.

The *soe* is struck on its front surface in the area between the center and outer rim. *Soe* technique is comprised of two basic strokes, open and closed. For the open stroke, the *soe* is struck and left to ring freely. This stroke is further divided into strong strokes and weak(er) strokes. At the general level these could be thought of as "loud" and "soft," though at more advanced levels of playing there are strong and weak strokes *within* both loud and soft sections. Common practice dictates an upward motion for strong strokes and a downward motion for weaker ones, though this is a matter of personal preference and by no means universal; when executed properly, however, it creates a visually exciting performance. The contrast between strong and weak (*kang* and *yak*) strokes is the lifeblood of the "left side" tradition. The path toward understanding this concept begins with a basic mastery and internalization of the oral mnemonics: strong strokes are represented by syllables ending in consonants, such as *kaeng, ken, kken, kaen,* or *p'aeng,* while weaker strokes are represented by syllables ending in vowels, such as *chi/ji, kae, kkae, ke,* or *kke.* A weaker stroke followed by a damping by the fingers of the left hand (*ŭng*) is represented by the syllables *kkae* (*ŭng*).

The mastery of left-hand damping, or *magŭmsoe* (from the verb *makta,* "to block [or stop up]," + *soe*), is the final and most advanced stage of the accomplished *soe* player. This technique is personal in that the decision of where to employ it is very much a matter of individual taste, with the exception of *kkae* (*ŭng*); the same rhythm can be damped in different ways by different players, even within the same group.

For the closed stroke, the *soe* is held firmly by the fingers and thumb of the left hand before and after striking, creating a muted sound represented by the syllable *kaet, kkaet,* or *tut.* This technique is highlighted in the *oemach'i chilgut* rhythmic pattern of the second movement, the *kajin yŏngsan* rhythmic pattern of the eighth movement, and during sections of the call-and-response *tchaksoe* (see chapter 5). According to Yi, the closed stroke is a relatively recent development.

The oral mnemonics presented above and in my discussion on *changgo* technique are clearly onomatopoeic in nature and are consistent to a certain extent with systems found in other genres of Korean music. As pointed out by the ethnomusicologist David Hughes in an article on Korean oral mnemonics and melodic instruments (1991: 307–8), the sharp attacks—in this case, of struck percussion instruments—are reflected at the beginning of each syllable with "voiceless obstruents" (*k, t, p, p,'* or one of these consonants doubled). The decay of the sound as well is accounted for at the end of each syllable: open strokes end with vowels or the consonant *n* or *ng* (nasals), both considered "continuants" in that air is allowed to keep flowing; closed strokes end with the consonant *k* or *t,* both of which are voiceless obstruents, indicating a stopped sound (see also Hughes 1989: 13). It is interesting to note in passing that other percussion traditions, particularly those employing sticks, also use the beginning consonant *t* or *d* to denote a drum stroke (Malm 1959: 122–27; Kunst 1973: 204–5; Diamond, Cronk, and von Rosen 1994: 69).

Later *soe* lessons involved Yi's and my trading off between the *soe* and *changgo* parts for the purpose of cementing the rhythmic relationship in my head. Traditionally, I was told, the lead *soe* player was responsible for playing the rhythmic variations (*pyŏnbak*) while the other *soe* players repeated the primary form (*wŏnbak*), though this was less true today. He also pointed out that in the *soe* line, and in the *changgo* to a lesser extent, strokes could be added or deleted as one wished, in either the *wŏnbak* or the *pyŏnbak.* The previous section on *changgo* technique distinguished three levels of rhythmic construct, the second being a more rhythmically involved elaboration on the *wŏnbak,* or "performance form." The same was not true of the *soe*—the *wŏnbak* was played in the form directly transmitted by oral mnemonics.

Changgo and *soe* (Dancing)

No new playing technique was introduced in dance lessons, except for the purely practical matter of attaching the drum to the body. Where Kim had favored looping the cloth cord at each stage of tying, with the exception of the final knot, Yi preferred tying knots, giving a more secure feeling. As I had become more comfortable with Kim's method of securing the instrument, I was advised not to change.

In rather marked contrast to that of "right side," the "left side" style of dance is distinguished by its relative simplicity and consistency. All rhythmic patterns begin with the foot located directly under the instrument (left foot for right-handed players). Steps are taken at a "comfortable" pace and tend to coincide with beats. The heel strikes the ground first, followed by the rest of the foot; the motion is accompanied by a slight bend in the knee. Yi maintained that the gesture should resemble, both in energy flow (slow and smooth) and weight, a farmer trudging through a deep rice paddy: it should have a feeling of heaviness or rootedness. *Changgo* players add the movement mentioned by Kim: turning the upper body to the left or right to accommodate the path of the mallet moving from the back to the front drumhead. Steps for both the *changgo* and *soe* were practiced with *hwimori* and *samch'ae* rhythmic patterns.

Official lessons at the individual level ended at this stage. Further training came in the form of observation and participation in rehearsals and impromptu performances with groups Yi regularly taught. A final note: progress during every step of the lesson process was assessed primarily by technical ability, which was intimately linked to memorization. Only when a rhythmic pattern could be sung and played properly *and without referring to notation* was I allowed to move to the next pattern or movement.

Beyond the Formal Lesson

Chŏnsugwan: P'ungmul Training Institutes

Like most serious students of p'ungmul of his generation, Yi had received most, if not all, of his initial and/or continuing training at a regional p'ungmul training institute. Institutes operated by p'ungmul (*nongak*) troupes designated as cultural assets gained the upper hand on account of their national status, attracting student groups during the winter and summer breaks not only from all over the country, but from the United States and Europe as well. Troupes that had not been so designated also set up their own training institutes, though their market was considerably diminished in scope and was often confined to their own particular county or province.

North Chŏlla province in the late 1990s had four major centers for the study of p'ungmul: Kim Hyŏngsun's "right side" cultural asset troupe in Iksan city (previously Iri city, Iksan county); Pak Hyŏngnae's "left side" cultural asset troupe in P'ilbong village, Kangjin subcounty, Imshil county; Yang Chinsŏng's "left side" troupe in Naktong village, Chusaeng subcounty, Namwŏn county (which has since joined the P'ilbong troupe); and Kim T'aehyŏng's "left side" troupe in Chungp'yŏng hamlet, Tot'ong village, Sŏngsu subcounty, Chinan county. The fact that three of the four training institutes taught the "left side" performance style most likely reflected the local trend amongst p'ungmul circles on university campuses. Interviews with circle presidents from the three leading campuses of p'ungmul activity in North Chŏlla province revealed that Usŏk University had thirteen "left side" groups and two "right side" groups (Yi Sangbaek 1995: personal communication); Chŏnbuk University had ten "left side" groups and one "right side" group (Shin Chun'gyu 1996: personal communication); and Chŏnju University had nine "left side" groups and one "right side" group (Pak Hyŏngyŏl 1995: personal communication). Yi's explanation for this phenomenon, one with which I readily agree, was twofold. First, "left side" rhythmic patterns and dance steps were, on the surface level, simpler and thus easier to learn. And second, "left side" performance style was perceived to have had deeper roots in traditional communal village practices, making it essentially more "politically correct" (a leftover from *minjung* ideology—refer again to chapter 3).

Though Yi had received much of his training from personnel at the P'ilbong cultural asset institute, he had lost touch with its leader and human cultural asset, Pak Hyŏngnae, over the past few years. During the early months of my study with Yi, however, he rekindled his relationship with Pak and was invited to be a teaching assistant for a high school p'ungmul group from Puan for a ten-day program over the winter break (January 1996). The mountainous area surrounding the village of P'ilbong, according to local knowledge, has always been considered one of the poorest regions in all of North Chŏlla province, both historically and in the present. P'ilbong's troupe used two buildings for their training institute, an "official" main building and an abandoned elementary school a few miles down the road (most local residents had moved to urban areas). The main building, however, had been without water and heat for months, so Yi's group was trained and housed in and around the school. Pak still lived in P'ilbong village, in the same home as the previous six generations of his ancestors had, despite the lack of modern conveniences and of easy accessibility from the main road.[23] Yi felt it was important for me to see a "typical day" at a training institute, as well as to get acquainted with "grandfather" Pak. The only condition was that I not mention to Pak that I was a regular pupil of Kim Hyŏngsun and the "right side" school.

I arrived in the early afternoon, in time to observe the session overseen by Pak himself. As Yi mentioned in his interview (chapter 1), the main teachers tended to give only an hour or two of personal instruction a day; for the remaining time students were supervised by the teaching assistant(s). As a general rule, Pak showed up early in the afternoon and stayed from one to three hours, leaving Yi to oversee the remaining hours of the day. Students were relaxed yet respectful with Pak, reserving the majority of their questions and observations for the sessions spent alone with Yi. The daily schedule was tightly organized and was as ambitious as it was strenuous, as figure 4.5

Figure 4.5. Daily schedule, P'ilbong winter training institute (March 1996) and Iri summer training institute (July 1996)

P'ilbong		Iri	
12 A.M.	Sleep	12 A.M.	Sleep
1	↓	1	↓
2		2	
3		3	
4		4	
5		5	
6	Wake up (6:30)	6	
7	Clean, breakfast, rest	7	Wake up, exercise, wash
8	↓	8	Breakfast
9	Technique (seated)	9	Practice
10	↓	10	↓
11		11	
12 P.M.	Lunch, rest	12 P.M.	Finish, prepare lunch
1	↓	1	Lunch
2	Technique (seated, standing)	2	Practice
3	↓	3	↓
4		4	
5		5	Finish, prepare dinner
6	Dinner	6	Dinner
7	↓	7	Talk, learn folksongs (*minyo*)
8	Technical evaluation	8	↓
9	Mask dance (*t'al ch'um*)	9	
10	Learning and evaluation	10	
11	Rest/free time	11	

Figure 4.6. "Rules to Live By," posted at the P'ilbong winter training institute and Iri summer training institute

P'ilbong	Iri
1. You must be punctual	1. Obey the leader's instructions
1.* Food must not be wasted	2. Individualism is prohibited
1. Treat the instrument as your body	3. Laugh
1. The leader's words are law	4. Make people laugh
1. You are responsible for anything entrusted to you (food duty)	5. Laugh for others
1. The teacher is God†	6. Play the music enthusiastically (this is the most basic requirement)
	7. Be punctual (especially waking)
	8. Don't be lazy

*The instructors at P'ilbong wanted every rule to be "number 1."
†The wording here is literally, "The teacher is the same year, same school as God" [Sabu-nŭn hananim-kwa tonggi tongch'ang ida].

---

shows. I have included the daily schedule from Iri's summer institute for comparison. It is interesting to note in passing that both daily regimens involved a component of older "traditional" culture—the learning of mask dance in P'ilbong and of folksongs in Iri.

Students followed a strict code of conduct, which included cooking and cleaning up after the teachers (see figure 4.6). This behavior was expected and consistently repeated time and time again as I traveled between the various training institutes observing lessons and personal interactions. This relationship, based on respect, very much resembled that of child to parent in the traditional Confucian filial sense of the meaning. The continuation of this form of transmission will most likely safeguard p'ungmul from the threat of extinction now facing many other traditional Korean performing arts.

In early 1996 Yi decided to increase his public profile back in his home county of Puan in anticipation of his eventual return after graduation from university. His invitation to teach at the cultural asset training institute in P'ilbong, and, to a lesser extent, my presence as a foreign researcher accompanying him on many of his teaching trips, served as the foundation for what would later become for Yi a relatively lucrative semiprofessional career. In the month of April alone, Yi taught between three and five student and amateur groups at any one time, all in Puan, for which he received 3.6 million wŏn (approximately $4,500 at the time; see plate 14). On May 20, 1996, he was elected vice president and educational director of the newly formed group Puan P'ungmulp'ae, a position he held for the next seven years.

Ham chinabi

Throughout Korea there is a special ceremony that continues to be practiced, in various guises, under the name of *ham chinabi* (literally, "father [or married man] [*abi*] carrying [*chin*] a chest [*ham*] on his back"). The custom involves the male friends of the bridegroom taking a box or chest (*ham*) of presents from the groom to the bride's family the day or evening before the wedding is to take place. One person is usually officially designated to carry the chest on his back and is called the *hamjaebi*. The tradition has roots in Korean Confucian marriage customs, though the manner in which it is performed varies by the participants and locale (compare the account below with Kendall 1996: 204–9).

One of Yi's close friends from his hometown in Puan county was to be married. The bride's home was in Chŏnju, very close to where I was living, so late one afternoon in February 1996 I received a call from Yi telling me to put on some nice clothes and to bring my *soe*. An hour or so later ten of the groom's friends had gathered on the street a block away from the prospective bride's home. Yi had brought the core set of p'ungmul instruments— two drums and two gongs—and two others had brought traditional candles and a mask made of dried squid for the *hamjaebi*. The evening began with a slow procession down the main street by the candle holders, followed immediately by the p'ungmul musicians playing *chilgut* and *pan p'ungnyu* rhythmic patterns (see chapter 5). As the group arrived in front of the bride's home, tables laden with food and drink were set up in the street for friends and relatives who had already gathered. It was at this point that I was encouraged to join the musicians in playing *pan p'ungnyu,* a pattern Yi felt had the proper feeling to get everyone in a good mood. Breaks were taken periodically for guests to yell "Ham saseyo!" (Please buy the chest!), after which the musicians would begin to play again and those gathered would dance or clap along. Twice during this portion of the evening the owner from the inn across the street came out to complain about the noise and how it was disturbing her business, but some older men—not related to the wedding party—who had come to watch shut her up, saying, "How do you expect for there to be any *hŭng* [enthusiasm or excitement] without the instruments playing?"

An hour or so later came the high point of the evening. Male members of the bride's party engaged in a mock battle with the *hamjaebi* and groom's friends, attempting to thwart any forward movement into the apartment

Figure 4.7. Yi Sangbaek with *ham chinabi* (wedding) musicians, Chŏnju city

building. The *hamjaebi* was challenged every step of the way, each forward progression being rewarded by a 10,000 wŏn bill (approximately $12.50 at the time). This continued until the *hamjaebi* had reached the front door of the bride's quarters, at which point the p'ungmul musicians began playing to announce the arrival of the groom's party (see figure 4.7). After ten to fifteen minutes of playing, the door was opened and all were invited in to eat and drink with the bride's family. The evening ended with singing, dancing, more drinking, and the playing of p'ungmul.

As I was being driven home early the next morning, Yi told me why I had been invited to attend. The primary reason was so I could observe a custom he had grown up with in the countryside, to see how p'ungmul was an integral part of it and how it continued to have meaning for modern-day Koreans. The secondary reason was to see how my *soe* playing was coming along by giving me a chance to play outside with others in a noisy and chaotic atmosphere away from the sterile practice room. He thought my contribution of playing really lifted the level of energy (*shinmyŏng*) among the other guests, not because of any technical proficiency achieved, but because of my willingness, even as a foreigner, to participate as a member of the group. That evening remains one of my fondest memories and most valuable lesson experiences.

SUMMARY AND REFLECTION

A summary in the form of a comparison of teaching methodologies is presented in figure 4.8. A number of general trends merit special attention. Kim promoted a familiar, communal lesson atmosphere through group practice and participation, while Yi favored one that was more individualistic (points 1–3). Kim taught almost exclusively by direct example and imitation, with little or no background explanation; Yi employed a highly integrated strategy involving verbal, visual, and recorded materials (points 4–6). Both teachers placed special emphasis on memorization (point 7), though Kim assessed progress primarily by time, with obvious constraints imposed on him in the form of institute policy. This was in contrast to Yi, who marked progress principally by the achievement of a certain technical level (points 8 and 9). Both teachers encouraged outside activities as part of the broader lesson process (point 10).

As we look back at Kim's past, we see learning as a one-to-one, more intimate activity that was only a smaller part of the larger whole of living with and serving the teacher. The structure was much less formal, often with no fixed time or designated location. Rhythmic patterns were introduced according to difficulty, with new opportunities being earned over a long period of time proving oneself. This outlook and approach changed partly because of his being accorded the status of human cultural asset later in life—a recognition that required him to teach others—but more likely can be attributed almost solely to financial necessity, reflected in his acceptance of the teaching position in Chŏnju, away from his home group and institute. Lessons were now held at a set place and time, and rhythmic patterns were standardized and taught in blocks to large groups of predominantly amateur students who received little or no personal attention. Kim was even required to produce promotional literature as well as notation owing to his students' changing needs, projects to which he was fundamentally opposed.

Yi, in contrast, received his earliest training as part of a group, albeit a much smaller and more intimate one. The location was often agreed upon beforehand, though in many cases the schedule and timing of the lessons were not. Learning took place over a longer period of time, and progress in

Figure 4.8. A comparison of teaching methodologies

Kim Hyŏngsun	Yi Sangbaek
1. Daily lesson (class period = 1 hour)	1. Weekly lesson (3–4 hours)
2. Group lesson (occasionally an individual student is singled out for personal criticism)	2. Individual lesson (though circle members often pass through and participate)
3. Lessons and practice considered essentially the same activity	3. Individual practice expected away from the lesson
4. Tape recording not encouraged	4. Lessons were tape recorded
5. Lesson process:	5. Lesson process:
a. Name of rhythmic pattern not always given; often no explanation as to where it fits into overall scheme	a. Name of rhythmic pattern given with oral mnemonics, along with its position within the overall piece
b. Rhythmic pattern demonstrated, followed by everyone playing together	b. Rhythmic pattern demonstrated, followed by teacher and student playing together, student playing alone, and student accompanied by *changgo* or *soe* (depending on stage)
c. Background of rhythmic pattern seldom if ever given	c. Background explanation of rhythmic patterns given with similarities to other patterns (in either repertoire)
d. Teaching of rhythmic patterns almost exclusively by demonstration (rote)	d. Teaching of rhythmic patterns split equally between demonstration and verbal instruction/notation
e. Repetition as main tool for learning	e. Emphasized necessity of repetition
f. Questions by students kept to a minimum	f. Questions allowed and encouraged at any point during the lesson
6. Piece taught in order but with certain rhythmic patterns omitted (see chapter 5 on performance and analysis); variations often taught later	6. Rhythmic patterns taught in basic order; variations taught in conjunction with first learning of the patterns
7. Emphasis on memorization	7. Emphasis on memorization

8. Progress assessed by time (primarily)	8. Progress assessed by ability (primarily)
9. Order of progression: a. *Changgo* (seated) b. *Changgo* (dancing) * *Soe* never encouraged nor dissuaded	9. Order of progression: a. *Changgo* (seated) b. *Soe* (seated) c. Review of *changgo* and *soe* (seated) d. *Changgo* (dancing) e. *Soe* (dancing)
10. Outside activities encouraged for learning process	10. Outside activities encouraged for learning process

the form of the introduction of rhythmic patterns was achieved only after the mastery of previously introduced material. Teachers came and went as they pleased and served more the role of an overseer. As Yi and I established our working relationship, however, he began to become comfortable with the concepts of a set lesson time and place and a previously agreed-upon lesson content, though it must be said that though I did learn the patterns in a shorter amount of time than that normally allotted, I was nonetheless still required to memorize everything before moving on. As time passed, he even began adopting some of the approaches gleaned from my lesson experience to outside groups and individuals. Like Kim, he could not ignore these outside offers, because of his need for a secure financial base.

It is tempting to assume that a move from the less structured pedagogical style characterized by Kim to the more formalized one characterized by Yi is a natural and inevitable trend in a rapidly developing country such as Korea, with its attendant imported religious, political, and educational structures; but we are still at a point in time in which any form of conclusive pronouncement would be premature. Kim's influence at the CTK in Chŏnju will continue until at least the early twenty-first century and will extend well beyond this time at his home institute in Iri and in the teaching strategy of his son Kim Ikchu. There is not enough data yet on the younger generation of performers such as Yi, who are operating essentially outside official institutional settings and are on the brink of commencing individual teaching careers. There is also the question of the extent to which my presence as a foreign researcher influenced Yi's decisions regarding the format and content of our lessons together, and whether or not he will continue to employ such changes in his role as educational director of Puan P'ungmulp'ae back in his hometown.

If you play the rhythmic patterns of *nongak kut* [p'ungmul] without leaving anything out, it is almost limitless. On the surface this playing may seem joyous or amusing, but deep down it penetrates your very soul.

—Shin Kinam, *Ŏttŏk'e hŏmŏn ttokttok hŏn cheja han nom tugo chugŭlkko?* [What Do I Have to Do to Get a Single Smart Disciple before I Die?] (1992), 32

5

The Repertoire

In contrast to previous chapters, which dealt primarily with activity surrounding the production of p'ungmul, I now look to document and examine the material of the music itself. Although further contextualization and general performance practice will be touched upon, the central discussion will revolve almost solely around the nature and construction of the rhythmic patterns. The repertoire of North Chŏlla province p'ungmul is rich in its breadth and diversity, providing yet another vantage point from which to view the tradition as a broad cultural repository. Its collection of rhythms reflects a fertile meeting ground of local and pan-Korean influences, borrowings from village ensemble and itinerant troupe performances that draw on such diverse sources as shamanistic and Buddhist ritual, communal labor activity, and aristocratic music and dance genres. The end result is in many ways a grand process of democratization, as previously dichotomous or even hostile elements of elite and commoner culture coalesce into a unified and seamless whole.

Individual performances by Kim Hyŏngsun's and Yi Sangbaek's p'ungmul groups will serve as the primary source material for the discussion that follows. The choice to concentrate my gaze in such a manner is motivated by a desire to firmly root such observations in concrete, historical circumstance. This tack is taken intentionally to run counter to prevailing trends in the Korean academic community that portray the p'ungmul oeuvre in abstract, archetypal models, with little reference to the lived, performed experience (e.g., Pak Sangguk et al. 1999; Yi Sora and Chŏng Sumi 2000). The clarity achieved in such models comes at the expense of missing p'ungmul's overall structural complexity, the flow between rhythms, transitions, and cadential passages, and the pacing and symmetry found within and between the various movements. The chapter will then conclude with a summary analysis that provides my rationale for the choice of the English gloss "rhythmic pattern"—versus "rhythmic cycle" most often encountered in the literature—with an attempt to establish a working definition of Korean rhythm that affords us a greater appreciation of its intricacies and inner workings.

IRI NONGAK

Official literature provided by Kim Hyŏngsun stated that historically Iri Nongak had six separate but related performance contexts in their total repertoire: the *mun kut* (gate ritual), *tangsan kut* (village shrine ritual), *saem kut* (well ritual), *tŭltangsan kut* (field shrine ritual), *madang palki* (January fund-raising, literally, "treading on the earth"), and *p'an kut* (entertainment-oriented performance). In recent times, however, they put on performances only of the *p'an kut,* a trend that apparently began in the mid-1980s (O Chongsŏp 1989: 8). These public appearances were split almost evenly between Chŏlla province and the capital, Seoul, with Kim receiving additional invitations to perform the *changgo* dance alone. Table 5.1 shows a typical year in the life of Iri Nongak.

The following account of Iri Nongak is based on the group's performance at the Seoul Norimadang on April 7, 1996. All of the trips to Seoul I witnessed over the year followed a similar routine. Early in the morning, the majority of the group would congregate at Iri Nongak's training institute in Iri (Kim's home) to eat and help with the loading of the team bus. In addition to the care of the instruments, clothing, and flags, alcohol and food had to be prepared and packed for the day's main meal, generally consumed in Seoul an hour or so before the performance commenced. The bus then departed on its three-hour journey north, stopping every so often along the side of the highway to pick up additional members who lived in other cities or provinces. The group would usually arrive in Seoul early in the afternoon, which left two to three hours for everyone to relax, eat, and change into their outfits at a leisurely pace. It never ceased to amaze me how much food was eaten beforehand; Kim and others assured me that this was the only way to survive a complete *p'an kut,* particularly in the hot summer

Table 5.1. Iri Nongak performance schedule, 1995–96

Date	Location	Function	Group (G) / Individual (I)
Sept. 10, 1995	Seoul	September Traditional Arts Performance, Seoul Norimadang	G
Oct. 27, 1995	Iri (Iksan)	Eleventh Annual Iri Nongak Public Performance, Fourth Chŏlla/Kyŏngsang Province Traditional Culture Exchange Performance	G
Nov. 5, 1995	Kwangju	1995 Kwangju Biennial Celebratory Performance	I
Apr. 7, 1996	Seoul	April Traditional Arts Performance, Seoul Norimadang	G
Apr. 13, 1996	Iksan	Cultural Asset Designation Ceremony	G
Apr. 16, 1996	Chŏnju	1996 Chŏnju Cultural Festival	G
May 4, 1996	Kunsan	1996 Kunsan Athletic Festival	G
May 5, 1996	Seoul	Children's Day Festival, Olympic Park	G
May 10, 1996	Iksan	First Annual Iksan Citizen's Day, Mahan Folk Arts Festival	G
May 11, 1996	Iksan	First Annual National College Student Samullori Competition	I
May 12, 1996	Seoul	May Traditional Arts Performance, Seoul Norimadang	G
June 15, 1996	Taejŏn (S. Ch'ungch'ŏng)	Canceled	G
July 13, 1996	Seoul	July Traditional Arts Performance, Seoul Norimadang	G
Aug. 10, 1996	Seoul	August Traditional Arts Performance, Seoul Norimadang	G

months. After playing, group members changed back into their street clothes and shared a quick cup of rice wine before loading the bus for the return to Iri (see plate 15).

The composition of Iri Nongak has been in a constant state of flux. This was so even prior to its official recognition as a cultural asset troupe in 1985. Table 5.2 shows two group rosters side by side, one compiled by the Office of Cultural Assets in 1982 (Chŏng Pyŏngho et al. 1982: 77), the other,

Table 5.2. Iri Nongak group rosters, 1982 and 1996

	1982	1996
Soe	Kim Mundal (male, 74)	Pak Yongt'aek (male, 44), Iri
	Yi Sunam (male, 65)	Yi Tongju (male, 32), Chŏnju
	Pak Hŏnjong (male, 74)	O Ŭisŏn (male, 70), Osan
	Pak Yongt'aek (male, 30)	Kim Iksang (male, 32), Iri
	Ch'oe Yongjin (male, 68)	Kim Suam (male, 49), Chŏnju
		Yi Hosun (male, 48), Chŏnju
Ching	Paek Sŭnggi (male, 67)	Chŏng Changsun (male, 55), Iri
	Pak T'aejun (male, 37)	Pak T'aejun (male, 51), Iri
Changgo	Kim Hyŏngsun (male, 49)	Kim Hyŏngsun (male, 63), Iri
	Kim Kaptong (male, 64)	Kim Ikchu (male, 27), Iri
	Kang Subong (male, 63)	Kim Kyŏngsuk (female, 32), Seoul
		Yi Oksun (female, 48), Chŏnju
		Shin Chaeja (female, 47), Taejŏn [SC]
		Yi Chŏngja (female, 54), Kunsan
		Han Sŏngja (female, 53), Kunsan
Puk		O Chongsŏp (male, 33), Seoul
Sogo	Kim Panghyŏn (male, 71)	Kim Chŏngnye (female, 28), Iri
	Pak Haengnam (male, 41)	Cho Myŏngja (female, 53), Chŏnju
	Yang Unyŏng (male, 55)	Kwŏn Munil (male, 46), Chŏnju
	Sŏ Sŭnghyŏn (male, 55)	Kim Ch'ŏngja (female, 52), Chŏnju
	Yi Tongil (male, 48)	Cho Kyŏngch'ae (female, 46), Chŏnju
	Chŏng Changsun (male, 41)	Kim Sŏni (female, 59), Chŏnju
	Han Illye (male, 26)	Yi Kamnye (female, 43), Chŏnju
	Han Ssangnye (male, 26)	Cho Yŏngja (female, 54), Kunsan
	Yi Kwangnye (male, 33)	Kim Sunik (female, 44), Chŏnju
	Yi Kilsun (female, 33)	Ch'ŏn Yangja (female, 53), Chŏnju
	Chŏng Kŭmman (male, 32)	Yi Sun'gŭm (female, 63), Iri
	Pak Yŏnggŭm (female, 34)	Kim Sundŏk (female, 59), Chŏnju
	Kim Yesun (female, 36)	Hŏ Hyangdŏk (male, 41), Chŏnju
	Yi Poksun (female, 37)	Yi Yŏngsun (female, 58), Chŏnju
	O Sundŏk (female, 37)	
	Kang Ch'ŏngja (female, 36)	
Ch'ae sangmo		Yang Sŭngnyŏl (male, 43), Iri
Taep'osu	Kim Ssangbok (male, 63)	Im Wŏnsŏp (male, 38), Chŏnju
Yangban	Hwang Kisŏng (male, 71)	Kim Chaegwŏn (male, 52), Iri
Kakshi		Yi Myŏnghŭi (female, 65), Iri
Chorijung		Kim Hyŏngsŏn (male, 51), Chŏnju
Nonggi	Yu Shinok (male, 21)	Kim Chongho (male, 42), Iri
Yŏnggi	Yi Kwangsaeng (male, 62)	
	Ch'oe Ch'ŏnnyŏl (male, 62)	
Team flag		An Chŏngsun (male, 65), Chŏnju
Hojŏk	Yi Chongt'aek (male, 77)	Yun Kubyŏng (male, 56), Tongsa [SC]

Note: [SC] = South Ch'ungch'ŏng province

by Kim Hyŏngsun in a 1996 private manuscript. The rosters are arranged hierarchically, with the lead player listed at the top of each category. Name, age, and gender are given in all instances; information regarding place of residence was available only for the 1996 list (unless otherwise indicated, all locations are in North Chŏlla province). What is so astounding about this comparison is that the Iri Nongak organization of the mid-1990s had only three of the same members as the group of fourteen years earlier: Pak Yongt'aek (soe), Pak T'aejun (ching), and Kim Hyŏngsun (changgo). Personnel listings as a reliable indicator of steady membership are made further problematic by the fact that Kim apparently also allowed unregistered players to participate in performances, provided he was confident that the event would not be attended by a member of the Cultural Assets Committee. I was invited by Kim to play with Iri Nongak as part of the changgo section on three separate occasions, including the April 7 Norimadang performance. The next month, on May 5, at the Olympic Park I was even introduced to the crowd via the loudspeaker system.

An examination of table 5.2 also reveals the obvious yet curious demarcation of instrument families by gender. P'ungmul traditionally was a male performance art, a practice that came to an end in the 1960s when women began slowly to be integrated into performing ensembles. In my own experiences with Korean drumming groups (college and professional) and those in the United States made up of mostly overseas Koreans, I have noticed a general trend for women to gravitate toward the drums and men toward the gongs—though I have no hard-and-fast data to substantiate this observation. The reason this is curious to me is that no teacher, performer, academic, or fellow student ever referred to an individual instrument as particularly "male" or "female"—usually such gendering was part of the total identity of each drum or gong (often in terms of ŭm and yang, as documented in chapter 2). Korean folklore and geomancy tell us that the drums and the sound of their leather are rooted in the "female" earth, while the gongs and their composition of metal reflect the "male" domain of the heavens; yet again, no one ever provided this explanation to me when I took up the various instruments. I have asked many students and performers over the years for some kind of clarification on this matter; the only answer I have received—and though it is a partial one, it is one with which I agree more and more—is that there is a strong association of playing the changgo strapped to the body with the professional female entertainer (kisaeng) tradition of changgo ch'um (changgo dance), which perhaps scares off the males. My own contribution to this debate is that the gongs often occupy a position of leadership, a role most men are accustomed to filling.

THE RHYTHMIC PATTERNS

Various terms, often linked to genre and social class, are used to denote rhythmic patterns in the Korean language. The two most common are *changdan* and *karak,* though their specific usage and meaning have been open to debate. The p'ungmul scholar Ryu Muyŏl saw these terms as essentially synonymous (1986: 39), while Robert Provine (1975: 6) and Han Manyŏng (Chang Sahun and Han Manyŏng 1975: 27) considered *changdan* appropriate for rhythmic patterns, in direct contrast to Kim Hyŏnsuk, who preferred *karak* (1991: 78). There are examples as well of Buddhist and shamanistic genres of music employing instrument names for rhythmic patterns, in place of the more commonly used terms above (Yi Pohyŏng 1991: 125–26). Kim Hyŏngsun used the two most common p'ungmul terms for rhythmic patterns, *karak* (literally, "strand" or "finger") and *changdan* (literally, "long and short"), with little differentiation in meaning at the general level. If pressed to make a distinction, Kim favored the term *changdan* for rhythmic patterns at the broadest level, reserving the use of the designation *karak* for individual phrases or "strands" within the particular pattern.

Iri Nongak's entertainment-oriented performance (*p'an kut*) proper is made up of four movements (*madang*), each of which can be considered a discrete and self-contained piece composed of a set series of rhythmic patterns and accompanying danced ground formations (*chinbŏp*) performed in an invariable order. Performance practice dictates playing through an entire movement without breaks and taking a short pause before moving on to the next movement. It is also customary for the lead *soe* player (the *sangsoe*) to signal the beginnings and endings of each movement, provide cues for moving from one rhythmic pattern to another, and regulate the overall tempo. In the case of Iri Nongak, however, this role was split almost evenly between the lead *soe* player and Kim Hyŏngsun, most likely because of Kim's senior status and position as the sole human cultural asset in the group. Each movement is structurally complex, placing considerable demands on the performers' mental and physical abilities that require memorizing not only the numerous patterns and transitions, but also the accompanying dance steps and larger ground formations. Figure 5.1 gives a compositional overview of this scheme as realized in the April 7 performance.

Iri Nongak's rhythmic patterns are listed below in the order in which they were performed. A shorthand account of each rhythm in terms of its divisions and subdivisions is provided in the following manner: a pattern resembling Western 12/8 time, for example, or a single phrase of twelve eighth notes divided into four equal beats with triple subdivisions, is written 3 + 3 + 3 + 3; a rhythmic pattern made up of two phrases of twelve eighth

Figure 5.1. Compositional overview of Iri Nongak performance, April 7, 1996

[Introduction] (2 min. 56 sec.)

   ilch'ae ♩ = 63-208+

   [roll]

   ich'ae ♩. = 138-160

   ich'ae [transition] ♩. = 160

   ich'ae ♩. = 160-192

   [roll]

   insagut [truncated] ♩. = 63/72-160

   [roll]

   ich'ae ♩. = 120-152

   [roll]

   insagut [A] ♩. = 54

1. *Och'ae chilgut* (10 min. 27 sec.)

   och'ae chilgut ♪ = 116-132

   ujilgut ♩ = 132/ ♩. = 104

   chwajilgut ♩. = 104

   chilgut ♩ = 138-152

   yangsando ♩. = 104

   iŭmgut ♩. = 104

   maedoji [truncated] ♩. = 104

   kin samch'ae ♩. = 108

   kin samch'ae/maedoji [B:altered] ♩. = 108

   kin samch'ae ♩. = 112

   maedoji [B] ♩. = 112

   kin samch'ae ♩. = 112-116

   tchalbŭn samch'ae ♩. = 116

   toen samch'ae ♩. = 116-120

   kin samch'ae ♩. = 139-144

   maedoji [A] ♩. = 144

2. *Obangjin* (11 min. 32 sec.)

   obangjin [A] ♩ = 76-92

   obangjin [B] ♩ = 92

   obangjin [C] ♩ = 92

   obangjin [A] ♩ = 92

   chin obangjin [A] ♩ = 184-192

   obangjin [A] ♩ = 96

   chin obangjin [A] ♩ = 192-208+

   iŭmgut ♩. = 114

   maedoji [truncated] ♩. = 104-116

   kin samch'ae ♩. = 116-120

   toraganŭn maedoji ♩. = 120

   kin samch'ae/maedoji [B] ♩. = 120-116

kin samch'ae ♩. = 116
maedoji [B:altered] ♩. = 116
kin samch'ae ♩. = 116
tchalbŭn samch'ae ♩. = 116
toen samch'ae ♩. = 116-138
chajin samch'ae ♩. = 138-144
maedoji [C] ♩. = 152

3. Hohogut (7 min. 45 sec.)

ilch'ae ♩ = 69-132
[roll]
naendŭraemi ♩. = 138
hohogut ♩ = 88
chajin hohogut [A] ♩. = 100-108
chajin hohogut [B] ♩. = 108
chajin hohogut [A:altered] ♩. = 108
chajin hohogut [B] ♩. = 108
chajin hohogut [A] ♩. = 108
chajin hohogut [A:altered] ♩. = 108
chajin hohogut [B] ♩. = 108
chajin hohogut [A] ♩. = 108
chajin hohogut [A] / chajin hohogut [C]
♩. = 108
chajin hohogut [A] ♩. = 108
iŭmgut ♩. = 144-152
kin samch'ae ♩. = 152
maedoji [A] ♩. = 152
[roll]

4. Kaein nori (23 min. 14 sec.)

Sogo nori (4 min.)

ilch'ae ♩ = 88-200
[roll]
kukkŏri ♩. = 56-60
kin samch'ae ♩. = 112-120
maedoji [E] ♩. = 120

Ch'aesang nori (1 min. 33 sec.)

[roll]
maedoji [E] ♩. = 116
kin samch'ae ♩. = 116
maedoji [E] ♩. = 116
ilch'ae ♩ = 92-184
[roll]
maedoji [E] ♩. = 132

Sangsoe nori (3 min. 23 sec.)

    [roll]

    kukkŏri ♩. = 60

    iŭmgut ♩. = 116

    kin samch'ae ♩. = 116-126

    maedoji [E] ♩. = 126

    chajin obangjin [A] ♩ = 116-126

    [roll]

    insagut [A] ♩. = 60

Changgo nori (10 min. 28 sec.)

    chajin obangjin [A] ♩ = 92-112

    chajin obangjin [B] ♩. = 112-192

    hwimori [A] ♩. = 116-160

    hwimori [B] ♩. = 160-176

    hwimori [A] ♩. = 176

    pan hwimori [A] ♩. = 176

    pan hwimori [B] ♩. = 176

    pan hwimori [C] ♩. = 176

    chin obangjin [B] ♩ = 108-138

    suppadadŭm ♩ = 132/116-126/120

    pan hwimori [A] ♩ = 120

    pan hwimori [B] ♩ = 96

    pan hwimori [D] ♩ = 116-126

    chin obangjin [C] ♩ = 126

    chin obangjin [D] ♩ = 126-138

    chin obangjin [C] ♩ = 138

    obangjin [A] ♩ = 116

    obangjin [D] ♩ = 116

    chin obangjin [E] ♩ = 116

    obangjin [A:transition] ♩ = 116

    obangjin [B] ♩ = 116

    obangjin [C] ♩ = 116

    obangjin [A:transition + altered] ♩ = 116

    chin obangjin [B] ♩ = 116-144

    insagut [B] ♩. = 72-80

    pan hwimori [D] ♩ = 100-144

    chajin samch'ae [A] ♩. = 144-160

    chajin samch'ae [B] ♩. = 160

    chajin samch'ae [C] ♩. = 160

    sosam taesam ♩ = 168/ ♩. = 108

    chajin hohogut [A:first phrase] ♩. = 108

    kukkŏri [A:transition] ♩. = 116

    iopkut ♩. = 66

kukkŏri [A] ♩. = 60
chajin kukkŏri [transition] ♩. = 60
kukkŏri[A] ♩. = 60
chajin kukkŏri ♩ = 160-192/ ♩. = 132/138-126
kukkŏri [A] ♩. = 60
kukkŏri [B:transition] ♩. = 60
kukkŏri [B] ♩. = 60
kukkŏri [C] ♩. = 56
iopkut ♩. = 63
tasŭrŭm ♩. = 112-138
kukkŏri [transition] ♩. = 184
iopkut ♩. = 63
kukkŏri [D] ♩. = 63
kukkŏri [A] ♩. = 60
kukkŏri [E:transition] ♩. = 60
kukkŏri [E] ♩. = 60-63
maedoji [F] ♩ = 176/ ♩. = 108
kin samch'ae ♩. = 108-120
tchalbŭn samch'ae [A] ♩. = 120
tchalbŭn samch'ae [B] ♩. = 120
kin samch'ae ♩. = 120-132
maedoji [G] ♩. = 138/ ♩ = 138/176
kukkŏri [transition] ♩. = 112-116
kin samch'ae ♩. = 116-126
toraganŭn maedoji ♩. = 116
maedoji [H] ♩. = 116
chajin hohogut [D] ♩ = 112-120
chajin hohogut [C] ♩. = 112-144
kin samch'ae ♩. = 144
maedoji [A] ♩. = 132

Yŏltubal nori (1 min. 32 sec.)
kin samch'ae ♩. = 116-120
chajin obangjin [A] ♩ = 144-152

Kit *nori* + closing (1 min. 28 sec.)
kin samch'ae ♩. = 116-120
hwimori ♩. = 152
[roll]
insagut [A] ♩. = 58

notes would be 3 + 3 + 3 + 3 / 3 + 3 + 3 + 3 (and so forth). P'ungmul ensembles as a rule tend to play at a moderate speed throughout, with little or
no acceleration within the individual patterns (excluding closing portions),
and generally at full volume. Background notes on the patterns are a synthesis of Kim's spoken words in lessons and interviews with those recorded
by the scholar No Poksun (1994: 129–78). Kim had expressed a general dis-
taste for academics and the writers of books, especially those who could
not play the music in which they claimed to be experts. The work by No
Poksun, however, was an exception, for though No was a researcher at the
CTK in Chŏnju, she spent seven years learning how to play the *changgo* with
Kim. In his own words, "She had a gentle manner about her—she spent
a lot of time following me around. I became fond of her, like my own child.
I spent a lot of energy teaching her thoroughly."[1]

Introduction

The first movement is preceded by an introduction, which is not considered part of the *p'an kut* proper. The main function of this preliminary section is to usher the ensemble in from backstage (or someplace out of the
audience's sight) to the center of the performance space. Three rhythmic
patterns are played in alternation as the members enter in single file and
then form a large circle.

   Ilch'ae: 2 + 2 + 2 + 2. Many p'ungmul patterns are named after the
number of *ching* strokes occurring during the playing of a single cycle,
hence *il* (one) + *ch'ae* (stroke). *Ilch'ae* gradually increases in speed until it
becomes a roll.

   Ich'ae: 3 + 3 + 3 + 3. The literal meaning of this pattern, *i* (two) + *ch'ae*
(stroke), is misleading since the *ching* is struck only once per cycle. *Ich'ae* is
more commonly known by the name *hwimori* and is found in other folk and
aristocratic instrumental genres.

   Insagut: 3 + 3 + 3 + 3 / metrically free section / 3 + 3 + 3 + 3. *Insa*
(greeting or salutation) + *kut*/-*gut* (ritual or performance) is played only
one time through as a cadential passage, indicating to the audience that the
main performance is about to begin. *Insagut* in this form is found throughout the p'ungmul repertoire of Kyŏnggi, Ch'ungch'ŏng, and Chŏlla provinces (the Western side of the Korean peninsula).

First Movement: *Och'ae chilgut*

This movement is performed by the entire group and is named after its
opening pattern.

Och'ae chilgut: 2 + 3 + 3 + 2 / 2 + 3 + 3 + 3 + 2 / 2 + 3 + 3 + 2 / metrically free section / 3 + 3 + 3. *Och'ae chilgut* is considered a defining rhythm
of "right side" (*udo*) p'ungmul and is very likely one of the region's oldest
(Yi Pohyŏng 1995: personal communication). Meaning literally "five-stroke
(*och'ae*) road ritual (*chilgut*)," it was in the past a processional rhythm with
strong shamanistic ritual connotations. An alternate and perhaps older title
of the pattern is *kil kunak,* or "road military music," which further strength-
ens the link with group movement (*chil* is Chŏlla province dialect for *kil*).
The pattern is played as a cycle, repeated with little or no variation a number
of times, and is marked off structurally by five strokes on the *ching,* as the
name suggests. At the sound of the first stroke the ensemble begins to move
in a counterclockwise circle (as do the majority of North Chŏlla province
circle dances).[2]

Performers and researchers place special emphasis on *och'ae chilgut,*
viewing the pattern as a microcosm of the repertoire from which it is taken
with regard to subtlety and complexity. Although the current form of *och'ae
chilgut* as played by Iri Nongak features asymmetrical phrase lengths and
divisions of the beats, as well as a metrically free section, Kim nevertheless
pointed out to me that this was a recent, "simplified" version, as he expressed
it in a videotaping session conducted shortly before I left Korea in 1996:

> In my experience, the *p'an kut* was only done in places like regional festivals
> or markets [*nanjang*]. In normal villages, like the ones around here, they didn't
> perform the *p'an kut.* In a word, . . . even if you play p'ungmul all day long, if
> you omit *och'ae chilgut* rhythmic pattern, then it is not a *p'an kut.* A *p'an kut* is
> only a *p'an kut* when *och'ae chilgut* is played. These days *och'ae* has changed—
> this person plays this and that person plays that, they all play something, but no
> one can play the way the older people in the past did. Even if they've played for
> thirty years, they can't really play the real *och'ae.* If you asked someone to play
> the older way, no one would be able to do it. I put out a lot of effort and tried
> to make my group [Iri Nongak] play that older style, but whenever they got to
> *och'ae chilgut,* it became chaotic. They couldn't do it.

Ujilgut: 2 + 3 + 3 + 2 / 2 + 3 + 3 + 2 / 2 + 3 + 3 + 2 / 3 + 3 + 3 + 3 /
3 + 3 + 3 + 3. Meaning literally "right (*u*) road ritual (*jilgut*)," the designation "right" is determined by facing the center of the circle, then moving to
your right (counterclockwise). Performers thus continue dancing in a circle
formation in the same direction as the previous rhythmic pattern. *Ujilgut*
also features unequal phrase lengths and divisions of the beat, and is played
as a cycle until the lead small gong player signals the change to move to the
next pattern.

Chwajilgut: 3 + 2 + 3 + 2 / 2 + 3 + 3 + 2 / 2 + 3 + 3 + 2 / 2 + 3 +
3 + 2. The group as a whole changes direction and rotates as a circle to the
left, or clockwise (*chwa* [left] + *jilgut*). *Chwajilgut* is played as a cycle and is
constructed by adding a 10/8 opening phrase (3 + 2 + 3 + 2) to the first
three phrases of the previous *ujilgut* pattern.

Chilgut: 2 + 2 + 2 + 2 + 2 + 2 / 3 + 3 + 3 + 3. In village (*maŭl*) ritual
p'ungmul the rhythm is played as the group moves from one location to
another walking along a path or road (*chil / kil*), which accounts for the alternate name of *kil nori*, or "road play." In Iri Nongak's *p'an kut* the ensemble
switches direction again and dances in a counterclockwise circular formation. *Chilgut* is composed of two phrases of equal length—but with different
internal subdivisions—and is performed as a cycle.

Yangsando: 3 + 3 + 3 / 3 + 3 + 3 / 3 + 3 + 3 / 3 + 3 + 3. This pattern is named for the *yangsando* rhythmic pattern heard in the folksongs of
Kyŏnggi province, to the north of North Chŏlla province. It is composed of
four equal phrases and is very similar in stroke order and feel to the *semach'i*
rhythmic pattern found throughout Korea in other folksong and instrumental genres. It is played as a cycle a number of times, with p'ungmul performers continuing to dance in a counterclockwise direction but adding a "spin"
move during the playing of the first phrase.

Iŭmgut: 3 + 3 + 3 + 3 / 3 + 3 + 3 + 3. From the noun *iŭm*, meaning "joint,
juncture, or seam," this rhythmic pattern is played one time through as a transition when moving to the *hanbat'ang* closing section. In North Chŏlla province it is known by the additional names of *tŏngdŏkkungi* and *chŏngjŏkkungi*.

[*Hanbat'ang*]. *Hanbat'ang,* meaning literally "scene, round, or bout," refers to the closing segment of the first three movements of Iri Nongak's
p'an kut and is always preceded by *iŭmgut*. It is not considered a rhythmic
pattern itself, but rather refers to a series of various *samch'ae* and *maedoji*
rhythmic patterns that combine to create a fluid form. The actual ordering of patterns is decided during the course of the performance by the lead
small gong player, so other members must be particularly alert during this
portion of the performance. The inner logic of *hanbat'ang* is given as a flowchart in figure 5.2; below I have listed the patterns in the order in which
they are most often encountered (refer again to figure 5.1 for the specifics
of the April 7 performance). During *hanbat'ang* the ensemble breaks away
from the circle and performs intertwining ground formations that isolate
the various instrumental families.

Kin samch'ae: 3 + 3 + 3 + 3 / 3 + 3 + 3 + 3. Made up of two phrases
of equal length, the misnomer *kin* (long) *samch'ae* (three strokes)—at least
with regard to contemporary performance practice—is a cycle marked by
two strokes of the large gong (*ching*). *Kin samch'ae* is also called *nŭjŭn* (slow)

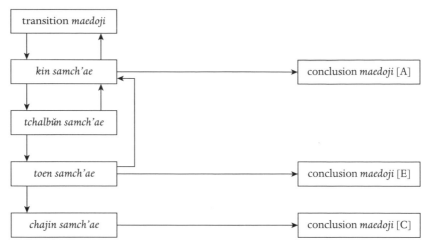

Figure 5.2. *Hanbat'ang* flowchart

samch'ae and is found in one form or another in all Korean p'ungmul regional traditions.

Tchalbŭn samch'ae: 3 + 3 + 3 + 3. *Tchalbŭn* (short) *samch'ae* is played as a cycle and represents a shortening of the previous *kin samch'ae*.

Toen samch'ae: 3 + 3 + 3 + 3. The cycle *toen samch'ae,* which takes its name from the verb *toeda* (thick or intense), creates tension by increasing the number of drum strokes in the *changgo* line, as well as by pushing the overall tempo.

Chajin samch'ae: 3 + 3 + 3 + 3. *Chajin* (fast or rapid) *samch'ae* is generally not encountered in Iri Nongak's *p'an kut* until the second movement (*obangjin*). This pattern is played as a cycle and is rhythmically identical to *toen samch'ae* in the *soe* line (with the difference that the instrument is played fully damped). *Changgo* players, however, switch to a new rhythm.

Maedoji: various. This cadential rhythmic pattern, which takes its name from the verb *maetta* (meaning to conclude, finish, or close), relaxes or unwinds the tension (*kinjang-ŭl p'urŏjunda*) that has been built up by the previous patterns. There are two basic forms of *maedoji* according to function: (1) transitional *maedoji,* marked as *maedoji* [truncated], *toraganŭn maedoji, maedoji* [B], or *maedoji* [D]; and (2) conclusion *maedoji,* marked as *maedoji* [A], *maedoji* [C], or *maedoji* [E] (refer to the notation at the Web site provided in the author's note). All forms of *maedoji* are played only one time through, and nearly all feature the alternation of duple and triple subdivisions of the beat, similar to a hemiola. This interplay of two and three is a common strategy for signaling a cadence in many Korean folk and ritual music genres.

Second Movement: *Obangjin*

The second movement is similarly named after its first rhythmic pattern.

Obangjin: 2 + 2 + 2 + 2 / 2 + 2 + 2 + 2. The name of this pattern is a direct reference to the geomantic five directions (*obang*) of east, west, south, north, and center in which the ensemble winds and unwinds, forming "drops" (*pangul*).[3] *Obangjin* is considered one of the most diverse patterns in North Chŏlla province, with many more variations possible than other rhythmic patterns in the first three movements of the *p'an kut*. It is to be played powerfully (*himch'age*), yet should give the feeling of exquisiteness or subtle charm (*sangdanghan myomi*). *Obangjin* proper is one of the few duple-meter cycles in the repertoire and is found in three related versions: [A], [B], and [C].

Chin obangjin: 2 + 2 + 2 + 2 / 2 + 2 + 2 + 2. Also a duple-meter cycle, *chin* (strong?) *obangjin* is composed of two phrases of equal length.

Iŭmgut: 3 + 3 + 3 + 3 / 3 + 3 + 3 + 3. *Iŭmgut* again signals the arrival of the *hanbat'ang* closing section.

[*Hanbat'ang*]. Refer to figure 5.1 for the specific patterns and their ordering. By the end of the second movement the group has reformed as a circle.

Third Movement: *Hohogut*

This movement begins with two introductory rhythmic patterns, then moves to the pattern from which the name of this movement is taken.

Ilch'ae: 2 + 2 + 2 + 2. This cycle is the same one that opens the introduction.

Naendŭraemi: 3 + 3 + 3 + 3 + 3 + 3. The name of this rhythmic pattern has the meaning of "to present or exhibit" (*naenot'a*). It is played as a cycle three times before *hohogut* proper.

Hohogut: 2 + 2 + 2 + 2 / 2 + 2 + 2 + 2 / 3 + 2 + 3 + 2 / 2 + 3 + 3 + 2 / 2 + 3 + 3 + 2 / 2 + 3 + 3 + 2. This rhythm is named for the nonsense syllables *ho ho* exclaimed by the entire group during the opening two phrases of the pattern. Along with *och'ae chilgut* of the first movement, *hohogut* is considered a representative rhythm of North Chŏlla province p'ungmul and is compositionally one of its most complex. Phrases alternate between duple and composite meters and are played as a cycle a number of times. In the past, *hohogut* was believed to have served as a code or password (*amho*) by the military.

Chajin hohogut: 3 + 3 + 3 + 3 / 3 + 3 + 3 + 3. Although the *chajin* (fast) *hohogut* cycle has become regularized to two phrases of straightforward compound meter, the level of complexity remains the same when the numerous ground formations and types of footsteps used are taken into account. Four versions of *chajin hohogut* exist: [A], [A: altered], [B], and [C].

Iŭmgut: 3 + 3 + 3 + 3 / 3 + 3 + 3 + 3.

[*Hanbat'ang*]. Refer again to figure 5.1 for the specific patterns and their ordering.

Fourth Movement: *Kaein nori—Changgo nori*

This movement is composed of a series of group dances named after the individual instrument families that perform them (*kaein* = individual, *nori* = play or performance). Iri Nongak features performances by the *sogo* (hand-held drum) players (*sogo nori*), a spinning-tasseled-hat specialist on the *ch'ae sangmo* (*ch'aesang nori*), the lead small gong player (*sangsoe nori*), the *changgo* players (*changgo nori*), a spinning-tasseled-hat specialist on the *yŏltubal sangmo* (*yŏltubal nori*), and a mock battle staged between the farming and dragon flags (*kit nori* or *kinnori*). Kim Hyŏngsun taught only the *changgo nori,* the longest of all the dances and the most complex in terms of number of rhythmic patterns and variations.

Kim explained that in the past the *changgo* dance featured the playing skills of the lead *changgo* player only, hence the alternate title of *sŏlchanggo*. After the emancipation from the Japanese in the mid-1940s, however, the practice underwent a gradual metamorphosis. In the case of Chŏngŭp (county) Nongak, the most prominent performing troupe in North Chŏlla province at that time and a group with which Kim had intimate ties, three performers would play the *changgo* dance, with the lead *changgo* player standing in the middle. The reasons were mostly practical: three was still a small enough number for all to be able to see and hear each other clearly. So when Kim began his own troupe, even if there were ten *changgo* players, he would select the other two players in advance. Nowadays, however, because of growing group sizes and the rise of individual egos, Kim feels he must include everyone; in this manner the performance act has become more communal (see plate 16).[4]

Very few new rhythmic patterns are introduced in the *changgo nori;* the majority are taken from the previous three movements but are presented in a different order (see figure 5.1 for the complete listing and their ordering). Many new and considerably more involved hand and foot movements, however, are required of the performer, making the North Chŏlla province "right side" version of the *changgo nori* the most well respected and emulated on the peninsula. Below are listed only those patterns not previously discussed.

Pan hwimori: Various. All versions of *pan* (half) *hwimori* are one phrase in length and played as a cycle. The "beat" in all cases is the same length, though the number of subdivisions may differ, which indicates the absence of composite meter: *pan hwimori* [A] (2 + 2 + 3 + 3), *pan hwimori* [B] (3 + 3 + 3 + 3), *pan hwimori* [C] (2 + 2 + 2 + 2), and *pan hwimori* [D] (2 + 2 + 2 + 2).

Suppadadŭm: Fifteen phrases of 2 + 2 + 2 + 2. Played one time through, the meaning of the name is unclear to me.

Sosam taesam: Phrases of 2 + 2. I was first introduced to the concepts of *sosam* ("small three") and *taesam* ("large three") in a *soe* lesson with Yi Ch'ullae, lead *soe* player of Chŏnju's semiprofessional p'ungmul group Kkach'imadang and master artist (*isuja*) under the regional human cultural asset Na Kŭmch'u (see chapter 1, n. 32). According to Yi, *sosam* and *taesam* had the broader meanings of "weak" and "strong," respectively (1996: personal communication; see also Korean Conservatorium of Performing Arts 1992: 186). The *sosam taesam* rhythmic pattern does feature an alternation of identical phrases played on the left and then the right drumhead, creating a subtle yet noticeable echo effect moving from loud to soft.

Kukkŏri: 3 + 3 + 3 + 3. From the nouns *kut* (ritual) and *kŏri* (section or portion), the basic form of the pattern represents a single phrase of 12/8 that is played as a cycle. *Kukkŏri* is found in both sacred and secular contexts throughout the folk vocal and instrumental repertoire and is considered an excellent rhythmic pattern for dance (see further Howard 1993). It has traditionally been viewed as the true testing ground of a drummer's full range of artistic skill, and many I spoke to promoted it as the specialty of the "right side" p'ungmul *changgo* performer. *Kukkŏri* exists in many versions: [A: transition], [A], [B: transition], [B], [C], [D], and [E].

Iopkut: 3 + 3 + 3 + 3. This pattern is considered a rhythmic variation of *kukkŏri* (the meaning of this name is unknown to me).

Tasŭrŭm: Phrases of 3 + 3 + 3 + 3; 3 + 3; 3. *Tasŭrŭm*, which takes its name from the verb *tasŭrida* (to regulate or order), is played as a series of sections that repeat internally, each successive phrase being half the length of the previous one. The name is more commonly used to refer to the prelude or warm-up passage of the folk solo instrumental suite *sanjo*.

PUAN P'UNGMULP'AE

As director of education of Puan P'ungmulp'ae (Association), Yi Sangbaek felt it was his responsibility to teach the local North Chŏlla province repertoire he had learned in P'ilbong village with his cultural asset instructors in as direct and untainted a manner as possible. This constraint was partially enforced upon him by association rules; he was, in fact, quite capable of teaching a number of pieces from the urbanized *samul nori* repertoire as well.[5] His first goal was to teach the first half (*apkut*) of the *p'an kut* to a core set of members, who would later aid him in the capacity of teaching assistants. More ambitious plans included the learning of the second half (*twikkut*) of the *p'an kut,* as well as raising money to build a permanent institute.

Because the group was still in its fledgling stage during my stay, Yi felt it was premature to schedule any public performances before the majority of the members were secure in their knowledge of the rhythmic patterns and ground formations. Unofficial "performances," however, occurred almost weekly. Association rehearsals were held twice a week in a studio located in the basement of an abandoned factory in downtown Puan. The end of the second weekly rehearsal was usually reserved for serious practice, which often meant a one- to two-hour run-through of the entire first half of the *p'an kut*. The discussion that follows is based on one of these occasions, held June 17, 1996.

At the time of the taping session, Puan P'ungmulp'ae was composed of fifteen core performers, with a total membership numbering forty-nine. With the exception of Yi as lead *soe* player, internal hierarchies had not yet been established within the ensemble. The group roster presented in table 5.3 lists only those who participated in the actual event, with the same gender divisions by instrumentation being followed as previously identified (males on gongs and females on drums). The layout is essentially the same as that of Iri Nongak, minus a listing of the place of residence, since all members of Puan P'ungmulp'ae were from the environs of Puan city. Yi pointed

Table 5.3. Puan P'ungmulp'ae core group roster, 1996

Soe	Yi Sangbaek (male, 30)
	Ko Isŏk (male, 32)
	Im Changho (male, 29)
	Ch'oe Kyŏngsam (male, 47)
	Song Kwangsŏp (male, 34)
	Yun Hyŏnjŏng (female, 20)
	Kim Chŏmnye (female, 42)
Changgo	Pak Yŏngsun (female, 20)
	Han Okkyŏng (female, 30)
	An Chongsŏn (male, 45)
	Song Chŏmsun (female, 51)
	Yi Kŭmsun (female, 45)
	Kim Yŏngsuk (female, 45)
	Kim Pyŏngguk (male, 450)
Ching	Chŏn Yongho (male, 31)

out afterward that a "true" performance would of course include *puk* and *sogo* players, as well as the full complement of characters (*chapsaek*).

THE RHYTHMIC PATTERNS

It is necessary again to briefly return to the topic of definitions. As stated earlier, Kim Hyŏngsun favored the term *changdan* for rhythmic patterns at the general level, reserving the use of the word *karak* for individual phrases or "strands" within a particular pattern. Yi, in contrast, used the terms *changdan* and *karak* interchangeably and synonymously for rhythmic patterns, with phrases roughly identified by their relative location, such as "the beginning of *samch'ae*" or "the ending section of *chilgut*." He was of the opinion that it was more appropriate to use *changdan* with vocal genres, such as *p'ansori* (storytelling through song) or *minyo* (folksong), and *karak* with p'ungmul. Nevertheless, the meaning was the same and the distinction not worth worrying about.

Yi was quick to warn against the dangers of reducing the art of "left side" p'ungmul to a mere collection of rhythmic patterns, as documented in the taping of one of my earliest lessons:

> The order of the strokes of a particular rhythmic pattern, either of the "left side" style or of other traditional music, is not important. To properly understand p'ungmul, you must first begin by personally playing it. Only then do you begin to grasp the feeling of the rhythmic pattern and the overall performance. When we speak of our music, we talk of a common mind [*kongdongch'e shim*], a unified performance [*taedong kut*], or communal spirit [*kongdongch'e shinmyŏng*]; the purpose of the performance is to establish a communal spirit through unified play [*taedong nori*]. . . . You slip into an alternate state of consciousness[6] — this is the level attained by the true performer. When you reach this level, you can no longer say p'ungmul is simply the playing of rhythmic patterns.
>
> As you already know, the playing of the basic patterns is not all that difficult, is it? To hit or strike the drum this way or that way, it's not difficult. Even so, it's not good to think of this music as simple. Why do we play this rhythmic pattern at that particular point in the performance? What feeling does this rhythmic pattern convey? When you personally "feel" the answers to these questions, then you can say you have learned a little bit about the performance. These days young people look at p'ungmul and think the road to mastery is just a short one. They feel that learning the strokes of the rhythmic patterns is all that there is. This is not right. If this were true, then there would be no reason to learn our p'ungmul. If p'ungmul is just playing *tŏng*, followed by another *tŏng*, then a *k'ung*, followed by a *tta*, then who can't play it? If rhythmic patterns

are just a collection of *tŏng* and *k'ung*, you could practice for a month or two and learn everything. This is, of course, absolutely not true.

It's like the proverb about the watermelon: Someone has a large piece of juicy watermelon, but only licks the surface of the fruit and then stops. They will never know the true flavor.

Yi reminded me that the form of the *p'an kut* most commonly taught today and presented here was originally only the first half, or the front *kut* (*apkut*). The front *kut* features music and dance and is rhythmically more complex. The second half of the performance, or the back *kut* (*twikkut*), in contrast, showcases dancing, singing, and theater (*yŏn'gŭk*) and is rhythmically quite basic or simple. The folk music scholar Yi Pohyŏng pointed out that in the past both Iri and P'ilbong p'ungmul traditions had front *kut* and back *kut*, with an intermission between the two sections for performers and other participants to eat and drink (1996: personal communication). The "left side" style also used to include individual dances (*kaein nori*) at the end of the front *kut*, but today the practice has for the most part been discontinued.[7]

The following movements and rhythmic patterns are presented in the order in which they were performed. As with Iri Nongak, regular performance practice dictates playing through a single movement without breaks, taking a pause before moving on to the next. All cues, whether to begin a movement or to cross over from one rhythmic pattern to the next, are likewise signaled by the lead *soe* player. As figure 5.3 shows, Puan's *p'an kut* is composed of eight discrete movements, some of which have counterparts (if only by name) in the Iri repertoire. Structurally the movements tend to end with the same series of closing rhythms—in the fashion of Iri's *hanbat'ang* section—with performers similarly being required to memorize and execute a number of patterns, individual dance movements, and group ground formations (for more specifics, see the Web site provided in the author's note).

First Movement: *Mŏrigut*

Mŏrigut, meaning literally "beginning [or introduction] ritual," serves as a warm-up for the entire ensemble before it enters the main performance space; it is performed while the group is standing in place. This brief period of time allows the lead *soe* player to test or hear the condition of the group and the performance surroundings. The lead *soe* is primarily concerned with whether or not the proper spirit (*ki*) is present.

Figure 5.3. Compositional overview of Puan P'ungmulp'ae performance, June 17, 1996

1. Mŏrigut (2 min. 55 sec.)

    ŏrumgut [I]

    hwimori ♩. = 160

    hwimori [trailer]

    iŭmsae [I] ♩. = 144

    toen samch'ae ♩. = 144

    iŭmsae [II] ♩. = 144/66

    nŭrin kaenjigen ♩. = 66-84

    iŭmsae [III] ♩ = 84

    hwimori ♩ = 84-92

    ŏrumgut [I]

    insagut [I] ♪ = 138

2. Oemach'i chilgut (4 min. 5 sec.)

    kilgut ♪ = 152-208+

    nŭrin kaenjigen ♩. = 100-108

    iŭmsae [III] ♩. = 80

    hwimori ♩. = 80

3. Ch'aegut (2 min. 35 sec.)

    ch'ilch'ae ♩. = 132-138

    tumach'i ♩. = 138

    iŭmsae [II:altered] ♩. = 138/72

    nŭrin kaenjigen ♩. = 72-80

    iŭmsae [III] ♩. = 80

    hwimori ♩. = 84

4. Hohŏgut (7 min. 40 sec.)

    chindadŭraegi ♩ = 72-144/144-160/

    ♩. = 80-138

    ŏrumgut [I]

    hohŏgut ♩. = 100-108/84-92/100-108

    tol hohŏgut ♩. = 120/72/112

    chajin hohŏgut ♩. = 112

    chung samch'ae ♩. = 112

    iŭmsae [III] ♩.= 144

    hwimori ♩. = 144

    tchaksoe ♩. = 144-160

    hwimori ♩. = 160-168

    tchaksoe ♩. = 168-200

    hwimori ♩. = 100

5. P'ungnyugut (7 min. 30 sec.)

    insagut [II] ♩. = 52

    p'ungnyu ♩. = 52-54

    pan p'ungnyu ♩. = 104-108

pparŭn kaenjigen ♩. = 108-116

iŭmsae [IV] 𝅗𝅥. = 76

hwimori ♩. = 76-92

6. Pangulchin'gut (14 min. 35 sec.)

ŏrumgut [II] ♩. = 76-120

hwimori 𝅗𝅥. = 96

ŏrumgut [II] ♩. = 92-116

hwimori 𝅗𝅥. = 88-100

iŭmsae [I] ♩. = 192

toen samch'ae ♩. = 168

iŭmsae [II] 𝅗𝅥. = 84/♩. = 84

nŭrin kaenjigen ♩. = 84-96

iŭmsae [III] ♩. = 192

hwimori ♩. = 192

tchaksoe ♩. = 192

hwimori ♩. = 192-200

iŭmsae [V] ♩. = 92 96

pan p'ungnyu ♩. = 96-100

pparŭn kaenjigen ♩. = 100-120

iŭmsae [IV] 𝅗𝅥. = 72

hwimori 𝅗𝅥. = 72-100

7. Mijigi (6 min. 5 sec.)

ŏrumgut [I]

tchaksoe ♩. = 144-160

hwimori ♩. = 160

tchaksoe ♩. = 160

hwimori 𝅗𝅥. = 84-108

iŭmsae [V] ♩. = 96-104

pan p'ungnyu ♩. = 104

pparŭn kaenjigen ♩. = 104-112

iŭmsae [IV] 𝅗𝅥. = 66

hwimori 𝅗𝅥. = 66-80

8. Yŏngsan (14 min. 5 sec.)

ŏrumgut [I]

kajin yŏngsan ♩. = 92-126

tadŭraegi yŏngsan ♩. = 126

hwimori ♩. = 152-176

tchaksoe ♩. = 176-200

hwimori ♩. = 200

ŏrumgut [I]

insagut [I] ♪ = 126

Ŏrumgut [I]: metrically free. *Ŏrumgut*, whose name comes from the verb *ŏrŭda* (literally, "to play with [or coax]"), begins with two strokes played very close together, followed by individual strokes that gradually increase in speed until they become a roll.

Hwimori: 3 + 3 + 3 + 3. Rhythmically identical to Iri Nongak's *hwimori,* this single-phrase pattern is played as a cycle. "Left side" p'ungmul groups tend to play *hwimori* at a faster overall speed, hence many *changgo* players will drop the "extra" strokes of the performance form and play only the primary form. *Hwimori* is a closing rhythmic pattern played at the end of every movement and is used more than any other. Yi felt that it was important to accent subdivisions 1, 4, and 9 in the *changgo* line so that they are heard from a distance; this gives the pattern its distinctive flavor. *Hwimori* is considered one of the most difficult rhythmic patterns for the *soe* to play. The dynamic contour of the *soe*'s strong strokes is as follows:

O	O	O	O
kaen-ji	*kaen-ji*	*kaen-ji*	*kaen-ji*

Hwimori [trailer]: 3 + 3. This two-bar phrase is played one time through by the lead *soe* player as a signal to move to the next rhythmic pattern.

Iŭmsae [I]: 3 + 3 + 3 + 3 / 3 + 3 + 3 + 3. Similar in meaning and function to Iri Nongak's *iŭmgut* ("joint," "juncture," or "seam"), *iŭmsae* in various forms serves as a bridge when moving from one rhythmic pattern to another (the verb *nŏmŏganda* is used as well, meaning "to cross over"). *Iŭmsae* plays a much more important structural role in "left side" p'ungmul, serving as the glue that holds the movements together. According to Yi, "Without *iŭmsae*, moving from one pattern to another is unbalanced [Yi used the English word] or strange [*isang hada*]." *Iŭmsae* are played through only once.

Toen samch'ae: 3 + 3 + 3 + 3 / 3 + 3 + 3 + 3. Performance practice suggests that the direct meaning of *toen* (from the verb *toeda,* or "thick" or "intense") *samch'ae* (three strokes) is misleading, since currently it features only two strokes on the *ching. Toen samch'ae* is composed of two phrases of compound meter and is performed as a cycle.

Iŭmsae [II]: 3 + 3 / 3 (this last set of subdivisions is in a slower tempo).

Nŭrin kaenjigen: 3 + 3. The second half of the name of this rhythmic pattern is taken from the oral mnemonics of the *soe* line (*nŭrin* means "slow"). Despite outward appearances, *kaenjigen* (like *hwimori*) is also considered a very difficult pattern for the beginning *soe* player. Yi told me that he felt he performed *kaenjigen* improperly for the first five years of study. He stressed that this rhythm cannot be learned in isolation—it must be played with the entire group to see how it fits into the overall scheme. *Kaenjigen* is played as a cycle and is considered unique to the "left side" tradition.

Iŭmsae [III]: 3 + 3 + 3 + 3.

Hwimori.

Ŏrumgut [I]: metrically free.

Insagut: 3 + 3 + 3 + 3. "Left side" *insagut* is identical in meaning, stroke order, and function to the first phrase of its counterpart in the "right side" repertoire; thus, it signals that the performance proper is about to begin.

Second Movement: *Oemach'i chilgut (Kilgut)*

Oemach'i (one stroke) *chilgut* (road or lane ritual), or just simply *kilgut*, is played as the group enters the performance space and forms a large circle moving in a counterclockwise direction (*chil* is local dialect for *kil*).[8] The movement is so named for its opening rhythmic pattern, though the reference to a single stroke of the *ching* is most likely a remnant of a playing tradition or style now extinct. *Kilgut* is also played during ritual p'ungmul performances when the ensemble moves from one location to another.

Kilgut: 3 + 3 + 3 + 3 / 3 + 3 + 3 + 3 / 3 + 3 + 3 + 3 = *apkut;* 3 + 3 + 3 + 3 = *pon'gut. Kilgut* the pattern is compositionally unique with regard to repeat structure in all of North Chŏlla province p'ungmul. It is made up two larger phrases: (1) the "front phrase" (*apkut* or *apkarak*), which is played straight through once and immediately followed by (2) the "main phrase" (*pon'gut* or *pon'garak*), which is repeated an unspecified number of times until the lead *soe* player signals to return to the front phrase (the entire process then repeats itself).

Nŭrin kaenjigen.

Iŭmsae [III].

Hwimori.

Third Movement: *Ch'aegut*

The term *ch'ae* in "left side" p'ungmul is also a reference to the number of strokes played on the *ching* within the duration of a single pattern. In the context of P'ilbong village tradition, rhythms so named are considered a direct remnant of *ture kut,* music played as accompaniment to the work of communal labor teams. *Ch'aegut* (stroke ritual or performance) theoretically contains the full complement of such patterns, progressing numerically from *ilch'ae* (one stroke) through to *ch'ilch'ae* (seven strokes), though standard procedure dictates that only a few patterns be selected during an ongoing performance due to time constraints. A further twist on this practice is that the order of the *ch'ae* rhythmic patterns is generally decided by the lead *soe* player, with considerable variation from performance to performance. Members, therefore, tend to let the lead *soe* play through the new pattern once alone in order to determine which one has been selected, as was the case for the June 17 performance.

Ch'ilch'ae: 3 + 3 + 3 + 3 / 3 + 3 + 3 + 3 / 3 + 3 + 3 + 3 / 3 + 3 + 3 + 3. In spite of the name of this pattern, *ch'ilch'ae* (seven strokes) only features four strokes of the *ching* that occur at the beginning of each of phrase. All *ch'ae* patterns are repeated as a cycle.

Tumach'i: 3 + 3 + 3 + 3 / 3 + 3 + 3 + 3. It is standard performance practice to follow each *ch'ae* pattern with the two-phrase cycle *tumach'i* (two strokes).

Iŭmsae [II: altered]: 3 + 3 / 3.

Nŭrin kaenjigen.

Iŭmsae [III].

Hwimori.

Fourth Movement: *Hohŏgut*

Within the "left side" tradition, *hohŏgut* is known as a movement of numerous transitions and complex ground formations. The title is derived from the rhythmic pattern of the same name, so called because of the nonsensical syllables *ho hŏ* exclaimed during the playing of the cycle.

Chindadŭraegi: 2 + 2 + 2 + 2 (1st); 2 + 2 + 2 + 2 / 2 + 2 + 2 + 2 (2nd); 3 + 3 + 3 + 3 (3rd). This pattern is actually a series of three separate cycles, each repeated and gradually increasing in speed until moving to the next. The ensemble now for the first time breaks into two families: the *changgo* and *puk* drum players, who continue moving in a counterclockwise circle, and the *soe* and *ching* gong players, who begin tracing an *ŭm-yang* (*yin-yang*) pattern.

Ŏrumgut [I].

Hohŏgut: 3 + 3 + 3 + 3 / 3 + 3 + 3 + 3 / 2 + 3 + 2 + 3 + 2 / 3 + 3 + 2 / 2 + 3 + 3 + 2 / 3 + 3 + 3 + 3. Though not identical to the Iri Nongak pattern of the same name (*ho hŏ* is a linguistic variant of *ho ho*), it nevertheless occupies the same position in terms of complexity, featuring asymmetrical phrase lengths and composite meters. *Hohŏgut* is one of the few rhythms in either regional style that omits the sound of the *ching*.

Tol hohŏgut: 2 + 3 + 2 + 3 + 2 / 3 + 3 + 2 / 2 + 3 + 3 + 2 / 3 + 3 + 3 + 3 / 3 + 3 + 3 / 3 + 3 + 3 + 3 + 3 + 3. Equally difficult in structure and execution, the cycle *tol* (from the verb *tolda,* "to rotate") *hohŏgut* is so named because of a spinning move added to the fifth phrase.

Chajin hohŏgut: 3 + 3 + 3 + 3 / 3 + 3 + 3 + 3. Yi and most of Puan P'ungmulp'ae considered *chajin* (fast) *hohŏgut* the most fun pattern to dance. The drum and gong groups at this point have formed opposing semicircles moving toward one another; as the head of each line approaches each other, they kick their respective right feet together, then move to the back of the line (the entire process then repeats itself a few times). The *ching* begins to play again.

Chung samch'ae: 3 + 3 + 3 + 3 / 3 + 3 + 3 + 3. *Chung* (medium) *samch'ae* (three strokes) marks the return of the ensemble to the counterclockwise circle formation. This two-phrase pattern is played as a cycle.

Iŭmsae [III].

Hwimori.

Tchaksoe: series of 3 + 3 + 3 + 3 phrases. The title of this rhythmic pattern is a combination of the words *tchak* (pair or couple) and *soe* (small gong). It is considered one of the most exciting sonic events in the entire "left side" repertoire and is eagerly awaited by all. As the rest of the ensemble plays a variation of *hwimori,* the lead *soe* begins to play a kind of dynamic interlocking or hocketing pattern with the other *soe.* Theoretically speaking *tchaksoe* can occur any time *hwimori* is played, though lead *soe* players tend to reserve its use for later movements to build to a greater climax.

Hwimori.

Tchaksoe.

Hwimori.

Fifth Movement: *P'ungnyugut*

Yi considered *P'ungnyugut* the most difficult to master in terms of playing style or feeling, versus technique per se. The rhythmic patterns within this movement are regarded as the best for dancing.

Insagut [II]: 3 + 3 + 3 + 3 / 3 + 3 + 3 + 3. This pattern is played one time through as a transition to the following *p'ungnyu.*

P'ungnyu: 3 + 3 + 3 + 3 / 3 + 3 + 3 + 3. *P'ungnyu* at the broadest level means "refinement," but in the context of traditional arts refers more specifically to aristocratic chamber music. The p'ungmul rhythm by the same name—oddly *not* used in the aristocratic genre—may appear technically simple on the surface, yet is believed to have the most flavor or character of any of the slower rhythms. *P'ungnyu* is similar in feeling to "left side's" *oemach'i chilgut* and "right side's" *kukkŏri* rhythmic patterns and is performed as a cycle.

Pan p'ungnyu: 3 + 3 + 3 + 3 / 3 + 3 + 3 + 3. Played at roughly double the speed of *p'ungnyu* (or in half the amount of time), *pan* (half) *p'ungnyu* is a two-phrase compound meter cycle. When Yi learned *pan p'ungnyu* and *pparŭn kaenjigen* (the following rhythmic pattern) from Yang Sunyong, the late lead *soe* player of P'ilbong Nongak, Yang would spend two hours on these two patterns alone—he considered them this fun or interesting. *Pan p'ungnyu* is similar to "left side's" *samch'ae* rhythmic pattern.

Pparŭn kaenjigen: 3 + 3 + 3 + 3. Also named after the *soe* oral mnemonics, *pparŭn* (fast) *kaenjigen* retains the same *soe* stroke order as the slower (*nŭrin*) version but doubles the length and increases the speed. Both fast and slow *kaenjigen* cycles were considered by Yi to be the most important rhythmic patterns in the "left side" repertoire, so much so that without them the meaning of the performance is lost. Yi made regular visits to P'ilbong to ensure his *kaenjigen* still had the proper character, since, according to his teachers, if one can play *kaenjigen* and *hwimori* well, particularly the *soe* player, others will then say "There is a truly great 'left side' player." The dynamic shape of the *soe*'s strong strokes matches the contour of its counterpart *nŭrin kaenjigen:*

   O   O   O   O

kaen—jigen *kaen—jigen* *kaen—jigen* *kaen—jigen*

Iŭmsae [IV]: 3 + 3 + 3 + 3.
Hwimori.

Sixth Movement: *Pangulchin'gut*

The title of this movement is taken from the verb *pangul chida,* "to form a drop." It is a reference to the ground formations the group makes during the playing of the opening rhythms, coiling and unwinding twice and producing two large teardroplike figures within the performance space. The rhythmic material of the first half is borrowed almost directly from the first movement (*Mŏrigut*).

Ŏrumgut [II]: 3 + 3 + 3 + 3; metrically free section. The first phrase in each instrument line is repeated and increased in speed until coming to a near roll, at which point the second phrase is played once through.

Hwimori.
Ŏrumgut [II].
Hwimori.
Iŭmsae [I].
Toen samch'ae.
Iŭmsae [II].

Nŭrin kaenjigen.
Iŭmsae [III].
Hwimori.
Tchaksoe.
Hwimori.
Iŭmsae [V]: 3 + 3 + 3 + 3 / 3 + 3 + 3 + 3 / 3 + 3 + 3 + 3 / 3 + 3 +
   3 + 3.
Pan p'ungnyu.
Pparŭn kaenjigen.
From this point on in the movement, the ensemble alternates between dancing in parallel lines and congregating freely in the center of the performing space.
Iŭmsae [IV].
Hwimori.

Seventh Movement: *Mijigi*

The title of this movement is taken from the ground formation of the same name featured during its performance. *Mijigi* (thrust and fall back) is generally recognized as a remnant of p'ungmul's military past—ensemble members form two opposing lines that face each other, then "march" forward and backward. Only at the end of the movement does the group return to a circle.
Ŏrumgut [I].
Tchaksoe.
Hwimori.
Tchaksoe.
Hwimori.
Iŭmsae [V].
Pan p'ungnyu.
Pparŭn kaenjigen.
Iŭmsae [IV].
Hwimori.

Eighth Movement: *Yŏngsan*

Yŏngsan is the highlight and culmination for the skilled performer of the "left side" tradition. It is that section of the performance in which the instrumentalists, particularly the *soe* players, are truly able to enjoy themselves while showing off their technical ability. Yi pointed out that in years past the movement included an additional *yŏngsan* rhythmic pattern called *chaenŭnggi* (literally, "talent" or "ability") *yŏngsan*. It was distinguished by its lack of any set rhythm, allowing the lead *soe* player to improvise freely while the *changgo* attempted to follow (Yi called this "oriental jazz"). *Chaenŭnggi yŏngsan* was no longer formally taught in North Chŏlla province.[9]

Ŏrumgut [I].

Kajin yŏngsan: Phrases of 3 + 3 + 3 + 3. There is no real set rhythmic pattern for the cycle *kajin* (collected) *yŏngsan* (the meaning of this word is unclear),[10] with phrases being added or deleted as the lead *soe* player wishes. Standard practice dictates that the lead *soe* player perform the pattern one time through alone, followed by the remainder of the *soe* players, who attempt to mirror his or her efforts directly. The resting performers are then given the opportunity to dance freely. The *ching* is not played during *kajin yŏngsan*.

Tadŭraegi yŏngsan: 3 + 3 + 3 + 3 / 3 + 3 + 3 + 3 / 3 + 3 + 3 + 3. *Tadŭraegi* (a term for which there is no good translation) *yŏngsan* is composed of the last three lines of *kajin yŏngsan* and is similarly performed as a cycle. The *ching* begins playing again.

Hwimori.

Tchaksoe.

Hwimori.

Ŏrumgut [I].

Insagut [I].

SUMMARY ANALYSIS

Throughout this book I have used the translation "rhythmic pattern" as a gloss for the Korean terms *karak* and *changdan*. In this section I will explain the rationale for my choice. Below are listed the primary rhythmic patterns found in Iri Nongak's and Puan P'ungmulp'ae's *p'an kut* performances, combined and rearranged to create fourteen categories based on metric structure, presence or absence of repetition, stability of tempo (the integrity of the eighth note or smallest unit), and number of phrases within a single occurrence of the pattern. Tempo is identified by either the capital letter S, meaning each phrase within the pattern is played at essentially the same tempo, or the letter C, indicating a change in tempo from phrase to phrase. This is directly followed by the phrase length, provided in brackets. Repeat structure, when applicable, is marked by the letter X, followed by the number of repetitions, with the lowercase letter *n* representing free repetition. The rhythmic pattern *hwimori,* for example, transcribed as a single phrase of four beats composed of triple subdivisions, repeated over and over at essentially the same tempo, is written: *hwimori* S[1] / 3 + 3 + 3 + 3 / X*n*.

Category 1: Single Meter, Free Repetition

"Right side":   *ilch'ae* S[1] / 2 + 2 + 2 + 2 / X*n*

ich'ae S[1] / 3 + 3 + 3 + 3 / X*n*

chwajilgut S[4] / 3 + 2 + 3 + 2 / 2 + 3 + 3 + 2 / 2 + 3 + 3 + 2 / 2 + 3 + 3 + 2 / X*n*

yangsando S[4] / 3 + 3 + 3 / 3 + 3 + 3 / 3 + 3 + 3 / 3 + 3 + 3 / X*n*

kin samch'ae S[2] / 3 + 3 + 3 + 3 / 3 + 3 + 3 + 3 / X*n*

tchalbŭn samch'ae S[1] / 3 + 3 + 3 + 3 / X*n*

toen samch'ae S[1] / 3 + 3 + 3 + 3 / X*n*

obangjin [A] S[2] / 2 + 2 + 2 + 2 / 2 + 2 + 2 + 2 / X*n*

obangjin [B] S[2] / 2 + 2 + 2 + 2 / 2 + 2 + 2 + 2 / X*n*

chin obangjin ⌊A⌋ S⌊2⌋ / 2 + 2 + 2 + 2 / 2 + 2 + 2 + 2 / X*n*

chajin samch'ae S[1] / 3 + 3 + 3 + 3 / X*n*

chajin hohogut S[2] / 3 + 3 + 3 + 3 / 3 + 3 + 3 + 3 / X*n*

kukkŏri S[1] / 3 + 3 + 3 + 3 / X*n*

iopkut S[1] / 3 + 3 + 3 + 3 / X*n*

"Left side":   *hwimori* S[1] / 3 + 3 + 3 + 3 / X*n*

toen samch'ae S[2] / 3 + 3 + 3 + 3 / 3 + 3 + 3 + 3 / X*n*

nŭrin kaenjigen S[1] / 3 + 3 / X*n*

ch'ilch'ae S[4] / 3 + 3 + 3 + 3 / 3 + 3 + 3 + 3 / 3 + 3 + 3 + 3 / 3 + 3 + 3 + 3 / X*n*

tumach'i S[2] / 3 + 3 + 3 + 3 / 3 + 3 + 3 + 3 / X*n*

chajin hohŏgut S[2] / 3 + 3 + 3 + 3 / 3 + 3 + 3 + 3 / X*n*

chung samch'ae S[2] / 3 + 3 + 3 + 3 / 3 + 3 + 3 + 3 / X*n*

p'ungnyu S[2] / 3 + 3 + 3 + 3 / 3 + 3 + 3 + 3 / X*n*

pan p'ungnyu S[2] / 3 + 3 + 3 + 3 / 3 + 3 + 3 + 3 / X*n*

pparŭn kaenjigen S[1] / 3 + 3 + 3 + 3 / X*n*

kajin yŏngsan S[20] 20 phrases of / 3 + 3 + 3 + 3 / X*n*

tadŭraegi yŏngsan S[3] / 3 + 3 + 3 + 3 / 3 + 3 + 3 + 3 / 3 + 3 + 3 + 3 / X*n*

Category 2: Single Meter, Set Repetition

"Right side":   *iŭmgut* S[2] / 3 + 3 + 3 + 3 / 3 + 3 + 3 + 3 / X1

obangjin [C] S[2] / 2 + 2 + 2 + 2 / 2 + 2 + 2 + 2 / X1

toraganŭn maedoji S[6] 6 phrases of / 3 + 3 + 3 + 3 / X1

          naendŭraemi S[1] / 3 + 3 + 3 + 3 + 3 + 3 / X3

          chajin hohogut [B] S[2] / 3 + 3 + 3 + 3 / 3 + 3 + 3 +
            3 / X2

          suppadadŭm C[15] 15 phrases of / 2 + 2 + 2 + 2 / X1

"Left side":   *iŭmsae* [I] S[2] / 3 + 3 + 3 + 3 / 3 + 3 + 3 + 3 / X1

          iŭmsae [III] S[1] / 3 + 3 + 3 + 3 / X1

          insagut [II] S[2] / 3 + 3 + 3 + 3 / 3 + 3 + 3 + 3 / X1

          iŭmsae [IV] S[1] / 3 + 3 + 3 + 3 / X1

          iŭmsae [V] S[4] / 3 + 3 + 3 + 3 / 3 + 3 + 3 + 3 / 3 + 3 +
            3 + 3 / 3 + 3 + 3 + 3 / X1

Category 3: Single Meter, Irregular Free Repetition[11]

"Right side":   *insagut* [truncated] C[?] / 3 + 3 + 3 + 3 / [3 + 3 + 3 + 3]
            Xn / X1

          maedoji [truncated] S[?] / 3 + 3 + 3 + 3 / 3 + 3 + 3 + 3 /
            [3 + 3 + 3 + 3] Xn / [3 + 3 + 3 + 3] Xn / 3 + 3 + 3 +
            3 / X1

"Left side":   *kilgut* S[?] / 3 + 3 + 3 + 3 / 3 + 3 + 3 + 3 / 3 + 3 + 3 +
            3 / [3 + 3 + 3 + 3] Xn / Xn

          tchaksoe S[?] / [3 + 3 + 3 + 3] Xn / 3 + 3 + 3 + 3 / [3 + 3 +
            3 + 3] Xn[12] / 3 + 3 + 3 + 3 / X1

Category 4: Single Meter, Sequential[13]

"Right side":   *sosam taesam* C[4] / 2 + 2 / X2 → / 2 + 2 / 2 + 2 / X2 → /
            2 + 2 / X8 → / 3 + 3 + 3 + 3 / X1

"Left side":   *chindadŭraegi* C[3] / 2 + 2 + 2 + 2 / Xn → / 2 + 2 + 2 +
            2 / 2 + 2 + 2 + 2 / Xn → / 3 + 3 + 3 + 3 / Xn

Category 5: Two Meters, Free Repetition

"Right side":   *ujilgut* C[5] / 2 + 3 + 3 + 2 / 2 + 3 + 3 + 2 / 2 + 3 + 3 +
            2 / 3 + 3 + 3 + 3 / 3 + 3 + 3 + 3 / Xn

          chilgut S[2] / 2 + 2 + 2 + 2 + 2 + 2 / 3 + 3 + 3 + 3 / Xn

          hohogut S[6] / 2 + 2 + 2 + 2 / 2 + 2 + 2 + 2 / 3 + 2 + 3 +
            2 / 2 + 3 + 3 + 2 / 2 + 3 + 3 + 2 / 2 + 3 + 3 + 2 / Xn

Category 6: Two Meters, Set Repetition

"Right side":   *maedoji* [A] S[7] / 2 + 2 + 2 + 2 + 2 + 2 / 3 + 3 + 3 + 3
            / 2 + 2 + 2 + 2 + 2 + 2 / 2 + 2 + 2 + 2 + 2 + 2 /
            3 + 3 + 3 + 3 / 3 + 3 + 3 + 3 / 3 + 3 + 3 + 3 / X1

maedoji [C] S[8] / 2 + 2 + 2 + 2 + 2 + 2 / 2 + 2 + 2 +
2 + 2 + 2 / 2 + 2 + 2 + 2 + 2 + 2 / 3 + 3 + 3 + 3 /
2 + 2 + 2 + 2 + 2 + 2 / 3 + 3 + 3 + 3 / 3 + 3 + 3 +
3 / 3 + 3 + 3 + 3 / X1

maedoji [E] S[5] / 2 + 2 + 2 + 2 + 2 + 2 / 2 + 2 + 2 + 2 +
2 + 2 / 3 + 3 + 3 + 3 / 3 + 3 + 3 + 3 / 3 + 3 + 3 + 3 / X1

insagut [B] S[8] / 2 + 2 + 2 + 2 + 2 + 2 / 2 + 2 + 2 + 2 +
2 + 2 / 2 + 2 + 2 + 2 + 2 + 2 / 2 + 2 + 2 + 2 + 2 +
2 / 2 + 2 + 2 / 2 + 2 + 2 / 2 + 2 + 2 / 2 + 2 + 2 / X1

maedoji [F] C[6] / 2 + 2 + 2 + 2 + 2 + 2 / 2 + 2 + 2 +
2 + 2 + 2 / 3 + 3 + 3 + 3 / 3 + 3 + 3 + 3 / 3 + 3 +
3 + 3 / 3 + 3 + 3 + 3 / X1

maedoji [H] S[6] / 2 + 2 + 2 + 2 + 2 + 2 / 3 + 3 + 3 +
3 / 2 + 2 + 2 + 2 + 2 + 2 / 3 + 3 + 3 + 3 / 3 + 3 +
3 + 3 / 3 + 3 + 3 + 3 / X1

"Left side":   *iŭmsae* [II] C[2] / 3 + 3 / 3 / X1

Category 7: Two Meters, Set Repetition + Sequential

"Right side":   *maedoji* [G] C[5] / 2 + 2 + 2 + 2 + 2 + 2 / 3 + 3 + 3 +
3 / 2 + 2 + 2 + 2 + 2 + 2 / [2 + 2] X4 / → / [2 + 2]
X6 / X1

Category 8: Two Meters, Irregular Free Repetition

"Right side":   *maedoji* [B] S[?] / 2 + 2 + 2 + 2 + 2 + 2 / 3 + 3 + 3 +
3 / 2 + 2 + 2 + 2 + 2 + 2 / 3 + 3 + 3 + 3 / 3 + 3 +
3 + 3 / 3 + 3 + 3 + 3 / [3 + 3 + 3 + 3] Xn / [3 + 3 +
3 + 3] Xn / 3 + 3 + 3 + 3 / X1

chajin hohogut [C] S[?] / 2 + 2 + 2 + 2 + 2 + 2 / 3 +
3 + 3 + 3 / 3 + 3 + 3 + 3 / [3 + 3 + 3 + 3]
Xn / X1

tasŭrŭm S[?] / 3 + 3 + 3 + 3 / 3 + 3 + 3 + 3 / 3 + 3 +
3 + 3 / [3 + 3] Xn / X1

Category 9: Mixed Meters, Free Repetition

"Left side":   *hohŏgut* C[6] / 3 + 3 + 3 + 3 / 3 + 3 + 3 + 3 / 2 + 3 +
2 + 3 + 2 / 3 + 3 + 2 / 2 + 3 + 3 + 2 / 3 + 3 + 3 +
3 / Xn

tol hohŏgut C[6] / 2 + 3 + 2 + 3 + 2 / 3 + 3 + 2 / 2 +
3 + 3 + 2 / 3 + 3 + 3 + 3 / 3 + 3 + 3 / 3 + 3 + 3 +
3 + 3 + 3 / Xn

Category 10: Mixed Meters, Set Repetition

"Right side":   *chajin kukkŏri* C[8] / 2 + 2 + 2 + 2 + 2 + 2 / 2 + 2 + 2 +
2 + 2 + 2 / 2 + 2 + 2 / 3 + 3 + 3 + 3 / 3 + 3 + 2 +
2 + 2 / 3 + 3 + 3 + 3 / 3 + 3 + 3 + 3 / 3 + 3 + 3 +
3 / X1

Category 11: Metered + Unmetered, Free Repetition

"Right side":   *och'ae chilgut* S[6] / 2 + 3 + 3 + 2 / 2 + 3 + 3 + 3 + 2 /
2 + 3 + 3 + 2 / metrically free / metrically free / 3 +
3 + 3 / X*n*

Category 12: Metered + Unmetered, Set Repetition

"Right side":   *insagut* [A] S[3] / 3 + 3 + 3 + 3 / metrically free / 3 +
3 + 3 + 3 / X1

"Left side":   *insagut* S[2] / 3 + 3 + 3 + 3 / metrically free / X1 or X2

Category 13: Metered + Unmetered, Sequential

"Left side":   *ŏrumgut* [II] C[2] / [3 + 3 + 3 + 3]X*n* / → / metrically
free / X1

Category 14: Metrically Free

"Left side":   *ŏrumgut* [I] metrically free

In 1991 the theme of the national meeting of the Korean Musicological Society (Han'guk kugak hakhoe) was *"Changdan* in Korean Traditional Music." A number of papers were presented and were later published in volume 19 of the journal *Studies in Korean Music (Han'guk ŭmak yŏn'gu).* The opening offering of this publication, by the esteemed scholar Yi Hyegu, presented three definitions of *changdan* given by three different scholars over a sixteen-year period. The article serves as a valuable reference point for the discussion that follows, for to my knowledge no new research has expanded on these three related views or rendered them obsolete.[14] The first definition, by Robert Provine, was taken from his initial publication on rhythms in North Chŏlla province "farmers' music":

> All types of Korean folk music share a common fund of basic rhythmic patterns
> called *changdan*. Literally "long and short," the primary meaning of a particular
> named *changdan* is a tempo and length of time; secondarily, it implies a meter
> and typical rhythmic content. (1975: 5, expanded from citation in Yi Hyegu
> 1991: 12)[15]

The second, given by Paek Taeung ten years later, is really only a slight expansion of Provine's:

> Changdan of traditional music are determined according to four essential elements: meter [pakcha], tempo [pparŭgi], accent [kangyak], and pattern [hanbae]. (1985: 326–27, cited in Yi Hyegu 1991: 12)

The third definition is by Yi Hyegu himself:

> To reiterate, a collection of beats [pak] constitutes a rhythmic pattern [pakcha],[16] and a collection of rhythmic patterns constitutes a changdan. (1991: 29)[17]

If I substitute Provine's "rhythmic content" for Paek and Yi's "(rhythmic) pattern" and combine the three examples into a more or less tidy whole—taking into account Provine's admittance of "shading" through accents (1975: 8) and Yi's relative vagueness—I am then able to provide the following definition:

> Changdan in Korean traditional music are determined by the following parameters: a (set) tempo, length of time, meter, series of accents, and typical rhythmic content.[18]

Because in many ways the selection of changdan studied in the academy is narrow and because they are often presented in introductory works on Korean music, this working definition implies that Korean rhythmic patterns are composed of a single meter. Table 5.4 presents an overview of the sixty-five p'ungmul rhythmic patterns arranged according to category and performance style. What is immediately apparent is the existence of five different metric classifications, ranging from one meter to no meter at all. Although it is true that the majority of the patterns fall into the single-meter categories 1, 2, 3, and 4 (forty-three of the total sixty-five, or roughly 66 percent) and are distributed more or less evenly across the performance styles, it would nonetheless be unwise to underestimate the function and importance of the remaining patterns in any complete p'ungmul performance. What is also notable is the varied use of repetition, the structure of which is intimately linked to meter and which is a major criterion in the establishment of the above categories. It is an element mysteriously unaccounted for in the academic definition.

Another common assumption is that rhythmic patterns are of a basically set length and are played at more or less the same tempo, overlooking mi-

Table 5.4. Rhythmic patterns arranged by category and performance style

Meter	Repeat structure	"Right side"	"Left side"
1. Single meter	Free repetition	14	12
2. Single meter	Set repetition	6	5
3. Single meter	Irregular free repetition	2	2
4. Single meter	Sequential	1	1
5. Two meters	Free repetition	3	0
6. Two meters	Set repetition	6	1
7. Two meters	Set repetition + sequential	1	0
8. Two meters	Irregular free repetition	3	0
9. Mixed meters	Free repetition	0	2
10. Mixed meters	Set repetition	1	0
11. Metered + unmetered	Free repetition	1	0
12. Metered + unmetered	Set repetition	1	1
13. Metered + unmetered	Sequential	0	1
14. Metrically free	Not applicable	0	1
	Total	39	26

nor fluctuations inherent in any sensitive performance. A look at table 5.5, however, reveals that patterns in nine of the fourteen categories (2, 3, 4, 5, 6, 7, 9, 10, and 13) change tempo markedly during a single occurrence of the rhythmic pattern. A fixed or set length of time is difficult to establish in categories 11, 12, and 13, owing to the unmetered sections, and it is impossible to determine with metrically free rhythmic patterns (category 14) or patterns of an undetermined phrase length (categories 3 and 8). The number of phrases, though absent from the definitions found in Yi Hyegu's opening article, is discussed in the fourth article, by Kim Hyŏnsuk, of *Studies in Korean Music*. Kim outlines four types of rhythmic patterns (*karak*, in her text) based on number of phrases and repeat structure. Although valuable in its exploration of new territory, the article is unfortunately limited in outlook and unsupported by concrete musical examples.[19]

The reason for my choice of the translation "rhythmic pattern" over the oft-encountered "rhythmic cycle" should now be apparent. "Cycle" implies the repetition of a set model or unit of time, terminology inappropriate for a large portion of the North Chŏlla province p'ungmul repertoire. It is also quite clear that although the academic definition of a rhythmic pattern accurately describes most aspects of category 1 and isolated aspects of the remaining categories, it is misleading and ultimately unusable *when*

Table 5.5. Rhythmic patterns arranged by category, tempo, and phrase structure

1. Single meter, free repetition	Same tempo	1 phrase (10)
		2 phrases (11)
		3 phrases (1)
		4 phrases (3)
		20 phrases (1)
2. Single meter, set repetition	Same tempo	1 phrase (3)
		2 phrases (5)
		4 phrases (1)
		6 phrases (1)
	Changing tempo	15 phrases (1)
3. Single meter, irregular free repetition	Same tempo	Undetermined phrase length (3)
	Changing tempo	Undetermined phrase length (1)
4. Single meter, sequential	Changing tempo	3 phrases (1)
		4 phrases (1)
5. Two meters, free repetition	Same tempo	2 phrases (1)
		6 phrases (1)
	Changing tempo	5 phrases (1)
6. Two meters, set repetition	Same tempo	5 phrases (1)
		6 phrases (1)
		7 phrases (1)
		8 phrases (2)
	Changing tempo	2 phrases (1)
		6 phrases (1)
7. Two meters, set repetition + sequential	Changing tempo	5 phrases (1)
8. Two meters, irregular free repetition	Same tempo	Undetermined phrase length (3)
9. Mixed meters, free repetition	Changing tempo	6 phrases (2)
10. Mixed meters, set repetition	Changing tempo	8 phrases (1)
11. Metered + unmetered, free repetition	Same tempo	6 phrases (1)
12. Metered + unmetered, set repetition	Same tempo	2 phrases (1)
		3 phrases (1)
13. Metered + unmetered, sequential	Changing tempo	2 phrases (1)
14. Metrically free (1)		

employed universally, owing to its limited scope. The following definition is, therefore, presented as a synthesis of the above debate within the context of p'ungmul, but it is most likely applicable to the majority of Korean folk music genres as a whole:

> Korean rhythmic patterns are determined by rhythmic models consisting of a series of accented and unaccented strokes or beats, often varying in metrical and repeat structure, use of tempo, and phrase length (when applicable).

I may make a living by carrying an A-frame with a rake on my back and by digging in the earth, but I consider myself an artist. Even if there are those who might say, "What is there to be proud of in a life of beating the drum?"

—Shin Kinam, *Ŏttŏk'e hŏmŏn ttokttok hŏn cheja han nom tugo chugŭlkko?* [What Do I Have to Do to Get a Single Smart Disciple before I Die?] (1992), 158

6

Timely Reflections

It seems only appropriate to end this book with a series of interrelated and juxtaposed dialogues held between me, my two principal mentors, and members of their close inner circles recording their reflections and ruminations on topics of great personal and societal import. This chapter should not be read so much as a definitive conclusion as an examination and appreciation of a small piece of cloth—the fieldwork experience's fixed period of time and space—torn from a long, elaborate, multicolored tapestry—the Korean p'ungmul tradition—the end and design of which we cannot make out clearly as it stretches into the past and reaches into the future.

Central themes that emerged during the interviews include the character and upbringing of the accomplished performer, couched within the larger context of the nature of talent and the parameters of musical competence; perceived differences in "left" versus "right" performance aesthetics as viewed through the prism of ensemble and/ or audience relationships and expectations; and contested understandings of the place of p'ungmul in contemporary Korean life. These artists' various viewpoints and perspectives are informed to a great extent by the dual realms of logos and mythos, a synthesis of the idiosyncratic and the comprehensive, of that which has been accomplished and that which is as yet unattainable. I begin by providing brief biographical sketches of our additional participants, drummers and dancers from Kim Hyŏngsun's and Yi Sangbaek's troupes who had earned special admiration and respect from my mentors.

I first met Pak Yongt'aek in early 1996 on the bus ride up to Seoul for my first performance with Iri Nongak. In addition to his role as lead *soe* player (*sangsoe*), Pak was really the spiritual and motivational leader of the organization. He had been with Kim Hyŏngsun during Iri's formative years, and this long-standing relationship had given birth to a respect and trust that extended well beyond the regular confines of friendship. Pak was in charge of running the home training institute in Iri (now the city of Iksan) while Kim was away in Chŏnju teaching. Pak's duties at the institute included the grooming of Kim's son, Kim Ikchu, for his eventual ascent to lead *changgo* player. Pak to this day remains a commanding presence, both in physical and artistic stature, though this was tempered by an easygoingness and humility I seldom encountered among other lead *soe* players who had grown accustomed to life in the limelight (see figure 6.1).

Figure 6.1. Pak Yongt'aek (lead *soe* player), Seoul, Iri Nongak

Pak was born in 1952 and hails from a distinguished line of "right side" lead *soe* players, as shown in figure 6.2. His love of p'ungmul began at a very early age, owing partly to an active program at his elementary school and partly to his dentist-farmer father's being an amateur *ching* player. While in college in 1975, Pak was taken by a friend to see Kim Hyŏngsun perform (Iri Nongak was not yet a formal entity); Pak was apparently so enthralled with Kim's performance that afterward he went straight to Kim to ask if he could join Kim's troupe. Kim saw enough potential in Pak to begin training the young man, who was soon studying directly with the future Iri Nongak *soe* players Yi Sunam and Kim Mundal.[1] Over the next decade Pak would play with nearly every major group and performer of the "right side" tradition, and in 1985, when Iri Nongak was designated a cultural asset, Kim Hyŏngsun chose Pak to lead his group. It was fortunate for Pak that the group received this honor when it did, as he had been skipping out on his company day job for years to play with Kim and was fired only a few months after Iri was elevated to cultural asset status.

Since that first encounter Pak and I had met privately on numerous occasions—some of these in the form of informal *soe* lessons—but Pak was nevertheless reluctant to be interviewed, perhaps for fear that his comments would be perceived as threatening Kim's sovereignty. The opportunity to interview him came shortly before my last performance with Iri Nongak at the Seoul Norimadang on August 10, 1996, just a few weeks before I left Korea. After seeing me interview other *soe* players at an outdoor coffee shop, Pak decided that his own opinions should be included as part of my overall account.

It is nearly impossible to get close to Kim Hyŏngsun without getting to know Cho Myŏngja. Cho was unofficially the lead *sogo* player of Iri Nongak, though because of her advanced *changgo*-playing ability she was often called upon to assist in teaching when Kim was tired or unwell. Even though Cho was a part-time instructor of traditional dance at the CTK in Chŏnju, she spent most of her free time in the p'ungmul studio, acting as a teaching as

---

Figure 6.2. Pak Yongt'aek's teaching lineage

Pak Manp'ung (b. 18??, deceased)
|
Kim Tosam (b. 1875, deceased)
|
Kim Mundal (b. 1909, deceased)   Yi Sunam (b. 1918, deceased)
| |
Pak Yongt'aek (b. 1952)

Figure 6.3. Author with Cho Myŏngja (lead *sogo* player), Seoul, Iri Nongak

well as personal assistant to Kim. On occasion she even filled in on *soe* for the advanced class. Over the years her relationship to Kim slowly changed from one of student and disciple to something like a family member (see figure 6.3).

Born in 1943 in Seoul, Cho moved to Chŏnju in 1986 because of her husband's work. Her background differed in almost every respect from that of Pak Yongt'aek. Raised in a Christian household, her fondest childhood memories included touring with a Western-style children's dance troupe that made the rounds of the local churches and U.S. army bases. Until her move to Chŏnju she had mainly studied Western classical music, though she was aware of Chŏnju's reputation as a "city of [traditional] arts" (*yesul ŭi toshi*) and so felt inclined to search out opportunities to study traditional song and dance upon her arrival. Cho discovered the CTK in 1987. She instantly felt drawn to traditional dance—much more so than she had been drawn to Western musical performance—and so quickly progressed within the ranks of that studio. It was during this period that Kim Hyŏngsun noticed something special about Cho's overall deportment, so he invited her to study p'ungmul with him when time allowed. From the early 1990s on Cho has suffered some physical setbacks because of health problems, which most likely kept her from being named an official assistant instructor (*chogyo*) under Kim.

I interviewed Cho on May 17, 1996, on the grounds of the CTK. Cho had taken it upon herself to be my secondary teacher during my fieldwork stay, often singling me out in class for individual praise or criticism. She, perhaps more than any other member of the Iri Nongak organization, had regular contact with foreign researchers and dignitaries. Frequent travel with her businessman husband, alongside considerable personal study, was rewarded by her self-admittedly modest Japanese and English language skills, as well as her awareness of academic life and its requirements. Cho arranged many of my private interviews with center students and was especially pleased to be included as part of this research.

The last voice to join in this chapter's discussion is Pak Yŏngsun. Born in 1977, Pak was one of the youngest regular members of Puan P'ungmulp'ae, the group to which Yi Sangbaek had been elected director of education. Her main love and focus was the *puk,* though she was an accomplished *changgo* player as well. She had played p'ungmul since elementary school and as a high school performer was introduced to Yi by her brother, one of Yi's closest friends. Pak was one of Yi's most devoted pupils: in addition to accompanying him on many of his teaching excursions around the county, she was largely responsible for organizing the high school group residency at the P'ilbong winter training institute, outlined in chapter 4. Pak was born and raised in Puan and was fiercely proud of her regional culture. Though many of her friends had made plans to move to larger urban areas such as Chŏnju or even Seoul after graduation, Pak was resolute in her decision to make a life for herself in her home county.

I interviewed Pak at the group's studio in downtown Puan on August 17, 1996. Although most of her responses were short and unadorned, they nevertheless were valuable for their insight into many of the views held by performers of her generation.

MUSICAL COMPETENCE

My interest in delving into overt and underlying attitudes regarding musical competence is twofold. From the beginning I had wanted to understand the role played by talent in Korean institutional frameworks that often seemingly ignored individual aptitude in matters of promotion and recognition. As outlined in chapter 4, progress at the CTK in Chŏnju was primarily assessed by the amount of time one had spent studying in the studio. And at the CTK and among Yi Sangbaek's p'ungmul groups at home and in college, members were keenly aware of what term or year someone had joined, intelligence that then served as a basis for assigning the person a place in the pecking order (though this latter custom was surely influenced by similar university and business practices). On a more personal and philosophical level, however, I needed to know whether Koreans engaged in the classic Western-style debates of "nature versus nurture" and/or of skill or technique versus musical feeling, with an unspoken yearning for understanding my own possibilities as a "foreigner" within the tradition.[2]

As the interviews that follow will illuminate, the idea of talent is conceptualized through a small lexicon of related terminology that moves from the general to the more specific. At the broadest level is *ki*, a word associated with a constellation of meanings in the Korean language that in the current context refers more narrowly and specifically to general innate artistic ability. For some this inborn and at times even intangible quality is credited to genetic disposition; for others it is viewed and accepted as a gift, akin to the receiving of grace. Actual skill or proficiency in a particular discipline is represented more directly by the words *chaejil* and *chaenŭng*, which literally mean "talent." From here a few participants further sharpened their terminological focus by using the phrases *yesulchŏgin kamgak* (artistic sense) and *ŭmakchŏgin kamgak* (musical sense), which, like *ki, chaejil,* and *chaenŭng,* were believed to be inherent in one's artistic makeup.

In spite of the aforementioned policies of CTK and college drumming circles, all five p'ungmul performers interviewed for this chapter directly linked a student's success to innate artistic ability, though some individuals allowed that hard work and certain kinds of family backgrounds provided additional benefits. Kim Hyŏngsun was quite forward and obvious in the attention he paid, in the form of extra coaching and advice, to a select few students who showed unusual promise. These chosen few were consistently invited to private parties, special performances, and p'ungmul competitions held throughout the province where Kim often served as a judge. I myself enjoyed such privileged treatment firsthand: within four months (and twenty months prematurely, according to CTK regulations) I was asked to join the advanced class; and within six months, Iri Nongak itself. Kim reflected on these issues:

> If I had to verbally explain it, when I first see a student, I think to myself, "If I train this person, will they take an active interest in this kind of music, or will it just be a hobby, a momentary entertainment?" We all have those kinds of thoughts. I have many disciples here, but there are definitely a few among them who will be more active than the others in this profession. And I do pay more attention to those few.
>
> Regarding family background, I can't really choose a disciple according to their family background or financial situation, but if it's possible, I think it's

better if he or she is from a well-to-do family. I say this because people can only make time to study and be active in p'ungmul if their family financial situation is settled. Otherwise, well, if their family financial situation is unstable, then they will have to work. There are those sorts of problems.

In general, in this profession—of course other professions could be the same, I suppose—I can tell whether this person or that person will have a future or not, because I've been teaching for so long. You know how teachers are—by looking at their student's appearance, dance style, personality, and the way in which they play the rhythmic patterns, they can judge whether or not this person will be able to make it with some effort. I suppose even a bit slower person can make it if they try endlessly. But there are those who are more diverse, those who by nature are artistic—I guess that's what they call *ki*. Those kinds of people may learn faster. In the case of the CTK, as you know, we are divided into three classes: beginner, intermediate, and advanced. But in the intermediate class, there are many better performers than in the advanced class. It's also possible that in the beginner class there could be better performers than some in the intermediate class. There are many students whose actual ability is beyond their level. They are in those particular classes because of institute formalities.

There is no question that one must be talented [*chaejil-i itta*]. I have observed this throughout my sixty years of life, to the extent that I've been able to guess just by looking at a person's face and appearance,[3] almost always, whether or not the person will be able to do it. As I told you earlier, even if someone studies a long time—five, six, seven, even eight years—they may not do as well as someone who has been studying only a year and a half. This was the case with you, how you memorized everything so quickly. This is why students from the advanced class ask you about the rhythmic patterns, and why they are not embarrassed.

Pak Yongt'aek shared Kim Hyŏngsun's belief in the existence of this natural or inborn *ki*, though, like his other colleague from Iri Nongak, Cho Myŏngja, he adds hard work as an additional essential ingredient for the making of a professional p'ungmul performer:

I strongly feel that the person without *ki* can't do it. You must have the interest. No matter how long or loud you bang a rhythm for someone, some people will never get it. I've taught so many university students, so I know. The dumb ones are always dumb—I'm a dumb one as well, so I got yelled at quite a bit. "Can't you even do this?!" they would scream. I was scolded every day. These days, being a teacher, I see those who can't learn, those people who really can't learn. There are a few with talent [*chaenŭng itta*] who play better than I do. But often they don't continue after college, though I wish they would. That's how we lose a lot of the talented ones. Good body movement, and those people who soak everything up quickly, they are the talented ones. If I teach them one rhythmic pattern, they can play two. I play *kaegaeng,* and then they play *kkaegaeng* [with more confidence]. That's the way they do it. So after observing for a couple of minutes, I can judge whether or not they will be able to do it. I think to myself: "You won't be able to teach them, no matter how many hundreds of times you try." This is because they can't play it the way I tell them to do it. Out of ten students, there are usually about two or three of them who are good—the rest of them are incompetent.

Talent is important, but one must work hard if one is going to go anywhere. It takes time, it can't be done quickly. For example, if everyone starts from the first movement, the talented ones will progress quickly on to the third. The person who works hard, however, can still progress—it just takes a very long time. People are born with *ki,* and they are the ones who are fast at learning. You know, honestly it can't be done without either *ki* or effort. I guess you need both, for those who become professional.

I've said that people who are considered talented are faster at learning. Definitely they are faster. Without musical talent it will be difficult. My daughter is studying p'ungmul with me now. She has been good at singing ever since she was little, and now this talent has carried through to her playing. She does the *changgo* dance [*sŏlchanggo*] and everything else, and also a bit of *samul nori* [urban form of p'ungmul]. It's difficult for the rest of the students her age—out of ten students, three will be good, and seven won't progress at all, no matter what you do. The others come only because their fellow students come. It's useless to push those kinds of kids to learn. It's like studying—no matter how well you teach them, they won't learn if they don't want to learn.

Cho mirrored these sentiments from the related perspective of a dancer:

Artistic feeling or sense [*yesulchŏgin kamgak*], they call this *ki* around here. I've had this *ki* since I was little. When I was little, in elementary school, I learned a bit of dancing, music, and singing. Then came entrance examinations in middle school. I graduated from Inch'ŏn Teacher's College—I graduated from a school that trains teachers. At that time, it was very difficult to get accepted. Back then it was a two-year college—one had to study extremely hard to get into college. My family tried to stop me. Those were certainly trying times—my parents would definitely not have approved of a career in the arts.

I don't particularly like the word "talent" [*chaejil*]—I think we should call it "musical sense" [*ŭmakchŏgin kamgak*]. People with this sense are faster, they get things faster than those who don't have it. If you look at the *changgo,* it requires a lot of time and effort. In many ways, the sound that comes out becomes mature through time, it has a different taste. Anybody can play, but everyone's taste is different. We can't play like Kim Hyŏngsun because we haven't matured as much. Of course we don't practice as much, either; we do this as a hobby, and he does it as a job. We all started this as a hobby. These ladies [fellow classmates] all started after a certain age, so it's either a hobby or exercise. There are many who play for the exercise—as you know, it's very physically demanding, running for an hour straight. If you want to become professional, you must possess a superior sense and must put in a lot of effort.

Again, I think it depends on the individual—they must have basic *ki*. I have a daughter, and my dance teacher wanted me to bring her in to see whether or not she could be trained at an early age. So I brought her in twice, and both times she was sent home. My teacher told her: "Go home, you don't have *ki* like your mother." She didn't have *ki*, meaning artistic sense—this means no talent. My teacher wanted to teach her, so I brought her in twice, but there was nothing that could be done. So we gave up. In that sense, one must be born with *ki*. In addition to this, you must have endurance. Endurance is needed not only for athletes, but for artists and others as well. There are aspects you can develop with hard effort, but I can recognize those people who have *ki*. Because I've done this for a while, I can tell just by watching a few steps whether or not he or she has *ki* and will be able to have the endurance. That kind of person catches my eye. And without a doubt, Mr. Kim would have no problem seeing these sorts of things. That's why they say teachers become like psychics—part of you begins to pick up this ability.

Although Yi Sangbaek also believed in a certain level of innate feeling, ability, character, and talent, similar to that found in the previous responses—later he used the familiar term *ki*—he stressed as well the importance of environment and external support, factors distinct from genetic disposition. Yi often spoke of regretting having started learning p'ungmul so late in life, a concern with which many of us as musicians are all too familiar. He outwardly professed having a certain advantage over city kids who had grown up without the benefits and associations of a rural upbringing, though he privately confessed the jealousy he felt toward people like Kim Hyŏngsun's son, Kim Ikchu, who had had drumsticks in his hands from the age of three. Yi often took me on hikes or extended walks through the Puan hills and countryside in the hope that the landscape and its experiences would somehow soak into my body through physical contact alone. Yi reflected:

It's impossible for just anyone to become a p'ungmul performer. It requires individual feeling [*kamgak*], ability [*kiryang*], and a certain character [*sŏnggyŏk*]. It's the same as Western music: it wouldn't be possible without talent [*chaejil*]—in Korean we say one has to be born with what is commonly called *ki*. That's how it is with our music, too. You need a certain level of talent and self-effort. Even if you are talented, it isn't enough—if the person doesn't have focus, it will be impossible. I don't think just anyone can be a professional player.

Feeling is the most important aspect of the good performer. In other words, one must have talent—without talent, no matter how much one observes and/or listens, it can't be done. I now see how talent is strongly related to the person's natural personality and character. The next most important element is environment. I believe the environment makes a big difference. By environment I mean how one got started in p'ungmul. I think this is a very important matter. For example, people who started at an older age, like me, it's a disadvantage. But those people who've seen this kind of music since they were very little, or those whose parents participated in this music—they can enter into the professional world much more easily. How much support you receive is also important—the way in which people around you make opportunities for you determines how easy it will be to dive into the professional world. When I say "professional," I mean this becomes the person's job. Because these days playing *samul nori* or p'ungmul is getting to be treated more as a job, it's possible for a person to be a professional musician when all of these elements are integrated. Self-will [*chagi ŭiji*] is also important.

Though Pak Yŏngsun avoided the direct use of the term *ki,* she nevertheless clearly establishes herself as a disciple of Yi in her belief in innate ability and the importance of environment in terms of early childhood experiences. She also broadens the argument to include the necessity of possessing a certain brashness or thick skin, as well as the power to form connections between members of a group:

First of all, I think any Korean has this feeling of *hŭng* [enthusiasm or excitement]. I noticed that many of my friends who weren't so interested in p'ungmul in the beginning ended up finding their own *hŭng* the longer they played. But the more I observed, the more I found that a person has to have a certain brashness or sassiness. He or she can't be afraid to stand up in front of an audience. And also the person must be on good terms with the rest of the group. He or she has to know how to unite, how to form connections between the group's members. I say people have to have really thick skin. They can't be shy while they are learning, and afterward they must take what they've been taught and make it their own. I don't really think everyone can become a professional p'ungmul performer. The few who do are probably born with the ability. Those who are born with it can become professional players. And they must be devoted.

The good performer is one who can lead well.[4] It's someone who can read the mood of the audience as well as deal with the feelings of the group's members. They have to encourage those who are tired, and also push it a little when *hŭng* is present. The person who leads well reads the situation quickly—it has to be interesting for everyone. The person who leads must have a certain joyfulness and contentment. They have to have a special talent at reading other people's minds.

In some ways, every person has his or her own slightly different character— either the right side of the brain is more developed, or the left side is more developed. It's the person's aptitude, such as who can memorize things well. I think there are innate abilities. I guess it's possible for someone to put in a lot of hard effort, but there will still be a limit. Each person has their own limit, an area somewhat beyond their innate abilities. But there are also cases where the father plays p'ungmul, so the son is directly influenced by it. I have friends who are like that. Speaking of environment, if a child sees a lot of what his or her father does, it can influence that child. I'd say first is innate ability, and second the environment in which you grow up.

Kim Hyŏngsun, Cho Myŏngja, and Pak Yŏngsun all engaged the question of skill or technique versus feeling, framed within an arguably romanticized view of an artistic past distanced from a present perceived as mechanically and technically oriented (criticisms commonly leveled against younger generations of classical and jazz artists in Western musical culture as well). Kim and Pak both drew a comparison between older rural p'ungmul and its newer urban counterpart, *samul nori;* for Cho the concern has more to do with institutional moves toward more technique-based regimens. Beginning with Kim:

The true performer achieves all of this through musical feeling [*ŭmakchŏk(in) kamgak*] that has been soaked into the body. Everyone must go through this. I went through a learning period just like all the others, starting at an early age. My predecessors, they have all passed away. They all passed away, and now it's my turn—our turn has come. Watching the famous performers dance in the past, now that was real p'ungmul.

Musically speaking, p'ungmul is like singing a song: there is a tune [*karak*] and a voice.[5] The same is true of rhythmic patterns played on the drum. The same pattern can be played in a beautiful or ugly manner. One can play it in a basic or diverse way. When the sound is composed of strong and weak, then you can say there is musicality. The melody of the rhythm comes out when you play strong when strong is needed and play soft when soft is needed. It can't become music if you just strike the drum without any thought. The same is true with singing—a song is a song when there is a melody. Otherwise it's just like reading a book, just hearing the text. It requires the same principle. And with dancing, the moment the dancer lifts up his or her foot, one can see this balanced gesture. One can often see a dancer who is clumsy—this kind of dancer may know the proper gesture in his or her head but isn't able to express it physically.

When I see young players today—generally speaking, that is—they are playing in a style that is much too mechanical [*kigyejŏk-ŭro*]. In the older tradition, my predecessors played in an artistic [*yesulchŏk-ŭro*] way. Playing mechanically is like a soldier training—five to ten people will form a group and practice the same rhythmic pattern all day long, taking breaks only to eat [a reference to *samul nori*]. Of course they end up being able to play it really fast, since that is all they are striving for. And they practice varying the pattern this way and that way, so that everyone plays it exactly together.

Pak continues in this vein:

These days, playing technique is seen as the most important aspect of train- ing, since p'ungmul is developing toward becoming more technique-oriented. Playing isn't possible without the support of musical sense [*kamgak*], however. I think technique has its limits.

Anything contrived is bad. Doing something just for show—what I mean is that something like *samul nori* is done only as a display. It's all right if people show off their abilities if they express their own inner excitement or enthu- siasm [*hŭng*]. The performer is at least enjoying his or her own *hŭng*. The truly bad performance is just a pure display of technique, showing off through mechanics. If no *hŭng* is felt—that's not good. In order to feel *hŭng*, each performer must practice over a long period of time. The music has to be fully integrated—it has to be absorbed into the performer's body.

And Cho uses *samul nori* as a point of departure for addressing p'ungmul's roots (though I am not in total agreement with her assessment of p'ungmul's technical demands):

P'ungmul is not like *samul nori*—it doesn't require so much technique. Of course, if you play with sophisticated technique, it will be much more pleasant to watch. But as you know, p'ungmul should evoke *hŭng* and make people feel joyful. For the most part, p'ungmul started in a farming atmosphere. It was there to encourage physically demanding labor. It had the same effect as farming songs [*nongyo*]. For this kind of music, you don't really need technique, in my opinion. Nowadays it's formally taught, so the technical side is coming out. Really, p'ungmul is not such a technical thing—that's my personal feeling.

Yi Sangbaek's response suggests a more integrated approach to this debate, though it shares Pak's and Cho's emphasis on *hŭng:*

> Eventually musical sense and technique gain the same level of importance,
> because technique comes out of this sense. But if you have to separate the two,
> I think musical sense is more important. It doesn't really matter if you play
> technically well without *hŭng.*

"LEFT" AND "RIGHT" PERFORMANCE AESTHETICS

There is little question regarding the physical basis of the division made between "left side" (east) and "right side" (west), since the Chŏlla provinces divide rather neatly in half between the eastern mountain ranges and the western plains. Though the distinction is painted in broad generalities—plains do in fact exist in eastern counties, as do mountains in the west—it nonetheless reflects local perception and pervading geographical realities. The issue that must be addressed, however, is the accuracy of this division when applied to specific groups within each performance style. It continues to be common practice in the majority of the texts on p'ungmul to equate the "left side" school with such-and-such a city or region and the "right side" with another, but as the scholar Chŏng Pyŏngho accurately observes— though his is a minority view—these differences, even if they held in the past, have in the present day become largely obsolete (1994: 208). Very obvious examples are provided by the cases of Kim Hyŏngsun and Yi Sangbaek: Kim teaches and promotes the "right side" style in the city of Chŏnju, a city traditionally considered "left side,"[6] while Yi teaches and promotes the "left side" style throughout Puan county, the home county of Kim and an area historically considered a bastion of the "right side" orientation. "Right side" and "left side" student circles existed on all of the campuses I visited, both in eastern and western counties, and community groups affiliated with the organizations in P'ilbong or Iri have become established in "wrong" areas throughout the province.

In July of 1996 I met with Hwang Sunju, a teaching assistant at the "left side" p'ungmul summer training institute then located in Namwŏn county. I raised this issue of geographically based musical and sociological distinctions promoted in the literature and among my teachers, looking for some new perspective or fresh insight he might be able to provide. His response turned all my previous notions completely upside down: he began by emphatically stating that the contrast made between "left side" and "right side" was a complete fabrication by scholars, and that the true difference resided in the *context* of the performance. P'ungmul should properly encompass a broad spectrum, with rural performances put on by and for local residents in a communal setting occupying one end, professional touring groups looking toward a more national audience on the other.[7] Hwang was of the opinion—one with which I came to agree—that these days students and scholars tended to associate the rural style with the "left side" p'ungmul tradition, owing to the government designation of the P'ilbong troupe, and the touring style with that of the "right side," owing to its association with Iri (1996: personal communication).

In reality, however, both P'ilbong and Iri fall somewhere between these two extremes. Iri Nongak under the leadership of Kim Hyŏngsun acquired the reputation it has today through a series of highly publicized national tours and participation in numerous government competitions, yet it was formed by local residents in and around Saeshil village who at one time were intimately linked to the village's spiritual and material welfare. There is no question that there has been a long and sustained p'ungmul tradition in the village of P'ilbong, and that its contact with even neighboring counties has been limited at best, yet P'ilbong achieved its cultural asset status only after performing at the national level, a practice now regularly required of the group due to the requirements of this very status. P'ilbong, like Iri, now relies on "outsiders" to fill their ranks for out-of-town performances, a trend that will no doubt blur the initial distinction made between these two troupes.

The local Chŏlla province p'ungmul scene could have been radically different. If the Namwŏn-based "left side" touring ensemble directed by the virtuoso lead *soe* player Yu Myŏngch'ŏl had been designated a cultural asset, or if the amateur "right side" village ritual group from Koch'ang had been recognized (see Hesselink 1999), then nearly all currently accepted norms and truisms would cease to have any explanatory power. Though I have been mostly sympathetic to the cultural asset system throughout the writing of this book, this last observation reveals a negative yet very real consequence of relying solely on this institutional framework. Many of Yi Sangbaek's comments in chapter 4 under the lesson process would seem to reflect biases born of such cultural-asset "wisdom"—his pairings of group orientation, focus on free individual expression, flexible musical forms, and "original" village flavor with "left," in contrast to individual orientation, emphasis on fixed group coordination, set musical forms, and an assorted or "mixed" essence with "right"—whereas what he had really described was the communal-presentational continuum existing in *both* styles that Hwang Sunju outlined above. In many instances this created an artificial battle-ground in which "right side" and "left side" training institutes competed for students by overemphasizing the apparent differences between the traditions, obscuring or in some cases even obliterating "right side" local village traditions or more professionalized "left side" troupes in the process.

This brief revisiting of the left-right dichotomy was provided to contextualize my own attempts to make sense of the related interview responses of my mentors and their close colleagues. On the surface it seemed that members of Iri Nongak and Puan P'ungmulp'ae had different agendas when asked what they felt contributed to a moving and successful performance. Pak Yongt'aek and Cho Myŏngja (Iri) focused their gaze outward, speaking mainly of audience enjoyment and involvement. Yi Sangbaek and Pak Yŏngsun (Puan), in contrast, were more concerned with the internal workings of the group, hardly addressing external issues at all. I had initially credited these differences to the respective performance schools, though I now see it was the *nature* of the ensembles with which they were associated that helped mold their perspectives (touring group versus community-based organization). However, other differences aside—use of contrasting hats and some different naming of rhythmic patterns, for example—importantly, the binding aesthetic outlook of both sets of participants remained the same, namely the joy and collective spirit of p'ungmul as communal participation.

As the motivational leader of Iri Nongak, Pak Yongt'aek was always sensitive to the audience's needs in gauging the success of any particular performance. This attention to group or community concerns—the total event—not only finds its precedents in the better ethnomusicological literature, but reveals Pak's showman mentality, inherited from Kim Hyŏngsun and his contemporaries through repeated performances on the road (see Boyd 1992: 182; Radano 1993: 127). This deflection away from himself and Kim further speaks to a humility I seldom encountered among more professional p'ungmul players during my fieldwork experiences:

What is good depends on the particular conditions of the day. If there's a large audience and a lot of applause—a good reaction—that's of course good. It's more fun then, and the feeling of the rhythmic pattern would come out better. If I had planned on doing a ten-minute solo dance beforehand, I would then stretch it out to fifteen minutes without becoming bored. But if there aren't that many people in the audience and there is very little applause—no reaction from the audience—then the performance is no longer fun. It all seems meaningless then, meaningless. So that's why there has to be a connection with the feelings between the audience and the performers. It has to come together— it's no fun if there is no connection. If we play well, the audience's reaction is good, and at the same time, if the audience is enthusiastic, we players are energetic. It binds all of us together. We keep p'ungmul because it's ours. As soon as I start to play, the people's mood changes. That is p'ungmul.

I like p'ungmul; all Koreans do. I start to play and the other person becomes happy. And the other person laughs and I laugh, too. When someone else isn't happy or feeling well, I can make them laugh by playing. It's a kind of comedy—yes, it's comedy. If you play p'ungmul, you know it's a comedy.

Cho Myŏngja's more solemn answer takes us even further beyond the confines of a specific performance by looking to p'ungmul's broader political implications:

The performance should be considered cooperative because it has to be harmonious—nothing should stick out. P'ungmul itself is very much like how farming work was done, gathering many workers together. In other words, if your neighbors come help with the work on your own land, then you go help with their work later, because farming was done as a group effort among many households. It's meant to bring about a united spirit [hyŏptong shim]. For these reasons, this kind of music should be considered cooperative.

This is all very much connected to our past. For thirty-six years we lived under Japanese occupation, and somehow we are now moving toward a democratic society with diverse opinions. But often a hero is born during times of conflict. When our country is in a troubled situation, such as a war against communism—in such dramatic situations people become united. That was our people's special character. And in the same way, we became united after the long occupation. I can see this happening as a general trend. When people are well off and scattered, as they are now, they become individualistic and boastful, but if there's an emergency, they wish to join forces. Our country in peaceful times seems this way to me, which worries me, but when conflict arises the people become one. Koreans then become a unified people.

P'ungmul's real purpose is to bind people together as a collective power [kyŏlsŏngnyŏk]. When a group of people gather together, such as for a demonstration—though this is frowned upon these days—there is great strength. It can create this strength when there's a need for a large gathering of people. We Koreans have been oppressed, we have struggled. Our people have experienced this throughout time. The playing of percussion instruments has the function of uniting us, doesn't it? Instruments such as the kayagŭm [zither] may have a delicate sound, but p'ungmul has a grandiose sound—it envelops us. P'ungmul is successful at uniting large groups of people.

Occupying the same role as that of Pak Yongt'aek in the capacity of lead soe player of Puan P'ungmulp'ae, Yi Sangbaek similarly placed special emphasis on (internal) group harmony and emotional resolution. *Minjung* terminology and concepts from Kim Inu's reading passage in chapter 3 (communal play and spirit) resurface as well:

> If we look at the individual players, we see the *soe, changgo, puk, ching, sogo,* and characters—they are all there. Each person has his or her own role. It's not just performing. In the case of the *sogo,* when the rest of the troupe is playing at their peak level of energy, if the *sogo* players are dragging their feet, then the lead *soe* player must take care of the problem by saying, "Do it this way." Another example: if the lead *soe* player is moving about passionately but the rest of the troupe has no energy, then what good is it if the lead *soe* player is acting alone? In situations like these, the lead *soe* player needs to slow the rhythmic pattern down or do whatever is appropriate for the particular situation in order to fulfill his role. People will praise this kind of leader. Other performers such as the *sogo,* even if they play well, are not praised unless the lead *soe* player has done a good job.
>
> Our p'ungmul is, after all, communal play [*taedong nori*]—in the past it was called *nori* [play or entertainment]. We feel p'ungmul achieves a communal spirit [*kongdongch'e shinmyŏng*] through communal play. In the process of an ongoing performance, competitive aspects do take place—everyone starts together, but then scatters in the middle. It's very much the case, and at the end it becomes integrated once again. That's why if you look at something like *mijigi* [the seventh movement], it's a fight between the two sides. They fight, but at the end they join together again. In a performance, the idea of uncoiling always exists, as does the concept of tension and release, particularly the feeling of untangling. Because of this, I see that cooperative, well, democratic factors are also a big part. Competition exists in some way—yes, it's there, but the final goal is unity or harmony. Being harmonious—this exists only when one lets go of any uneasy feelings that are being kept inside. So even if we started the performance with bad feelings, through sweating and playing we eventually release everything. This is what determines a good p'ungmul performance.
>
> What is considered a good or bad performance—that changes with time. These days, that which is considered good is very much determined by how technical and brilliant the performer is. You almost must do something special or unusual in order to be considered "good." But in olden times the leader had to both embrace and lead a thirty- or forty-person troupe as well. Each member's given role was well harmonized with the others' in a successful performance. Body movement was part of technique, and technique and mind had to work together as one. You couldn't say it was "good" or "bad" just by looking at the technical side. These days what they consider good is judged solely by technique. I think, however, that technique has to be harmonized with the

person's mind and lifestyle for the person to be considered a good player. What good is skill if everyone speaks badly of you as a human being?

And Pak Yŏngsun's reflections as a *puk* player added a spiritual dimension to the larger discussion:

> It's first of all cooperative. If cooperation is not involved, it can't be called a performance. Competition exists as well, to a certain extent. People may learn together, but at some point there could be differences of opinion. It's not that there is always a right or wrong way of doing things, just that there could be different opinions. This doesn't happen in the earlier stages of learning—only after the people have reached a higher level of playing.
>   I heard that when there is *shinmyŏng* [spiritual state or state of oneness] you don't feel the tiredness.[8] Frankly, I can't say I've experienced *shinmyŏng*. I've only studied for a short period of time. But I heard that one doesn't feel tiredness when one reaches that particular stage. Even if you are tired, you should keep up with the lead *soe* player. The group has to be of one mind.

It is worth briefly noting that these interrelated aesthetic philosophies are mirrored and reinforced throughout much of American p'ungmul society, especially on college campuses with strong transnational connections to P'ilbong's "left side" troupe (a fuller discussion is beyond the immediate scope of this chapter). Almost without exception, these various clubs and organizations promote p'ungmul as a tightly knit, socially active, emotionally interactive, and community-building enterprise, in some cases even at the expense of improving musical skills. These organizations even reference the key *minjung* ideal of *kongdongch'e,* or heightened communal awareness, as conceptualized by Kim Inu in chapter 4 (see especially Kwŏn Hyeryŏn 2001; Park, Joo Won 2005).[9]

P'UNGMUL'S PLACE IN CONTEMPORARY KOREAN LIFE

Throughout this book I have attempted to reveal the multifaceted and ever-changing roles of p'ungmul in a society that itself continues to transform as it struggles to understand and redefine its own place in the world. Whether it be a national symbol of pan-Korean consciousness and wisdom that exists in the sphere of mythos, or a cultural leisure activity that enhances regional solidarity and operates under the rules of logos, p'ungmul adapts and is adopted anew by performers, audiences, academics, and consumers who draw from its deep well of traditional resources. This grand portrait, painted in the broad strokes of dichotomous and seemingly unified worldviews, however, conceals contested understandings within and across boundaries resulting from the often conflicting requirements of these dual worlds, especially as perceived by the performers themselves. I have chosen, therefore, to bring this narrative to a close with this chapter's participants speaking openly and passionately about these issues, concerns that highlight ongoing tensions yet point the way to future possibilities.

We begin with two separate but related accounts of shamanistic ritual (*kut*) accompanied by p'ungmul instruments, as recalled by Kim Hyŏngsun. The first emphasizes the power with which this music is believed to be imbued, especially within the context of healing. The notion of being able to either invite or expel spirits through the use of percussion instruments is well known and reiterated in shaman and other religious literature throughout the world, but what Kim does not tell us is that this very activity is largely responsible for the apprehension many Korean parents in the countryside feel about their children's taking up the drum (Yi Pohyŏng 1995: personal communication). By openly approving activity he acknowledges to be currently perceived as "superstition"—no doubt more so (potentially) by this foreign researcher born of Christian missionary parents—he removed a barrier of formality between us that can only be interpreted as an act of friendship. By exposing a facet of village society, a part of "hidden" Korea important to both his religious and his personal make-up, Kim executed a bold leap of trust, a move made all the more dramatic considering the somewhat recent historical trend in the area for musicians to distance themselves from shamanistic activity (see Howard 1990: 29):

When I was little there were no medical facilities. So whenever someone became sick, they would have a ritual called a *chudangmaegi* [literally, "to fetter (or confine) a malignant spirit"] performed. This is a story from the past, but I experienced it myself. It's a really strange thing that I'm going to tell you, though it's considered superstition [*mishin*]. If a person became ill from visiting a place or direction where they shouldn't have been, then they called this *chigol pannŭnda* [receiving a *chigol*],[10] meaning a *chigol* had been received from evil spirits. After returning from the wrong direction, a person could die from receiving the *chigol*. When something like this occurred, a shaman [*tan'gol*] who was responsible for a certain area within the village would be called out to heal.[11] When a person fell sick within the family, the shaman would first visit the home and determine the nature of the sickness. The shaman achieved this by a "scissors fortune" [*kasetchŏm*]. Probably you don't know what this is, but it's fortune-telling with a pair of scissors. Every family has a large pair of scissors, doesn't it? When the divination is to take place, a large bowl of water is prepared and the pair of scissors is suspended above it by two crossed pieces of thread. I know it seems strange, but the shaman puts a spirit into the scissors and asks, "How did this person get sick? If it's for such and such a reason, then shake the scissors back and forth. If this is not the reason, then remain still." This is how they do the scissors fortune—I often saw this kind of thing when I was little.

There was also something called a *chambap*. A *chambap* is what makes your head clear and free from headaches. A *chambap* is another word for a measuring cup. Nowadays measuring cups are square, but in olden times people used gourds that were cut and then emptied out. They would choose a gourd that was approximately a single measuring cup in size. Anyway, the shaman would fill this gourd with rice up to the top and cover it tightly with a piece of cloth. The shaman would then shake the gourd seven times each for seven different points near the area that was hurting [the head], for a total of forty-nine times. It was strange, but if it worked, when you uncovered the gourd, there was a little area where the rice had been eaten. These kinds of things were done often when I was little.[12]

There is another way I remember of treating someone who is sick because of having gone to a place he or she shouldn't have. They called this *chudang-maegi* as well. They would spread straw on the ground and pretend it was someone's funeral. They would then lay the sick person on the straw like a dead person and bind him with straw rope seven times. The shaman would then circle around the person and perform the ritual. You know, one day I would like to reenact this when the cultural asset committee members come visit.

Many people feel that this is all superstition, but I have experienced it twice personally as an adult. The first time was because of my second daughter, who now lives in Taegu [a city in North Kyŏngsang province]. When she was born, I adored her—I took her everywhere. I went around holding her hand, even buying her things, because I adored her so much. But one day she got an eye disease. We thought it was a normal kind of eye disease and took her to the hospital. The doctors said it wasn't anything too serious and gave her a shot to sanitize the area. But when she came back home, some kind of pus began coming out. It was so bad, you couldn't see the pupil or the white part, it was so covered with pus. We laid her on her side on a towel and the pus kept flowing out. I thought I was going to lose a daughter. Even the seventy- and eighty-year-old men in the neighborhood said they had never seen anything like it. They said, "What on earth is it?" I took her to hospitals all over the place looking everywhere for good medicine.

And then—maybe it was meant to be—I met one of my students from the past. This guy's name was Ch'oe Kangsŏk, and he'd studied *changgu* with me when he was a student. We were close—he called me older brother and my children nieces and nephews. Then he disappeared for a couple of years. Apparently he studied fortune-telling in a Buddhist temple somewhere. He now lived in Seoul and had become president of a fortune-teller [*chŏmbach'i*] association.[13] *Chŏmbach'i* refers to a man who plays the *changgu* and *soe* in order to heal someone. Under one *chŏmbach'i* there will be three or four fortune-tellers [*chŏmjaengi*]. That's how they make their living. So Ch'oe asked me how my daughter Yangsuk was doing. And I told him that she seemed to be dying from an eye disease. He stood quietly for a second or two, then said, "She will have to be healed with a ritual." I said goodbye, thinking that was a strange thing to say, so I turned and called back to him, "What was that you said?" And he said, "Older brother, it can be healed with a ritual." So I asked him to come to my house with me. He saw my child that day and decided on a day for the ritual.

The day came and we prepared the food. I told you how we used every possible medicine available. Pus was flowing out of her eye, and we had put a towel under it. The towel got so soaked we had to replace it. I just can't tell you how I felt—if I hadn't experienced it myself I wouldn't believe it. So we did the ritual. That night, villagers from all around came to watch. The shaman and the musician arrived soon after. The musician played a *changgu* with a *soe* hanging off the end of it—you have to practice a lot to be able to play both at the same time. The musician has to play very well in order for the shaman to be able to perform properly. In other words, the music has the ability to either invite or kick out the spirits. The musician banged and the shaman danced, and when the last stroke of the ritual had been played, my daughter was healed. It was so miraculous, I've told this story more than a hundred times in my life.

And I myself have gone through it once, too. This is how it happened: I was coming back from somewhere one day, and in order to get to my home I had to pass by Iri Elementary School. Since that time it's become a crowded street, but then it was a quiet, remote corner, a quiet, remote wooded area with lots of big trees. So one day I was coming back from somewhere and took a short-cut to get home quickly. As I was walking on the path, I felt a sudden shiver go through my body, a feeling as if someone was coming after me to hurt me. So I turned around to take a look, but nothing was there. I thought it was strange, but then I arrived home and didn't think much about it. I ate dinner, rested, and went to sleep.

But while I was sleeping, at around 2:00 A.M., I started to shake with the cold. I felt so cold—two to three blankets didn't even help. I was still shaking. After two to three hours of this I was soaking wet—my clothes were dripping with sweat. I thought it was odd and went to the hospital the next day. The doctor said there was nothing wrong and gave me a shot. After I went home I felt fine, so I did some work and ran some errands. But at exactly 2:00 A.M.

the next morning the shivering came back. Every night the shivering came back at exactly the same time. My body would start to feel cold, the chill would come, and my teeth would start to chatter. It was so strange. Hospitals were absolutely no use. Because I was sweating so much, I lost weight and began to wither away. That's how ghosts destroy a person. My wife thought there was no other way but to go see a fortune-teller. So we went to one and told our entire story. I was so weak then that I wanted a ritual performed. So the fortune-teller came with a musician—they always travel as a pair. They performed the ritual all day long, and afterward I felt so relieved.

So I've experienced this twice in my sixty years, and in the process I've changed my mind. I used to say that it was superstition, that it was useless. But since I've experienced it, I don't say that anymore. Even if the hospital can't fix it, there are other remedies that can cure a sickness. We call this *chudangmaegi* or *chudang-ŭl mangnŭnda* [blocking the malignant spirit]. So our music, we say "playing a ritual" [*kut ch'inda*] or "playing p'ungmul" [*p'ungmul ch'inda*]. They will change this word *nongak* [farmers' or farming music]. I hear the cultural asset committee will officially change this term. This is much more than music for just farmers.

Kim's second set of reflections on shamanistic activity reveals a similar sense of loss and perhaps even nostalgia as he describes how ritual contexts are disappearing from a society that has in many ways abandoned its trust and reliance on these older ways. From personal experience he traced the transformation of p'ungmul as a spiritual and community-affirming enterprise to one of truncated, largely sanitized spectacle:

There was once a time when p'ungmul musicians didn't know how to count numbers, which meant they had to draw lines on the wall one by one in order to remember what number it was. Because they couldn't count, the villagers would put pinecones in a big basket in front of the gate. As each performer passed through the gate, he or she would pick up a pinecone and put it into another basket placed just inside the gate. Each performer did the same, one by one. The villagers would then count the number of cones to find out how many outsiders had come into the village, in order to prepare the right amount of rice and food. As soon as the troupe had entered the village, they had to play greeting p'ungmul [*tangsan kut*]. The shrine [*tangsan*] was where the village's spirit resided.[14] This ritual was accompanied by set phrases, such as "Field shrine, sky shrine" [*Tŭltangsan, naltangsan*]. They played the village shrine ritual and would then play a well ritual by the village communal well. After this, the troupe would enter an individual house, playing a front-yard ritual [*madang kut*], a kitchen-god ritual [*chowang kut*], a god-of-the-home ritual [*sŏngju kut*], a storage-area ritual [*ch'ŏryung kut*], and so on. The lead *soe* player would say the appropriate phrases, and the performers would play the corresponding music.[15]

Nowadays performances have a time limit of twenty or thirty minutes. The p'ungmul [*kut*] they did in the past—you had to play for one or two days without any distractions. First you'd play, then have a drink, then go visit another house and play and have a drink—you'd do this for two days. You can't really do it these days; there are no opportunities left.

Though Kim Hyŏngsun never saw a lack of formal education or rural associations as a hindrance to p'ungmul's artistic standing or social status, Cho Myŏngja, in contrast, expressed what many performers in the more aristocratic or elite traditional genres felt but were usually reluctant to openly admit:

You see, in my case I'm not only doing p'ungmul but dance. I'm already at a certain level in dance. Traditional dance is considered high art and has a certain status. P'ungmul doesn't have that kind of status—it's not a high art form. Its status has improved, but in olden times p'ungmul performers were considered beggars who went around playing for food—you know, the fund-raising troupes [*kŏllipp'ae*]. In olden times, they were treated like beggars, kind of like the *namsadang* [itinerant performance troupes]. It was really difficult for them to feed themselves. Only now have they finally gotten over that sort of reputation. If you compare it with dance, it seems so behind. I think this way sometimes. One person can perform a solo dance, but p'ungmul needs a number of people.

Now our economy is better and we don't have to worry about food and clothing, but it was only twenty or thirty years ago that food and clothing weren't so easily available. If you look at the past, you see p'ungmul had a somewhat low standard compared to other art forms. The standard reached a higher level in the 1980s with the Olympic Games—interest in p'ungmul was renewed. It hasn't reached the level of high art, but it's improved a lot.

Demonstrations may have seemed like South Korea's major cultural export in the 1980s and 1990s, judging by the inordinate amount of attention they received in the Western press. A significant component of these mass movements not always picked up by the camera lens was the widespread use of p'ungmul instruments by students and/or laborers on the front lines. Their use was so prevalent in connection with these gatherings that large segments of Korean society—including many university faculty—are still often unable to mentally separate the two (Yi Sangbaek spoke of this in his interview in chapter 1). It is this sociohistorical context that Pak Yongt'aek reacts to so vehemently in the following passages. The underlying tension shared by many p'ungmul performers, both amateur and the more serious minded, now explodes onto the surface. His refusal to accept these types of students shows Pak to be an idealist. Iri's training institute relied heavily on student numbers during term breaks to stay financially solvent, and Pak's attitude put this fragile balancing act at risk. He eloquently expresses the rage and frustration felt by performers of his inclination who continue to work at promoting p'ungmul as an art form free from overt political and social agendas:

> In the past—well, if you look at university students these days, they participate in demonstrations and such things playing p'ungmul. In olden times, there were no such kinds of things. Kim Hyŏngsun told me that in the past, out on the battlefield, the Japanese thought people were gathering in large numbers to fight whenever they heard Koreans playing p'ungmul. So they took all the instruments away to keep the Koreans from playing. The Japanese thought they heard many people out in the fields, even if it was only two or three people playing. The Japanese ended up taking all of our instruments away.
>
> P'ungmul is now generally misunderstood because of university students and demonstrations. Students who have nothing better to do but play p'ungmul stand in front and bang away on their instruments, encouraging the spirit of demonstration. Many of the students who come to study with me tell me that people think they are studying *changgo* only to play in front of demonstrations. People would call them "demo bastards" [*temo hanŭn nom*]. That's not true at all—there are kids like that, but there are also students who do it to study our own folk art. They are the serious ones who will never use it to lead demonstrations. It really depends on what kind of university club it is. There may be twenty different clubs in a university, and among those there are folk art study groups and there are groups called *p'ae*. Always *p'ae* after their title—they are the ones who often stand in front of the demonstrations. This word *p'ae*, it's from *p'aegŏri* [gang or mob], and it sounds rough. Groups with names like "Minsokhak yŏn'guhoe" [Folklore Research Association], however, are not like that at all. Names like "Ssalp'ae" [Rice Gang] or "Turip'ae" [Round Gang]—these are the kinds of groups who go for the demonstrations. Folk associations never do such things.
>
> People's general understanding of p'ungmul is swayed by what they see. If we as performers play for a demonstration, then people will label us as a demo troupe as well. That is exactly what the situation is. We as performers never did such a thing. We really hate things like demonstrations. Why? Yes, I'm a Korean, too. I know that they protest to survive, but they don't need to—it just ends up getting people killed. I would never do it—I hate it. I just take care

of my own problems with my own hands. I know demonstrations don't change anything, anyway. Not in a thousand years. I studied this music because I love my people and their culture. That's why I studied it. I'm against demonstrations and such things. I won't teach those who want to learn p'ungmul to use it in a demonstration. I will tell them to leave. Why? Because I don't want to be called names or be labeled a certain way. I didn't study it with such a purpose. I have made up my mind, like Kim, that I will play p'ungmul until I die.

Like Pak, Yi Sangbaek began to study p'ungmul in earnest upon his return to university after completing nearly three years of military service, then required of all Korean males. I noticed, however, that Yi was always careful to sidestep any direct questions referring to this pre-p'ungmul collegiate phase. Only in the following brief response does he let his guard down: when Yi says he was a "live by the principle" kind of personality before starting to play p'ungmul, he is speaking of his first two years in university before military service, when he was an active leader in campus political organizations and public demonstrations, a part of his life he is reluctant to talk about in any detail even to this day. What is so profound about his course of action is that he actually moved *away* from demonstrations because of his love of and dedication to p'ungmul, contrary to the assumptions of individuals such as Pak Yongt'aek. P'ungmul in and of itself became Yi's personal and national salvation:

I think if p'ungmul is developed more in the future, it can serve many important functions. I'll tell you my story as an example. My personality has changed quite a bit since I started playing p'ungmul. Before, I was very edgy or sensitive and introverted. I was a "live by the principle" kind of personality. But since I started playing p'ungmul I've become more relaxed, gentler, and more easygoing. I think the problem with our society is that people are selfish and cruel to others. Playing p'ungmul would erase these aspects of our self-centered society. P'ungmul has the ability to take the role of cleansing or purifying society. You begin with p'ungmul groups of forty to fifty people. A lot of very difficult problems will most likely occur as the group develops in its own way. As they experience these problems, they get to practice cooperation through conversation and interaction. P'ungmul provides plenty of these opportunities. And as more and more groups continue to form, this society would change little by little into a happier one. I personally feel a sense of mission to revitalize p'ungmul. I think that through hard work I can steer the direction of this society.

The structure of our country will continually change. Our country suddenly became industrialized and Western culture rushed in, to the extent that our own culture regressed. But because our economy has become richer and stronger, people's sentiments and level of conscience and education are getting higher. And because of that, people will pursue satisfying cultural needs. Then our country will have no choice but to promote its own traditional culture. So I see a bright future for p'ungmul. I don't see anything else that has the potential to fulfill such a role. We eat, drink, and have a great time playing all day. Even if our group doesn't win a competition, the rest of the day we still keep our outfits on and play away. Our p'ungmul achieves that atmosphere—it's difficult to describe with words.

I have saved the final passages of this book for the youngest voice in our group, Pak Yŏngsun. Her observations connect the past with the present, the ideal with the practical, in summary fashion. Despite lingering biases, here expressed in the disapproving glare of her parents, Pak remains resolute in her efforts to pursue p'ungmul as a viable occupation and acceptable lifestyle. Her closing sentiments reflect my own enthusiastic and optimistic outlook on p'ungmul's future prospects as a mainstay of modern Korean society:

A lot of our society is reflected in p'ungmul, especially the older society. I think every culture is a reflection of its society. P'ungmul is the same. For a while it was neglected—especially after the Japanese occupation. They pretty much stopped playing. That's the process of change in the history of a society. Nowadays, many people want to rediscover their old things. People are beginning to participate again in traditional activities, looking to the past. This seems to be the general trend of society. These days people look to p'ungmul again to discover the flow of our past society.

P'ungmul has progressed beyond a hobby for me now. I want to play as much as I can, make it a part my life. It's difficult, but I'm learning and I'm very thankful for the opportunity. My family, however, is against it because they have old ideas about p'ungmul musicians being poor and starving. Older people still have those kinds of thoughts, but I think I can overcome their opposition. I'm still young and I have a lot of time, time to convince them. I have to try to please them a little, but still we have conflicts. . . .

P'ungmul is important for our future because of the simple fact that we are Korean. We are Koreans, and we should not forget this. A lot of foreign culture has come in through rapid globalization. If we stop our traditional ways, Koreans will disappear. I think p'ungmul could be an important influence on our people. We are Korean, and we need to have our own foundational culture that suits our own sentiment. Only then can we accept other cultures, Koreanizing them into something more suitable to our Korean aesthetic.

APPENDIX: INDIVIDUALS CITED

The following individuals were cited in the text under "personal communication":

Cho Myŏngja (female, b. 1943): Iri Nongak *sogo* player; fellow student at CTK.

Hong Chunp'yo (male, b. 1966): Owner of Chŏnju video game parlor; fellow student at CTK.

Howard, Keith (male, b. 1956): Ethnomusicologist.

Hwang Pyŏnggi (male, b. 1936): Korean musicologist, composer, performer.

Hwang Sunju (male, b. 1967): P'ilbong P'ungmulgut *puk* player; nationally designated cultural asset master artist.

Kim Hyŏngsun (male, b. 1933): Iri Nongak lead *changgo* player; nationally designated cultural asset holder.

Kwŏn Osŏng (male, b. 1940?): Korean musicologist; president of Korean Musicological Society.

Pak Hyŏngnae (male, b. 1927): P'ilbong P'ungmulgut lead *changgo* player; nationally designated cultural asset holder.

Pak Hyŏngyŏl (male, b. 1969): Chŏnju University p'ungmul circle president; fellow student at CTK.

Pak Ŭnha (female, b. 1960): *Changgo* and *soe* player; member of National Center for Korean Traditional Performing Arts *samul nori* team.

Pak Yŏngsun (female, b. 1977): Puan P'ungmulp'ae *changgo* and *puk* player.

Pak Yongt'aek (male, b. 1952): Iri Nongak lead *soe* player; nationally designated cultural asset assistant instructor.

Rector, Gary (male, b. 1950?): Performer; instructor.

Shin Chun'gyu (male, b. 1970): Chŏnbuk University p'ungmul circle president.

Song Pangsong (male, b. 1942): Korean musicologist.

Yi Ch'ullae (male, b. 1962): Chŏnju Kkach'imadang lead *soe* player; regionally designated cultural asset master artist.

Yi Hosun (male, b. 1948): Iri Nongak fourth *soe* player; assistant instructor at CTK.

Yi Oksu (male, b. 1950?): *Changgo* player; regionally designated cultural asset holder candidate.

Yi Pohyŏng (male, b. 1935): Korean musicologist, folklorist.

Yi Sangbaek (male, b. 1966): Puan P'ungmulp'ae lead *soe* player; Usŏk University p'ungmul circle president.

Yun Chigwan (male, b. 1954): Professor of English literature, Tŏksŏng Women's University.

NOTES

Introduction

1. See also Clifford 1986; Geertz 1988; Appadurai 1991: 193; Daniel and Peck 1996: 1–20; Clayton 2003.

2. This phenomenon has been referred to as the "hermeneutical arc" (Ricouer 1981: 145–64; see also Harnish 2001: 22–25).

3. See, as examples, Hsu 1973; Crapanzano 1980, 1986: 74; Dower 1986; Ringer 1991: 192.

4. A revivalist movement in anthropology views "the proper collection and description of primary data [as] at least as important as [the] rigorous subsequent analysis of them" (Henderson and Netherly 1993: 3). The insulation of American students from the raw materials of history in their high school textbooks presents a similar concern for educators (Loewen 1995: 5).

Chapter One

1. Two of today's most famous female lead small gong players (*sangsoe*) are remnants of this legacy, and both hail from North Chŏlla province: Yu Chihwa from Chŏngŭp county and Na Kŭmch'u from Puan county.

2. Two notable exceptions include Han'guk hyangt'osa 1994, 1997.

3. Kim Sunam, Im, and Yi 1986; Kim Inu 1993; Kim Hŏnsŏn 1994; P'ungmul/ ch'ump'ae kippal 1994; Ch'oe Chongmin 2002. See also Kim Yŏngt'ak 2002.

4. Cho Hŭngyun 1985: 122–42; Kim T'aegon 1985: 342–421; Ch'oe Kilsŏng 1987: 49–114; Kim Kwangil 1988: 131–61; Chu Kanghyŏn 1995.

5. Iri Nongak is the subject of numerous studies (e.g., Sŏng Chaehyŏng 1984: 68–87; Chŏng Pyŏngho and Yi Pohyŏng 1985: 29–57; Ryu Muyŏl 1986: 236–48; An Hyeyŏng 1986; Yu Kyŏngok 1987; O Chongsŏp 1989; Chŏng Pyŏngho 1994: 216–23; No Poksun 1994; Yi Sora and Chŏng Sumi 2000) and will be examined in detail in later chapters. It should be noted as well that the city of Iri and the surrounding county of Iksan have become the larger city of Iksan; there is, as a consequence, technically no

place remaining called "Iri" (though one still finds old signs along country roads leading you there).

6. According to tournament organizers and literature given by Iri Nongak itself, Iri Nongak officially won *second* prize (*ch'oeususang*) in 1981; it received the top prize (*taesang*) in 1983.

7. Yi Sunam (male) was born in 1918 in Hwabae village, Yongan subcounty, Iksan county, North Chŏlla province (Ch'oe T'aeyŏl 1984: 21).

8. My interview with Kim Hyŏngsun, one of my principal mentors and a central focus of this book, is reproduced later in this chapter.

9. Kim Mundal is the subject of a chapter in Kim Myŏnggon's collection of encounters with Chŏlla province musicians (1994: 305–14; a better picture of Kim appears in Chŏng Pyŏngho 1994: 73).

10. According to the folk music scholar Yi Pohyŏng, the origins of fund-raising troupes lie in village rituals with shamanistic roots. When a large sum of money was needed by the village itself for a special purpose, a nonprofessional troupe would be assembled by village members; the performers received no personal fee for their service in the ritual or performance. When a larger project on a grander scale between many villages was required, however, a professional troupe would be formed and employed. The formation of this professional group often involved a large competition held beforehand among p'ungmul players from all of the participating villages; the best players were then selected for the final troupe. Yi felt that most of p'ungmul heard in contemporary times came from this professional-style fund-raising troupe (1996: personal communication).

11. Kim Pongnyŏl and his group have been studied numerous times (Kim Hyŏnsuk 1987; Kim Hakchu 1987: 8–10 of notation; Han'guk hyangt'osa 1994: 108–72; Kim Myŏnggon 1994: 107–16; Pongch'ŏn norimadang 1995: 274–351). Kim was featured in the second annual performance of "Chŏlla Province Music and Dance" (*Chŏllado ŭi ch'um, Chŏllado ŭi karak*), held at Chŏnju's North Chŏlla Art Hall (Chŏnbuk yesul hoegwan) in 1993.

12. Chungp'yŏng's training institute (*chŏnsugwan*) has become quite popular, attracting students from the surrounding regions as well (see chapter 4). Kim Pongnyŏl, however, is no longer in charge, because of his advanced age.

13. *Mudong*, literally "dancing child," refers to children who are held on the shoulders of (male) adults, waving their arms in a prescribed manner. The topic is dealt with in more detail in chapter 2.

14. *Chŏllip* were felt hats formerly worn by soldiers; see chapter 2 for a full discussion.

15. *P'ungnyu* refers to instrumental chamber music dating from the latter part of the Chosŏn dynasty (1392–1910; see Chang Sahun 1986: 438–40). The local group Iri Hyangje Chulp'ungnyu was designated an important intangible cultural asset (*chungyo muhyŏng munhwajae*) in this genre in 1985 (a recording of this music is found on the compact disc Jigu JCD-9402, 1994).

16. Although the term *mae kut* (or *maegu, maegwi kut*, etc.) is at times used interchangeably with the terms *nongak* and p'ungmul (Hong Hyŏnshik 1969: 51; Lee, Po-hyŏng 1981: 69), in this passage it refers to a village-cleansing ritual performed by group members in which evil spirits are exorcised (see Chŏng Pyŏngho 1994: 285; Yu Kiryong 1975: 77).

17. This date, like the dates that follow, is according to the Korean lunar calendar (see Crane 1967: 197–201, 206–11 for a brief introduction to the calendar and its corresponding festival days).

18. The term translated here as "village ritual p'ungmul" is *sanshinje*, literally, "mountain spirit ritual." The synonymous terms translated here as "fund-raising p'ungmul" are *chŏngwŏl kŏllip* (January fund-raising) and *madang palbi* (literally, "treading on the earth"), also known by the linguistic variant *madang palki*.

19. The original text prints Ansŏng town (*ŭp*) and is incorrect; the proper reading is Ansŏng subcounty (*myŏn*), as is given in this translation.

20. Yi Hwach'un figures significantly in the history of Chŏlla province "left side" lead *soe* players; he claims both Yang Sunyong (Imshil) and Yu Myŏngch'ŏl (Namwŏn) as direct disciples (Kim Hyŏnsuk 1987: 8).

21. Though Shin Kinam settled and later died in Imshil county, it is his legacy with respect to "right side" p'ungmul that will be remembered. Shin was born in 1914 in Taeyong village, Sosŏng subcounty, Chŏngŭp county, and is the teacher of Yi Pongmun, who was the teacher of the esteemed lead *changgo* performer Yi Tongwŏn (see Kim Myŏnggon 1994: 339–49; Shin Kinam 1992). Yi Tongwŏn was Kim Hyŏngsun's teacher (see interview later in this chapter). Shin is quoted in the epigraphs to chapters 5 and 6.

22. Yang Sunyong and Imshil P'ilbong Nongak/P'ungmulgut have been the object of numerous reports (Chŏng Pyŏngho et al. 1980; Ch'oe T'aeyŏl 1984; Sŏng Chaehyŏng 1984: 31–68; Yang Chinsŏng [1980?]; Ryu Muyŏl 1986: 201–23; Kim Chiyŏng 1987; Kim Hakchu 1987: 5–7 of notation; Kim Hyŏnsuk 1987; No Poksun 1994; Chŏng Pyŏngho 1994: 23–51, 1995: 285–95; Honam chwado p'ungmulgut 1995; Yi Chongjin 1996; U Chwamiyangja 1999; Pak Sangguk et al. 1999; Yi Yŏngbae 2000). Yang Sunyong's sons were the primary teachers of Yi Sangbaek, my second principal mentor, who is interviewed later in this chapter. P'ilbong Nongak has also been photodocumented (Kim Sunam, Im Sŏkchae, and Yi Pohyŏng 1986: 53–77).

23. Kangnyul subcounty, as printed in the original text, is incorrect.

24. The term used in the text is *tangsanje*, literally, "mountain [or village] shrine ritual." *Tangsanje*, like the related designations *tangje, tangsan kut*, and *tang kut*, refers to a greeting ritual offered to the village's guardian spirit (*suhoshin*) as the group enters the village (Pak Sangguk et al. 1996: 76–7).

25. Yu Myŏngch'ŏl's life history is the subject of a chapter in Kim Myŏnggon's collection (1994: 259–68); his playing has been used as a starting point for analysis as well (Kim Hakchu 1987: 1–4 of notation). Yu was featured in the fifth annual performance of "Chŏlla Province Music and Dance" in 1996 (held in Chŏnju) and was advertised in the program as "the last Chŏlla province 'left side' lead *soe* player."

26. A similar activity was recorded by the scholar Yi Sugwang (1563–1628) in his sixteenth-century *Chibong yusŏl* (Topical Discourses of Chibong), believed to be the earliest such documentation. Apparently it was so popular in the capital (Seoul) that men and women were required to go on separate days (Ch'oe Sangsu 1988: 132–34).

27. The original passage only makes mention of *soe* players, though there is little reason to doubt the inclusion of all the instrumentalists.

28. The term *kukkŏri* (*kut* + *kŏri*, here properly romanized as *kukkŏri*, though in actual practice often sounding closer to *kutkŏri*) has a wide range of meanings,

including a rhythmic pattern and performance type (this text is most likely referring to the latter). See Howard 1993 for a discussion of both the secular and sacred contexts in which it is used.

29. This is a solo genre of the double-reed wind instrument *p'iri* accompanied by a *changgo*.

30. See n. 15 above.

31. This practice is most probably based on the folk entertainment (*minsok nori*) known as *nottari palki*, in which a woman walks over the backs of others (Ch'oe Sangsu 1988: 113–18). A picture of *nottari palki* is found in Kim Kwangǒn and Kim Sunam 1989: 36; a verbal description is found as well in an account of the song and circle dance genre *kanggangsullae* on the island of Chindo (Howard 1990: 137).

32. The situation has since changed—a newly formed Puan Nongak Group under the leadership of lead *soe* Na Kǔmch'u performed at the thirty-third annual "Day for the Citizens of Puan," held May 1, 1996. Na is a regional cultural asset (*chibang mun-hwajae*) and faculty member at the North Chǒlla Provincially Established Center for Korean Traditional Performing Arts (Chǒnbuk torip kugagwǒn), located in Chǒnju. Na was lead *soe* with Yi Tongwǒn (also a regional cultural asset) before his death and was the subject of a published study (Han'guk hyangt'osa 1994: 68–107). She was featured as well in the first annual performance of "Chǒlla Province Music and Dance" in 1992.

33. An expanded version of this text appears in Kim Iktu et al. 1994: 164–70.

34. The information that follows in the text is of particular interest, as Yi Tongwǒn was the primary teacher of Kim Hyǒngsun. Yi's son Yi Oksu, also a *changgo* player, continues to keep "right side" p'ungmul alive in Puan county, serving as the president of the "Puan Society for the Preservation of Nongak" (Yi Oksu 1996: personal communication).

35. Kim Pyǒngsǒp may very well be the highest-profile lead *changgo* performer in modern history, a status related in no small part to the number of publications featuring and/or analyzing his playing (Chǒn Inp'yǒng 1979; Chu Yǒngja 1981, 1985; Howard 1983, 1991–92; Provine 1975, 1985).

36. Chǒn Sasǒp was born in Ch'ǒnwǒn village, Ibam subcounty, Chǒngǔp county, in 1913. Considered a legendary performer of the "right side" school of p'ungmul, he passed away in 1993 (Yi Kyuwǒn and Chǒng Pǒmt'ae 1997: 92–95; a color photograph of Chǒn is reproduced on p. 26 of this work).

37. In 1986 Yi was leader of a Puan p'ungmul group that won first prize in Chǒlla province's National P'ungmul (Nongak) Competition (source: 1996 brochure provided by the organizing committee).

38. A considerably expanded text, including costuming, instrumentation, performance contexts, and rhythmic patterns, is found in Kim Iktu et al. 1994: 130–34.

39. Chǒng Hoegap's transcriptions of Hoch'ǒn hamlet, Sǒkch'ǒn village, Nangsan subcounty, Iksan county p'ungmul (*nongak*) and of Taemae hamlet, Samdam village, Nangsan subcounty, Iksan county p'ungmul are quite probably the earliest forms of documentation for this area (part of the *Chǒnbuk chibang nongak* series, most likely compiled in the late 1960s or early 1970s). A more current study has examined the "left side" p'ungmul tradition found in Sǒngdang village, Sǒngdang subcounty, Iksan county, under the leadership of Yi Insu (Han'guk hyangt'osa 1994: 26–67).

40. Notable exceptions are the volumes on folk musicians in the Deep-Rooted Tree Oral Histories Series produced by Ppuri kip'ǔn namu (Ch'oe Soshim 1992, interviewed by Kang Yunju; Ham Tongjǒngwǒl 1992, interviewed by Kim Myǒnggon and Kim Haesuk; Kim Myǒnghwan 1992, interviewed by Kim Haesuk et al.; and Shin Kinam 1992, interviewed by Kim Myǒnggon). Interest in oral literature and histories has increased since the mid-1990s (e.g., Sǒ Taesǒk 1997; Kim Yunho 2000).

41. Two major lists of famous Chǒlla province p'ungmul musicians have been compiled, one in 1967 and one in 1986, which include players mentioned in the following two interviews (see Hong Hyǒnshik, Kim, and Pak 1967: 199–200; Chǒng Pyǒngho 1994: 289–90).

42. *Li* or *ri* is an older unit of measurement for determining distances—one *li* is approximately 0.4 km (Han'gǔl hakhoe 1957: 956).

43. These two references are to Intangible Cultural Assets no. 68, *Miryang paekchung nori* (literally, "Buddhist All Souls' Day entertainment," but really a servant's festival, of Miryang, South Kyǒngsang province), and no. 69, *Hahoe pyǒlshin'gut t'allori* (shamanic mask dance drama from Hahoe, North Kyǒngsang province).

44. This is a reference to the 1982 report translated in part earlier.

45. The designation *yangban* originally referred to officials of the "two orders" (civil and military), an institution begun in the thirteenth century during the Koryǒ dynasty (918–1259) but expanded to include the upper classes in general in the early Chosǒn dynasty, under the considerable influence of the rise of Neo-Confucianism (Deuchler 1992: 12–13; Lee, Peter H. 1985: 490, 1993: 566–69).

46. The Japanese exploitation of mineral resources in Korea, particularly of copper, lead, zinc ore, and iron ore, increased dramatically after 1930, owing to expanded imperialism in continental Asia (Kim, Y. K. Kirk 1977: 93–99).

47. Kim would at times during lessons explain something to me in Japanese, if he felt I hadn't grasped the full meaning of the Korean.

48. A 1996 *Ssirǔm* Grand Tournament, broadcast on KBS 1 on lunar New Year's day, featured p'ungmul percussion instruments during intervals between matches, with the prize of a real bull being replaced by a trophy in its image. *Nanjang* has expanded to include various forms of entertainment, sports competitions, and sales by local vendors, and continues to be held annually in Chǒnju, North Chǒlla province (in 1996 it was held June 17–23, in conjunction with the Chǒnju Traditional Performing Arts Grand Competition, or *Chǒnju taesasǔp nori*). See Yi Sangil 1987: 138–40 for a brief discussion of *nanjang*'s origins.

49. Park Chung Hee came into power through a military coup d'état staged the morning of May 16, 1961.

50. First place is generally indicated by the Korean term *taet'ongnyǒng sang*, literally, "presidential award." Iri Nongak received this award in 1983 for a national p'ungmul (*nongak*) competition and in 1985 at the 26th Annual National Folk Arts Competition (*Chǒn'guk minsok yesul kyǒngyǒn taehoe*).

51. The relationship between student groups and cultural asset training centers is discussed at length in chapter 4.

52. Regional cultural assets are designated under national law as well, though they receive a considerably smaller monthly stipend and enjoy a perhaps slightly lower level of social prestige.

53. Cultural asset training centers are discussed in detail in chapter 4.

54. Although the relationship between p'ungmul and student political activism is an intimate one, it is, nonetheless, irresponsible and somewhat insulting to imply it is the sole motivational factor behind the study of the art form within university circles (as stated, for example, in Lee, Byongwon 1993: 125).

55. This comment would later fuel an ongoing inside joke, as Pak Hyŏngnae is still very much alive. At the time of this interview, Yi hadn't been to Imshil for almost a year and was speaking on hearsay. Chapter 4 outlines the special relationship rekindled between these two players (see also figure 1.10).

56. By 2003 the rift between these two schools had been mended.

57. Yi is referring to the seated version of the now widely popular urbanized genre of *samul nori* (also romanized as *samullori*), literally "four things at play," a reference to the two drums and two gongs used in p'ungmul ensembles. Though the topic will be brought to the surface sporadically throughout the remaining text, a general introduction in the English language is offered in Howard 1991; Kim, Duk Soo 1992: 7–11. More comprehensive treatment is found in Kim Hŏnsŏn 1994, 1995 (Korean); Park, Shingil 2000: 177–218 (English); Hesselink 2004 (English).

58. Yi had seen Kim Hyŏngsun perform on numerous occasions, and had taken a few lessons at the center in Chŏnju where Kim taught.

59. Keith Howard's *Bands, Songs, and Shamanistic Rituals* organizes an entire chapter around p'ungmul (*nongak*) bands' origins in the military (and by extension China), folk religious practices, Buddhism, and farming (1990: 217–39).

60. Chinese Communist forces entered the Korean War officially in October 1950, though direct intervention in North Korean affairs preceded this date by at least a year (Cumings 1990: 350–76). The earliest documentation of percussion instruments being used by the Chinese in an attack is recorded in an official U.N. report dated November 25, 1950: "When darkness fell, most of the EUSAK [Eighth U.S. Army Korea] units heard a sudden frighting [*sic*] uproar of noise. Bugles, whistles, and flutes were blown, cymbals clanged, and drums rattled. This weird cacophony signaled the beginning of the Red Chinese second offensive in a [*sic*] full-scale all along the western front" (War History Compilation Committee 1975: 386).

Chapter Two

1. The translation of this tale is taken from Ha, Tae Hung 1958: 114; an annotated English translation accompanied by the original text is found in Song, Bang-song 1980: 13–15, 157.

2. This system is arranged according to the materials from which the instruments are made: metal, stone, silk, bamboo, gourd, earth or clay, leather or hide, and wood (Yi Hyegu 1986: 14–15).

3. I have consulted the English translation of this work by A. Baines and K. P. Wachsman, as reproduced in Myers 1992: 444–61.

4. The word *changgu* is most likely a regional linguistic variant of *changgo*, though I have seen one source claim that the second syllable -*ku*/-*gu* is from the Chinese character for dog, ostensibly due to the widespread use of dogskin on p'ungmul drums (No Poksun 1994: 100).

5. In some provinces a clay drum is referred to as a *sajanggu* (Kim Yŏngun 1989: 45).

6. References here and throughout the remaining text of this chapter are to the 1610 edition of the *Akhak kwebŏm,* as reproduced in the appendix of Chang Sahun 1986: 627–738 (see Provine 1988: 57–59). Chang Sahun's pagination is immediately followed by a page reference to the 1610 edition.

7. The cloth was a light-yellow cotton blend. The head struck by the stick was double-layered, the side struck by the mallet triple-layered.

8. A picture of a rural *changgo* player using the bare palm of his left hand is found in Howard 1985: 132.

9. A teaching assistant to Kim Hyŏngsun made me a *kunggulch'ae* with a lacquered *wooden* handle, the first I had ever seen. As beautiful as the handle is, I must admit that a certain amount of playing comfort is sacrificed!

10. Page numbers provided for dynastic annals are references to the pagination of the original document, as reproduced through photographic reprints by the Committee of National History (the *Chosŏn wangjo shillok* [Annals of the Chosŏn dynasty] series; see Provine 1988: 29–34 for further historical and bibliographic details). Page references to original sources in this chapter use the following convention: 132.15*a,* for example, means chapter 132, p. 15, first half of the folio (the recto).

11. The passage from the *Samguk sagi* quoted near the beginning of this chapter would seem to lend weight to this account, at least in popular lore.

12. A general discussion of spirit poles, including the related terms *sŏnang* and *sottae,* is found in an English introduction by Im, Dong-kwon (1994: 8–9).

13. Yang Chinsŏng ([1980?]: 21) lists *kwangsoe* as another possible variation, which I had assumed was the combination of the onomatopoeic prefix *kwang-* followed by the standard term *soe.* A document dated March 27, 1957, from the village of Changjwa on Wando Island, South Chŏlla province, however, lists *kwangsoe* with two Chinese characters in an inventory of village instruments (Eikemeier 1980: 208). The characters have in all likelihood been chosen for their respective pronunciations, not their meanings (*kwang,* or "radium," and *soe,* "make efforts"). *Kwangsoe* also refers to the gong used in the Buddhist rite of *shiktang chakpŏp* ("Maigre Feast"; Kim Yŏngun 1989: 56; Lee, Byongwon 1987: 19).

14. In the *Akhak kwebŏm,* the *soe ch'ae,* like many of the various mallets, is called a *ch'u* (mallet; Chang Sahun 1986: 641; 8.9*b*).

15. Before my departure from Korea in 1996, I purchased a *soe* mallet with a modified rubber sponge handle, which seemed to me to be lighter and more comfortable to the touch. Professional players I showed it to, however, expressed very little enthusiasm.

16. The Changjwa village document cited in n. 13 lists the large gong with the Chinese character *chaeng,* meaning "metallic sound," though this is the only source I know of that uses this designation (Eikemeier 1980: 208).

17. A third method known as *pan pangja* (semi-forged) is used for lidded brass rice bowls or bowls whose edges slant inward (Lee, Hyoung-kwon 1997: 52). After the metal is taken from the mold, the finishing touches are applied by beating and smoothing the edges by hand.

18. Yi Yonggu is a professional *ching* maker born in 1937 in Hamyang county, South Kyŏngsang province. His recently published book is an entire work dedicated to the *ching*'s historical past as recorded in oral and written sources, as well as its specifications, method of construction, analysis of sound waves, famous makers, and performance

contexts. An account of the master gong maker Yi Pongju from Kyŏnggi province has recently been published in English as well (Lee, Hyoung-kwon 1997).

19. The beater depicted in the *Akhak kwebŏm* has a triangular point and is called a *ch'u* (mallet; Chang Sahun 1986: 641; 8.9*b*).

20. Use of the term *sogu* is particularly widespread along the east coast of the Korean peninsula (Kim Yŏngun 1989: 48).

21. A picture of the somewhat unusual *sogo* stick with a striking end in the shape of a *t'aegŭk* is found in Chŏng Pyŏngho 1994: 59.

22. The first syllable, *ho*, can be written alternatively with the Chinese character of the same pronunciation meaning "shout or cry out" (Paek Yŏngja 1994: 134).

23. Chang Sahun (1995: 44) gives the Chinese character compound *ch'onap*, literally "guardian silencer," a reading I have not encountered in any other literary or historical source.

24. Measurements in the *Akhak kwebŏm* are indicated by the Chinese characters *ch'ŏk* (a Korean foot), *ch'on* (0.1 *ch'ŏk*), and *pun* (0.1 *ch'on*), designations that continue to be used in the sources cited below. According to the research of Pak Hŭngsu, the *ch'ŏk* during the time in which the *Akhak kwebŏm* was written was equivalent to 31.2 cm (1967: 215); therefore, the measurement of the *hojŏk* cataloged reads one *ch'ŏk*, five *ch'on*, two *pun*—roughly 47.4 cm (Chang Sahun 1986: 655; 7.13*a*).

25. The instrument depicted in this treatise is the *taegak* (large horn), measuring two *ch'ŏk*, six *ch'on*, or roughly 81 cm (Chang Sahun 1986: 642; 8.8*b*).

26. The construction of the *nabal*, like that of many of Korea's traditional instruments, has undergone a process of modern "improvement" (*kaeryang*) under the sponsorship of the National Center for Korean Traditional Performing Arts (Kungnip kugagwŏn). A *nabal* made by Kim Hyŏn'gon in 1989, for example, features an instrument with detachable sections, three valves, and a trumpet mouthpiece (Mun Hyŏn 1996: 56).

27. This is in contrast to the full-length vest—usually of a tan, light blue, or orange color, worn by the common soldier—called a *kujong* (Sŏk Chusŏn 1992: 445).

28. An example of such a *chŏllip* is on display at the Onyang Folk Museum and is reproduced in Adams 1993: 66.

29. The term used here is *ch'anghoji*, paper used in the frames of windows and doors (*ch'angho*) in traditional Korean homes and architecture.

30. Pak raises this issue in the context of a certain amount of confusion he encountered when being evaluated by a group of scholars from Seoul who demanded to see his troupe's *ch'ae sangmo* hats (see Hesselink 1998b).

31. The paper used is called *ch'anghoji*, as described in n. 29.

32. More regional variants of the term *nonggi* are provided in Chŏng Pyŏngho 1994: 38.

33. This article summarizes a larger work published in 1976.

34. *Yŏnggi* depicted in the eighteenth-century "Illustrated Ceremonial Manual" displayed at the National Museum of Korea in Seoul are square and solid blue in color, and they include no Chinese characters.

35. Three other "guardian flags" (*ŭijanggi*) also feature the figure of a dragon: the *ch'ŏngnyonggi* (literally, "blue dragon flag"), a triangular flag with a yellow dragon printed

on a purple background (p. 33); the *osaek kŭmnyonggi* (five-colored golden dragon flag), a triangular flag with a gold-colored dragon printed on a five multicolored striped background (p. 63); and the *yongmagi* (dragon horse flag), a four-colored dragon horse printed on a white background, as recorded in the *Sejong shillok* (Annals of Sejong; p. 75).

36. The two flags depicted in this treatise are of two different sizes and have an asymmetrical rectangular shape.

37. No Poksun 1994: 45–47, 81–84, was the main source consulted for this list, though I have cross-referenced it with Chŏng Pyŏngho and Yi Pohyŏng 1985: 36–37, Chŏng Pyŏngho et al. 1980: 59, and Yang Chinsŏng [1980?]: 24–26.

38. Yang Sunyong, P'ilbong's lead *soe* player (now deceased), believed the *taep'osu* character was from the military and therefore not an ordinary hunter, as reflected in P'ilbong's use of the military *yŏpch'ong* weapon (quoted in No Poksun 1994: 83).

39. The methods by which scholars determine what constitutes a separate ground formation are often inconsistent. Pak Hŏnbong and Yu Kiryong, in the initial cultural asset report on p'ungmul, for example, listed twenty-seven total formations based primarily on shape and function (1965: 377–80), but the report on Chŏlla province p'ungmul, submitted only two years later by Hong Hyŏnshik, Kim, and Pak, listed a total of fifty-one; the same formations were often listed numerous times but under different names according to the rhythmic pattern played (1967: 150–80). It is difficult to ascertain whose criteria formed the basis for the various categories (scholar versus informant-performer).

Chapter Three

1. Three representative passages of Ch'oe's teachings translated into English are found in Lee, Peter H. 1996: 316–21.

2. In 1994 a special issue of *Korea Journal* was published commemorating the one hundredth anniversary of the Tonghak Peasants' Uprising (vol. 34, no. 4). Rules of behavior and proclamations of this movement have been translated into English (Lee, Peter H. 1996: 363–70).

3. In Korean cultural studies, as perhaps elsewhere, the idea of "people" suggests a conscious, political, and proactive entity, in contrast to "the masses," who are somehow unknowingly acted upon from above (Yun Chigwan 1998: personal communication). For this reason, I choose to translate *minjung* hereafter as "people('s)."

4. In this paragraph I am discussing an oppositional-culture *minjung* rooted in indigenous cultural practices, versus a politicohistorical *minjung* associated more with socialism and the international Left (Abelmann 1996: 23, 26; see chapters 2 and 6 of her book for a more comprehensive treatment of *minjung* ideology).

5. "Play," or *nori* in the Korean, refers to both action and practice as well as entertainment-based activity, though with a subtle leaning toward the "fun" aspect.

6. *Homi ssikki* (also known by the linguistic variant *homi ssishi*), literally "to wash the hoe," is a festival celebrated in lunar calendar July, in the middle of the agricultural cycle. Part communal feast, part dance, part mime, and part music, it encompasses both ritual and play elements. The nearly synonymous regional terms *nongsanggye*, *ch'oyŏn*, and *p'ukkut nori* are also listed in O's original Korean text. For a full discussion of *homi ssikki's* origins and performance structure, as well as comprehensive visual documentation, see Kim Sunam and Kim Misuk 1986.

7. *Tang kut* is a commonly abbreviated form of *tangsan kut*. The term *norip'an* was the subject of an entire article (Chŏng Pyŏngho 1988). Briefly, the *(nori)p'an* represents "any communal space in which people gather together to converse with each other and enjoy themselves" (1988: 9).

8. *Ture kut* is a function often associated with p'ungmul, even considered by one scholar to be the primary impetus behind its genesis (Shin Yongha 1985). Although the practice has been recorded as becoming extinct in the early twentieth century (Sorenson 1988: 3–4), there are photos and written documentation from the much more recent past (Chŏng Pyŏngho 1994: 25, 119, 211; Chŏng Pyŏngho 1995: front plates; Chu Kanghyŏn 1997: 200–246). I never personally witnessed a communal labor team (*turep'ae*) accompanied by music during my fieldwork period, nor did I meet anyone who had done so in recent memory.

9. The link between greeting rituals and the farming flag was established in the cultural asset report translated in chapter 1, entry 12a.

10. The term used here is *chinsan,* the mountain that stands to the north of the village.

11. Shim Usŏng 1978 is cited as a source by O for this paragraph.

12. I am taking poetic license with the translation of the Korean phrase *okkis-ŭl yŏmida,* literally "adjust one's dress," into the English as "reflective."

13. Compare this passage with Yi Sangbaek's interview in chapter 1, where he briefly alludes to the reflective nature of the *soe* (small gong) and its powers of healing.

14. Shamanistic ensembles do not always use the same percussion instruments as p'ungmul; see table 2.1 for a comparison of instrumentation across genres.

15. O cites Yi Man'gap 1980 at this point in the text.

16. The *kŭmjul,* also known by the names of *kŭmgijul* (taboo rope), *injul* (human rope), *chwasak* (seated rope), and *munsak* (gate rope), is a rope made of twisted straw used in ritual contexts to expel unwanted spirits. This rope is also hung in front of homes after a successful birth to announce the sex of the newborn child (Kim Sŏngbae 1998: 203–4).

17. *Wiji tongijŏn* is the popular name for the section of the third-century historical record cited at the beginning of chapter 2. This document also chronicles activity occurring in Japan during roughly the same period (Takashi 1986: 248–71).

18. The Chŏlla province regional variant *changwŏllye* is used here in the Korean text instead of *homi ssikki* (see Kim Sunam and Kim Misuk 1986: 99).

19. A comprehensive analysis of play culture (*nori munhwa*) is provided in Yi Sangil 1988.

20. Yi Sangbaek had felt this was one of the primary reasons the Japanese and sympathetic Korean government officials of the post-liberation period had degraded p'ungmul activity, labeling it as "superstition" (*mishin;* 1995: personal communication). This would begin to explain one of certainly many interrelated factors behind p'ungmul's popularity among student demonstration groups.

21. This view is shared by Kim Inu (1993) in the reading passage found at the end of this chapter, though Yi Sangbaek comments in chapter 4 that he feels individual satisfaction in playing is a worthwhile goal.

22. I was notified early in 2005 by the publisher Hangminsa in Seoul that the name Kim Inu was in fact a pseudonym, chosen at the time for personal and financial reasons (which were not provided to me in any detail). Kim finally published under his real name of Kim Wŏnho in the later 1990s when this essay was reprinted in a larger work on p'ungmul (Kim Wŏnho 1999: 293–344).

23. An earlier document does exist that extols the virtues of oral mnemonics in the learning process (No Kwangil 1985: 281–82).

24. Rice and rice-paddy stories figure significantly in more popular and/or political literature (Kim Chiha 1977: 11–12; Abelmann 1996: 15–19).

25. A number of scholars have written works on p'ungmul or *nongak* under the heading of dance (Kim, Yang-kon 1967; Kim, Mae-ja 1981: 80; Ch'oe T'aeyŏl 1984; Chŏng Pyŏngho 1985, 1995; Sŏng Kyŏngnin 1985: 364–66). The largest bookstore in Korea, Kyobo Mun'go in Seoul, displays the majority of its works on the subject on the dance shelf.

26. The term *shinmyŏng* is composed of two Chinese characters, *shin* (spirit or deity) and *myŏng* (shining or illumination). This rather abstract concept is believed to have roots in shamanism and group (dance) performance, evoked either through a heightened festive atmosphere (Song, Soo-nam 1990: 34) or by the descending of a deity and its possession of an individual or group, fusing the secular and the sacred into a single entity at the climax of the ritual event (Ch'ae, Hui-wan 1983: 5; a very rough Western equivalent is the "peak experience" as documented by Boyd 1992: 173–74). Therefore I will translate *shinmyŏng*, depending on the context, as spirit, spiritual state, enthusiasm, or state of oneness.

27. The *porittae ch'um* (literally, "barley stalk dance") is a dance that is ubiquitous throughout the Korean peninsula in which the arms are held loosely out to the sides, accompanied by a gentle up-and-down movement produced by bending the knees.

28. The *ttŭnsoe* were the first rank among the performers of the itinerant *namsadang* troupes (see Shim Usŏng 1994).

29. This section of the performance shows off the lead *soe* player's ability at manipulating the *pup'o* hat.

30. In the original text, the term translated in this section as "oral verse" is *ipchangdan*, literally, "mouth rhythmic patterns."

31. The terms *changdan* and *karak* are essentially interchangeable at the general level; the issue is dealt with in greater depth in chapter 4.

32. *Kuŭm* are analyzed in more detail in chapter 4.

33. *Hanbae*, depending on the context and the author, can refer to either general tempo (Han Myŏnghŭi 1994: 30–33), pattern (Paek Taeung 1985: 326–27), or space between the strokes or pitches (Cho Myŏngja 1995: personal communication).

34. This rhythmic pattern is composed of two phrases of twelve eighth notes (similar, but not identical, to Western 12/8 time): | *Ttang* | | *to* | *ttang* | | *to* | *nae* | | *ttang* | *i* | *da* | |, | *Cho* | *sŏn* | | *ttang* | | *to* | *nae* | | *ttang* | *i* | *da* | |.

35. *Ich'ae* as well is composed of two phrases of twelve eighth notes: | *Pyŏl* | | *tta* | | *se* | | *pyŏl* | | *tta* | | *se* | |, | *ha* | | *nŭl* | *chap* | | *ko* | *pyŏl* | | *tta* | *se* | | |.

36. This is a line by the female poet Mo Yunsuk (b. 1910), most likely from an extended poem titled "Ren ŭi aega" ("Wren's Elegy"), published in 1937 (see Suh, Doo Soo 1965: 84).

37. These are references to Sino-Korean pitch indicators used in Korean mensural notation (*chŏngganbo*) developed in the Korean court. Today their approximate Western counterparts are *chung* = A♭, *im* = B♭, *mu* = D♭, *hwang* = E♭, and *t'ae* = F (see Howard 1988: 20–21).

38. *Ch'uimsae* are interjections of encouragement from either the audience or accompanying instrumentalists and performers, the most standard being "Ŏlshigu" (excellent), "Chot'a" (nice), and "Chal handa" (well done). *Ch'uimsae* are a more prominent feature of *p'ansori* singing and recitation.

39. The term *ki* encompasses a broad range of meanings, including energy, strength, mind, spirit, heart, life force, and "material force" (see Choi, Min-hong 1978: 20, 114–15).

40. Other scholars use different terms—Yi Chaesuk, for example, though specifically in reference to the rhythmic patterns *chinyangjo* and *chungmori*, uses the Sino-Korean designations *ki* (rise), *kyŏng* (connect), *kyŏl* (tie or bind), and *hae* (culminate; 1979: 11–13).

41. *Kinjang* and *iwan* are Sino-Korean terms; their native Korean counterparts are *maetta, choeda,* or *choeida* (tension) and *p'ulta / p'unda* (release; Song Pangsong 1993: personal communication).

42. *Och'ae chilgut* of the "left side" tradition is transcribed in Hesselink 1998c, Appendix C.

43. *Oemach'i hŭtchilgut / oemach'i chilgut* is a processional rhythm played by ensembles when moving from one locale to the next, as well as in the context of entertainment p'ungmul (*p'an kut*); *chŏpchilgut / och'ae chilgut* is a specialized rhythmic pattern used only in the context of the *p'an kut*.

44. In this one instance I have translated *karak* as "phrase," which I feel more closely reflects the intent of this passage.

45. The idea of basic or primary forms of the rhythmic patterns versus rhythmic variants will be discussed at greater length in chapter 4.

46. The verb translated here as "intensely playing" is *pibida*, literally, "to rub."

47. This is actually the fourth phrase of the "left side" *chilgut* rhythmic pattern, which is repeated over and over, like a vamp. The rhythm of the above example is as follows: | *ching*—| *gil*—| *san*—| *don*—| *tat*—| *ton*—|, | *ching*—| *gi ri* | *san*—| *don*—| *tat*—| *ton*—|.

48. This sequence of rhythmic patterns, as well as the ones that follow, is from the "left side" p'ungmul repertoire; the patterns are listed in chapter 5.

49. Although it is true that rhythmic patterns from the section or movement (*madang*) titled *ch'aegut* are organized according to the number of *ching* strokes (see Yi Pohyŏng 1984 as an example), I am unable to find a source that bases its method of classification solely on this criterion.

50. From this point on, the text reads more smoothly leaving the Korean term *shinmyŏng* in the English translation.

Chapter Four

1. The Seoul Norimadang, opened in 1987 and sponsored by the Seoul city government and the Ministry of Culture and Sports, is an outdoor venue featuring free live performances of Korean traditional music and dance during the spring and summer months. One month out of each year is usually reserved for visits by cultural asset "holders" and/or troupes, which was the case for this particular event. During the summer of 2004 this space was temporarily closed for the construction of a roof that would cover both the performers and the audience, thus making for a longer season and one less prone to cancellations on account of weather.

2. The North Chŏlla Provincially Established Center for Korean Traditional Performing Arts was officially opened in 1986, in accordance with a law that increased the power of the provincial governments, though activity existed at the location some time before then. The institute was initially called the Chŏlla puktorip kugagwŏn, but the name was abbreviated to its current form, Chŏnbuk torip kugagwŏn, in 1996. In 1997 it launched its own academic journal, *Chŏnbuk kugak* (North Chŏlla Traditional Music/Dance).

3. The Iri institute offered classes in *soe, changgo,* traditional dance, *sangmo* (spinning-tasseled hat), and *samul nori* (an urbanized genre of p'ungmul). The primary music instructors were Pak Yongt'aek, Iri Nongak's lead *soe* player (interviewed in chapter 6), and Kim Ikchu, one of Kim's sons and Iri Nongak's second *changgo* player.

4. Use of the term *madang* may reflect a past relationship with shamanistic rituals performed outdoors (*madang kut*), but it should not be confused with the past designation for individual pieces within the *p'ansori* repertoire by the same name (see Cho Tongil and Kim Hŭnggyu 1978; Chŏng Pyŏnguk 1981: 34–35).

5. I have chosen the loose translation "primary form" for *wŏnbak* for clarity's sake, in order to avoid the reiteration of the word "rhythm" (*wŏn* = original or primary, *-pak/-bak* = beat or rhythm). One also sees references to the nearly synonymous terms *wŏnhyŏng* (Yi Chaesuk 1979: 11) and *kibonhyŏng* (Kim Hyŏnsuk 1987: 49).

6. My invention of the term *yŏnjubak* (literally, "performance beat or rhythm") for a Korean translation of a conference paper presented in Seoul met with little resistance by the local musicological community (Hesselink 1998a: 20).

7. The word *pyŏnbak* is made up of two Chinese characters: *pyŏn* (alteration or variation) and *pak/-bak* (beat or rhythm).

8. Yi Hosun was really Kim's right-hand man, taking attendance for all the classes, bringing him food and drink, repairing broken instruments, and coordinating parties and impromptu performances (no small task), in addition to his teaching assistant duties. Yi Hosun is seen in figure 6.1 standing directly behind Iri Nongak's lead *soe* player, Pak Yongt'aek.

9. This section is told from the perspective of a right-handed player, which accounts for the majority of both amateur and professional performers today. The concept of "left" and "right" handedness in drum playing as communicated to me during my fieldwork period may in fact signal a generational shift in attitude: Keith Howard pointed out that many of the older performers he had worked with played in a "reverse" style (with the mallet in the right hand), though it was not considered "left-handed" (1997: personal communication). It should be noted that Kim played in this manner, which created a useful mirror effect when he taught from the front of the room.

10. Perhaps owing to acoustics (see Provine 1975: 4), the right or stick hand strikes the drum slightly ahead of the left hand, at least as the stroke is taught by both Kim and Yi. Though the sequence is difficult to determine conclusively, it is my opinion that the stick strikes the drum *on* the beat and the mallet strikes a fraction of a second later.

11. Although it has been argued that Korean traditional dance is characterized by heel-first stepping and turning (Loken 1983: 80; Loken-Kim and Crump 1993: 14), there is some discussion of the specifically shaman dancer moving forward on the toes with the heel up (e.g., Huhm 1980: 43). Kim does admit to creating his own choreography, as well as to the obvious fact that the tightrope walker was a part of his traveling troupe.

12. The consumption of alcohol in conjunction with the playing of p'ungmul really deserves a separate study in its own right, though a general overview of Korean drinking customs has been published in English (Choi, Seung-beom 1996). Every performance, by either the CTK impromptu group or Iri Nongak, in which I participated was preceded and/or followed by the drinking of alcohol (almost invariably of the indigenous Korean type, such as *soju* or *makkŏlli*). This was true as well for first meetings with unfamiliar p'ungmul performers and groups, particularly those composed of students. A major exception to this rule was Kim himself, who quit drinking soon after his termination at the alcohol production plant (mentioned in his interview in chapter 1).

13. The Iri Nongak group was made up of Pak Yongt'aek on *soe* (lead *soe*), Kim Ikchu on *changgo* (second *changgo*), Yang Sŭngnyŏl on *puk* (*sangmo* spinning-tasseled hat specialist), and Yi Hosun on *ching* (fourth *soe*).

14. Circle members close to Yi were openly hostile toward the Japanese, often calling them "bastards" or "sons of bitches." The situation became worse during my sixth month of research, when the Japanese government declared its intention to "reclaim" the Tokto islands from South Korea.

15. Much has been written on the effects of the 1971 *Saemaŭl undong* on Korean communal village society (Lee, Man-gap 1973; Kim, Jong-ho 1977; MOHA 1979; Whang, In-joung 1981; Oh, Myung-Seok 1998). A collection of then-president Park Chung-hee's [Pak Chŏnghŭi] speeches on the concept of *saemaŭl* was published in 1979 (Park, Chung-hee 1979).

16. Yi cited the reading passage of Kim Inu translated in chapter 3 as one example.

17. He gave the *obangjin* rhythmic pattern as one example, stating it was actually an *uttari* rhythm (the *uttari* region is centered in Ch'ungch'ŏng and Kyŏnggi provinces, though with roots in Chŏlla province "left side"–style p'ungmul).

18. Flavor is a common synesthetic metaphor throughout Asia (in Japanese, for example, the phrase is *aji ga aru / aji ga nai*).

19. In a lesson in February 1996 with a beginning group from a local Puan county farming cooperative (*nonghyŏp*), Yi emphasized the importance of being able to sing the rhythms, but then proceeded to teach the rhythmic patterns in order of increasing complexity, moving from *hwimori* to *toen samch'ae* to *insagut* (not the regular order of instruction or performance; see plate 14).

20. The growing influence of *samul nori* on "traditional" p'ungmul performance practice and philosophy, though worthy of a lengthy in-depth study, is beyond the immediate scope of this book.

21. A group this size is more of an ideal; few ensembles these days are able to claim or support such a large number.

22. Examples of this older method of playing have been visually documented in Chŏng Pyŏngho 1994: 66; Chu Kanghyŏn 1995: 231; Kim Sunam, Im Sŏkchae, and Yi Pohyŏng 1986: 55.

23. Pak's past relationship with the village and troupe is recorded in an interview in Hesselink 1998b.

Chapter Five

Note on the epigraph: Shin Kinam was the renowned North Chŏlla province *changgo* player who included Kim Hyŏngsun as a first-generation disciple. Shin is mentioned in the 1982 cultural asset report translated in part in chapter 1 (section 6, under the passage on the village of Imshil).

1. The specific order of gong and drum strokes with accompanying footsteps and ground formations is recorded in notation on the Web site provided in the author's note (see above, p. xiv).

2. Ammann (1997: 65) has hypothesized that the counterclockwise movement originated in part in human physical development. This direction places the left-hand side to the center of the circle with protection by the right hand to the outer. In addition, right-handed people—the majority of the planet—take longer strides with their right leg (which is why people who are lost in the desert move in counterclockwise circles).

3. The five directions, each with corresponding colors and symbolic imagery, have significance in both folk and court religious practices (Hwang Pyŏnggi 1993: personal communication; Kim Ŭisuk 1993: 47; Paek Yŏngja 1994: 223–24; Hesselink and Petty 2004).

4. However, on two occasions Kim selected only three other players for the *changgo* dance, ostensibly because of the relative importance of the events: a special performance for the cultural asset committee in Seoul, and a concert at the Olympic Park for Children's Day.

5. Yi had spent a couple of summers at Kim Duk Soo's training institute in Puyŏ, where he and some college friends formed a *samul nori* quartet that performed on a regular basis.

6. The term used here is *muajigyŏng,* literally, "a state in which one's 'self' is annihilated."

7. A notable exception occurred in a performance by Imshil P'ilbong Nongak on August 24, 1996 at the Seoul Norimadang, when P'ilbong's acting lead *changgo* player Yang Chinhwan (one of Yi's mentors) played the solo *changgo* dance (*changgo nori*) near the conclusion of the front *kut.* Yi had learned a version of this dance as well, though he did not include it as part of the repertoire he regularly taught.

8. This is an alternate method of counting *ching* strokes: *oe* (or *hana*) is the number 1 in Korean numerals; *mach'i* comes from the verb *mach'ida,* or "to be struck [or hit]."

9. A transnotation of one *soe* performer's rendition is given in Hesselink 1998c: 535–38.

10. See Kim Hakchu 1987 for a discussion of the word's possible etymological roots.

11. Here and in category 4 "free repetition" refers to sections of free repetition, as well as to an entire rhythmic pattern.

12. Technically speaking the *changgo* players continue playing this phrase in triple subdivisions while the *soe* players switch to duple subdivisions.

13. "Single meter" refers to individual phrases within each sequence.

14. A considerable amount of research has been conducted by Yi Pohyŏng, however, concerning grouping and subdivisions within each cycle or pattern (1992, 1994, 1995; Lee, Bo hyung 2003).

15. A much simpler definition by the scholar Han Manyŏng appeared the same year: "A rhythmic pattern [*ridŭmhyŏng*] of fixed or uniform length is called a *changdan*" (Chang Sahun and Han Manyŏng 1975: 27).

16. Yi saw "meter" and "rhythmic pattern" as essentially synonymous terms (Yi Hyegu 1991: 13).

17. Conflicting usage of the words *pak, pakcha,* and related rhythmic terms is · rampant and beyond the scope of this analysis. The adventurous are invited to compare Pak Chongsŏl 1991 and Yi Hyegu 1987 with the works of Yi Pohyŏng cited in note 14 above.

18. In all fairness to Provine, he does speak of complex metric constructions later in the cited work above (1975: 5).

19. Kim's divisions are (1) *oe changdan hyŏng* (single-phrase form), a rhythmic pattern in which a single line or phrase is repeated over and over; (2) *ŭm-yang taebi hyŏng* (*ŭm-yang* contrasting form), a pattern in which two phrases, one male and one female, are repeated alternately over and over; (3) *kajin hyŏng* (collected form), a pattern in which the rhythm is set or uniform, composed of more than two phrases, and is repeated over and over; and (4) *hŏt'ŭn hyŏng* (scattered form), a pattern that constantly changes, with no fixed rhythm (Kim Hyŏnsuk 1991: 78).

Chapter Six

1. For Yi Sunam, see chapter 1, n. 7. Kim Mundal was then Iri Nongak's lead *soe* player; see chapter 1, section 2c of the cultural asset report.

2. These criteria are treated in considerable detail and insight in Brinner 1995 (see especially pp. 74–86).

3. This comment may be a reflection of an old Korean practice known as *kwansang,* character reading or fortune-telling based on a person's physiognomy, generally centered on the facial region (see Cho Sŏngu 1985; Kim Hyŏkche 1978).

4. She is now speaking of the role of the lead *soe* player (*sangsoe*).

5. The term *karak* can refer to either melody, tone, pitch, or rhythmic pattern, depending on the context.

6. According to the cultural asset report translated in chapter 1, "left side" p'ungmul in Chŏnju had already ceased to be transmitted by the year 1982, in large part because of the activities of the "right side" *sogo* player Paek Namyun (see Yi Hogwan et al. 1982: 10–11).

7. Hwang used the words *maŭl kut* (village ritual) and *ttŭnsoe* (professional performers in itinerant troupes) to refer to the rural and touring groups, respectively.

8. See chapter 3, note 26, for a brief discussion of *shinmyŏng.*

9. Kwŏn Hyeryŏn is the Korean name of Donna Kwon. Park Joo Won's 2005 survey can be downloaded at plaza.ufl.edu/joowon/jwpoongmul.zip (accessed August 3, 2005). The most valuable Web site related to the American p'ungmul scene is www .poongmul.com/.

10. *Chigol*, also known by the name *chibŏl*, is divine punishment for acting against the gods or spirits (Chŏn Sŏn'gi 1992: 3886).

11. *Tan'gol* belong to a hereditary class of shamans and are characteristic of Chŏlla and Kyŏngsang provinces (Kim T'aegon 1985: 147).

12. Also known as *chambap mŏgigi* (to feed *chambap*), this practice has its origins in folk remedies. A portion of the rice (beans may be substituted) is believed to be eaten by the evil spirit(s), which are mollified by the offering (Shin Chunho 1991: 1190).

13. The term *chŏmbach'i* refers to a ritual specialist who occupies a position somewhere between a shaman and a fortune-teller. The designation is characteristic of the Chŏlla provinces (Kim T'aegon 1985: 261).

14. Many in the Chŏlla provinces believe that the village spirit lives in a large tree called the *tangsan namu* (spirit tree), located near the entrance of the village. The ritual performance I witnessed and recount below in note 15 included playing this ritual twice, once for the grandfather's spirit tree, in front of the village, and once for the grandmother's spirit tree, planted in back (this is not an isolated example; see Han'guk hyangt'osa 1994: 65–66).

15. This account is essentially consistent with those found in the general literature (Howard 1990: 37–50; Kim Inu 1993: 134; Chŏng Pyŏngho 1994: 105–16). A ritual p'ungmul performance I attended on March 1, 1996, in Sŏngnam village, Taesan subcounty, Koch'ang county, was a day-long event sponsored by the local community, but its order in many ways mirrored Kim's story above. The day began at 10:00 A.M. with a gate ritual (*mun kut*), followed by greeting p'ungmul performed around the village's front spirit tree. The group then played a field shrine ritual (*tŭltangsan kut*), followed immediately by a well ritual (*saem kut*). Then everyone took a break for lunch, and at 12:30 individual houses were visited (this included the front yard [*madang*], kitchen [*chowang*], and storage area [*ch'ŏryung*] rituals). A tug-of-war was then enacted by the villagers and visiting onlookers, followed by a village shrine ritual for the back spirit tree. The day was concluded with a large entertainment-oriented performance (*p'an kut*), ending around 6:00 P.M.

BIBLIOGRAPHY

Abelmann, Nancy. 1996. *Echoes of the Past, Epics of Dissent: A South Korean Social Movement.* Berkeley and Los Angeles: University of California Press.

Adams, Edward B. 1993 [1987]. *Korean Folk Art and Craft.* Seoul: Seoul International Publishing House.

Ammann, Raymond. 1997. *Kanak Dance and Music: Ceremonial and Intimate Performance of the Melanesians of New Caledonia, Historical and Actual.* Nouméa, New Caledonia: Agence de Développement de la Culture Kanak.

An Hyeyŏng. 1986. "Honam udo nongak ŭi kusŏng hyŏngshik-e kwanhan yŏn'gu" [A Study of the Compositional Form of Chŏlla Province "Right Side"–Style *Nongak*]. Master's thesis, Sungmyŏng Women's University.

Appadurai, Arjun. 1991. "Global Ethnoscapes: Notes and Queries for a Transnational Anthropology." In *Recapturing Anthropology: Working in the Present,* edited by Richard G. Fox, 191–210. Santa Fe: School of American Research Press.

Applebaum, Herbert. 1984. *Work in Non-Market and Transitional Societies.* Albany: State University of New York Press.

Armstrong, Charles K. 2003. "The Cultural Cold War in Korea, 1945–1950." *Journal of Asian Studies* 62, no. 1:71–99.

Armstrong, Karen. 2000. *The Battle for God.* New York: Alfred A. Knopf.

Bakan, Michael B. 1999. *Music of Death and New Creation: Experiences in the World of Balinese Gamelan Beleganjur.* Chicago: University of Chicago Press.

Bock, Philip K. 1988. *Rethinking Psychological Anthropology: Continuity and Change in the Study of Human Action.* New York: W. H. Freeman.

Boyd, Jenny, with Holly George-Warren. 1992. *Musicians in Tune: Seventy-five Contemporary Musicians Discuss the Creative Process.* New York: Fireside.

Brinner, Benjamin. 1995. *Knowing Music, Making Music: Javanese Gamelan and the Theory of Musical Competence and Interaction.* Chicago: University of Chicago Press.

Ch'ae, Hui-wan [Ch'ae Hŭiwan]. 1983. "*Shinmyŏng* as an Artistic Experience in Traditional Korean Group Performance-Plays." *Korea Journal* 23, no. 5:4–14.

Chang Sahun. 1986. *Hanguk ŭmaksa* [A History of Korean Music]. Seoul: Segwang ŭmak ch'ulp'ansa.

———. 1989. *Kugak myŏnginjŏn* [Biographies of Famous Traditional Musicians]. Seoul: Segwang ŭmak ch'ulp'ansa.

———. 1995 [1986]. *Han'guk akki taegwan* [Korean Musical Instruments]. Seoul: Sŏul taehakkyo ch'ulp'anbu.

Chang Sahun and Han Manyŏng. 1975. *Kugak kaeron* [An Introduction to Korean Traditional Music]. Seoul: Han'guk kugak hakhoe.

Chen Shou. 1962. *Sanguo zhi* [A History of the Three Kingdoms], modern ed. Peking: Zhonghua shuju chuban.

Chernoff, John Miller. 1979. *African Rhythm and Sensibility: Aesthetics and Social Action in African Musical Idioms*. Chicago: University of Chicago Press.

Cho Hŭngyun. 1985 [1983]. *Han'guk ŭi mu* [Korean Shamanism]. Seoul: Chŏngŭmsa.

Cho, Hung-youn [Cho Hŭngyun]. 1987. "The Characteristics of Korean *Minjung* Culture." *Korea Journal* 27, no. 11:4–18.

Cho Sŏngu. 1985. *Kwansang taejŏn* [The *Kwansang* Canon]. Seoul: Myŏngmundang.

Cho Tongil and Kim Hŭnggyu. 1978. *P'ansori ŭi ihae* [An Understanding of *P'ansori*]. Seoul: Ch'angjak-kwa pip'yŏngsa.

Ch'oe Chongmin. 2002. "P'ungmul ŭi hyŏndaejŏk chŏn'gae yangsang" [P'ungmul's Present-Day Developmental Phase]. In *Saeroun chŏnt'ong ŭmak-ŭrosŏ ŭi p'ungmul* [P'ungmul as New Traditional Music], 11–20. Yesan: Yesan kukche p'ungmulche chojik wiwŏnhoe.

Ch'oe Kilsŏng. 1987. *Musok ŭi segye* [The World of Shamanism]. Seoul: Chŏngŭmsa.

Ch'oe Sangsu. 1988 [1985]. *Han'guk minsok nori ŭi yŏn'gu* [A Study of Korean Folk Entertainments]. Seoul: Sŏngmun'gak.

Ch'oe Soshim. 1992. *Shibang-ŭn an hae, kanggangsullae-rŭl an hae* [They Don't Do *Kanggangsullae* These Days], edited by Kang Yunju. *Ppuri kip'ŭn namu minjung chasŏjŏn 9: Chindo kanggangsullae apsorikkun Ch'oe Soshim ŭi hanp'yŏngsaeng* (The Deep-rooted Tree Oral Histories 9: The Life of the *Kanggangsullae* Performer Ch'oe Soshim). Seoul: Ppuri kip'ŭn namu.

Ch'oe T'aeyŏl. 1984. "Chŏnbuk chwa-udo nongak mu-e kwanhan yŏn'gu" [A Study of "Left Side"- and "Right Side"-style *Nongak* Dance in North Chŏlla Province]. Master's thesis, Chungang University.

Ch'oe Tŏgwŏn. 1990. *Namdo minsokko* [A Study of Chŏlla Province Folk Customs]. Seoul: Samsŏng ch'ulp'ansa.

Choi Seung-beom [Ch'oe Sŏngbŏm]. 1996. "Korean Drinking Customs." *Koreana* 10, no. 4:20–25.

Choi, Min-hong [Ch'oe Minhong]. 1978. *A Modern History of Korean Philosophy*. Seoul: Seong Moon Sa.

Chŏn Inp'yŏng. 1979. "Kukkŏri changdan ŭi pyŏnju pangbŏp: Kim Pyŏngsŏp changgu nori-e kihayŏ" [The Process of Variation in *Kukkŏri* Rhythmic Pattern: The *Changgu* Drum Dance According to Kim Pyŏngsŏp]. *Minjok ŭmakhak* 3:79–96.

Chŏn Sŏn'gi, ed. 1992. "Chibŏl." In *Uri mal k'ŭn sajŏn* [A Large Dictionary of the Korean Language], 3:3886. Seoul: Ŏmun'gak.

Chŏng Chaehwan, ed. 1971. *Yŏkchu Koryŏsa* [An Annotated Translation of the *History of Koryŏ*]. Seoul: Tonga taehakkyo ch'ulp'ansa.

Chŏng Hoegap. n.d. *Chŏnbuk chibang nongak* [North Chŏlla Province–Area *Nongak*]. Includes *Chŏnbuk Chŏngŭp-kun Ch'ilbo-myŏn Shisan-ri Haengdan-purak nongak* [*Nongak* of Haengdan Hamlet, Shisan Village, Ch'ilbo Subcounty, Chŏngŭp County, North Chŏlla Province]; *Chŏnbuk taep'yo* [Representative North Chŏlla Province (*Nongak*)]; *Chŏnbuk Iksan-kun, Nangsan-myŏn, Sŏkch'ŏn-ri, Hoch'ŏn-purak nongak* [*Nongak* of Hoch'ŏn Hamlet, Sŏkch'ŏn Village, Nangsan Subcounty, Iksan County, North Chŏlla Province]; *Chŏnbuk Iksan-kun, Nangsan-myŏn, Samdam-ri, Taemae nongak* [*Nongak* of Taemae, Samdam Village, Nangsan Subcounty, Iksan County, North Chŏlla Province]; *Chŏnbuk Namwŏn-ŭp nongak* [*Nongak* of Namwŏn Town, North Chŏlla Province]; and *Yi Chŏngbŏm changgo karak* (Chŏnbuk Chŏngŭp-kun, Naejang-myŏn) [*Changgo* Rhythmic Patterns of Yi Chŏngbŏm (Naejang Subcounty, Chŏngŭp County, North Chŏlla Province)]. Unpublished manuscript.

Chŏng Pyŏngho. 1985. *Han'guk ch'um* [Korean Dance]. Seoul: Ilchogak.

———. 1988. "Norip'an ŭi kusŏng-kwa kinŭng" [The Organization and Functions of the *Norip'an*]. In *Nori munhwa-wa ch'ukche* [Play Culture and Festivals], edited by Yi Sangil, 9–23. Seoul: Sŏnggyun'gwan taehakkyo ch'ulp'anbu.

———. 1994 [1986]. *Nongak.* Seoul: Yŏrhwadang.

———. 1995 [1992]. *Han'guk ŭi minsok ch'um* [Korean Folk Dance]. Seoul: Samsŏng ch'ulp'ansa.

Chŏng Pyŏngho and Yi Pohyŏng. 1985. *Nongak: Muhyŏng munhwajae chijŏng chosa pogosŏ 164* [*Nongak:* Report of Investigation 164 on Designated Intangible Cultural Assets]. Seoul: Munhwajae kwalliguk.

Chŏng Pyŏngho, Yi Pohyŏng, Yi Chuyŏng, and Chŏng Chun'gi. 1980. *P'ilbong nongak* [*Nongak* of the Village of P'ilbong]. Seoul: Munhwajae kwalliguk, Munhwajae yŏn'guso.

Chŏng Pyŏngho, Yi Pohyŏng, Kang Hyesuk, Kim Chŏngnyŏ, Chang Chugŭn, Ha Hyogil, Im Tonggwŏn, Pak Chŏnnyŏl, and An Ŭnhŭi. 1982. *Han'guk minsok chonghap chosa pogosŏ 13: Nongak, p'ungŏje, minyo p'yŏn* [Joint Report of Investigation on Korean Folk Practices 13: Volume on *Nongak, P'ungŏje,* and *Minyo*]. Seoul: Munhwa kongbobu, Munhwajae kwalliguk.

Chŏng Pyŏnguk. 1981. *Han'guk ŭi p'ansori* [*P'ansori* of Korea]. Seoul: Chimmundang.

Chu Kanghyŏn. 1995 [1992]. *Kut ŭi sahoesa* [A Social History of Shaman Ritual]. Seoul: Ungjin ch'ulpan.

———. 1996a. "Categories and Classifications of National Culture." Lecture presented at the Korea Foundation, Seoul, April 16.

———. 1996b. *Uri munhwa ŭi susukkekki* [The Enigma of Korean Culture]. Seoul: Han'gyŏre shinmunsa.

———. 1997. *Han'guk ŭi ture* [Communal Labor of Korea], vol. 2. Seoul: Chimmundang.

Chu Yŏngja. 1981. "Han'guk changgo ŭmak-e nat'anan rhythm-kwa movement yŏn'gu" [A Study of Rhythm and Dance Movement in Korean Drum Music]. *Hanguk munhwa yŏn'guwŏn nonch'ong* 38: 217–90.

———. 1985. *Minsogak rhythm yŏn'gu* [A Study of Folk Music Rhythm]. Seoul: Ihwa yŏja taehakkyo, Han'guk munhwa yŏn'guwŏn.

Clayton, Martin. 2003. "Comparing Music, Comparing Musicology." In *The Cultural Study of Music: A Critical Introduction*, edited by Martin Clayton, Trevor Herbert, and Richard Middleton, 57–68. New York: Routledge.

Clifford, James. 1986. "Introduction: Partial Truths." In *Writing Culture: The Poetics and Politics of Ethnography*, edited by James Clifford and George E. Marcus, 1–26. Berkeley and Los Angeles: University of California Press.

———. 1988. *The Predicament of Culture: Twentieth Century Ethnography, Literature, and Art.* Cambridge: Harvard University Press.

Cooley, Timothy J. 1997. "Casting Shadows in the Field: An Introduction." In *Shadows in the Field: New Perspectives for Fieldwork in Ethnomusicology*, edited by Gregory F. Barz and Timothy J. Cooley, 3–19. New York: Oxford University Press.

Crane, Paul S. 1967. *Korean Patterns.* Royal Asiatic Society, Korea Branch Handbook Series 1. Seoul: Hollym Corporation.

Crapanzano, Vincent. 1980. *Tuhami: Portrait of a Moroccan.* Chicago: University of Chicago Press.

———. 1986. "Hermes' Dilemma: The Making of Subversion in Ethnographic Description." In *Writing Culture: The Poetics and Politics of Ethnography*, edited by James Clifford and George E. Marcus, 51–76. Berkeley and Los Angeles: University of California Press.

Cumings, Bruce. 1990. *The Origins of the Korean War*, vol. 2, *The Roaring of the Cataract, 1947–1950.* Princeton: Princeton University Press.

———. 1997. *Korea's Place in the Sun: A Modern History.* New York: W. W. Norton.

Daniel, E. Valentine, and Jeffrey M. Peck, eds. 1996. *Culture/Contexture: Explorations in Anthropology and Literary Studies.* Berkeley and Los Angeles: University of California Press.

DeNora, Tia. 1995. *Beethoven and the Construction of Genius: Musical Politics in Vienna, 1792–1803.* Berkeley and Los Angeles: University of California Press.

Deuchler, Martina. 1992. *The Confucian Transformation of Korea: A Study of Society and Ideology.* Cambridge, Mass.: Council on East Asian Studies, Harvard University.

di Leonardo, Micaela. 1998. *Exotics at Home: Anthropologies, Others, American Modernity.* Chicago: University of Chicago Press.

Diamond, Beverly, M. Sam Cronk, and Franziska von Rosen. 1994. *Visions of Sound: Musical Instruments of First Nations Communities in Northeastern America.* Chicago: University of Chicago Press.

Dower, John W. 1986. *War Without Mercy.* New York: Pantheon.

Eikemeier, Dieter. 1980. *Documents from Changjwa-ri: A Further Approach to the Analysis of Korean Villages.* Weisbaden: Otto Harrassowitz.

Feld, Steven. 1984. "Sound Structure as Social Structure." *Ethnomusicology* 28, no. 3: 383–409.

Friedmann, Georges. 1960. "Leisure and Technological Civilization." *International Social Science Journal* 12:509–20.

Geertz, Clifford. 1988. *Works and Lives: The Anthropologist as Author.* Stanford, Calif.: Stanford University Press.

Ha, Tae Hung [Ha T'aehŭng]. 1958. *Folk Tales of Old Korea.* Seoul: Yonsei University Press.

Ham Tongjŏngwŏl. 1992. *Mul-ŭn kŏnnŏ pwaya algo, saram-ŭn kyŏkkŏ pwaya algŏdŭn* [To Understand Water, You Must Cross It; To Understand a Human, You Must Experience Him], edited by Kim Myŏnggon and Kim Haesuk. *Ppuri kip'ŭn namu minjung chasŏjŏn 15: Kayagŭm myŏngin Ham Tongjŏngwŏl ŭi hanp'yŏngsaeng* (The Deep-rooted Tree Oral Histories 15: The Life of the *Kayagŭm* Virtuoso Ham Tongjŏngwŏl). Seoul: Ppuri kip'ŭn namu.

Han Myŏnghŭi. 1994. *Uri karak uri munhwa* [Our Music, Our Culture]. Seoul: Chosŏn ilbosa.

Han'guk hyangt'osa yŏn'gu chŏn'guk hyŏbŭihoe [National Research Council on Korean Local History]. 1994. *Han'guk ŭi nongak: Honam p'yŏn* [Korean *Nongak*: Volume on Chŏlla Provinces]. Seoul: Tosŏ ch'ulp'an susŏwŏn.

———. 1997. *Han'guk ŭi nongak: Yŏngnam p'yŏn* [Korean *Nongak*: Volume on Kyŏngsang Provinces]. Seoul: Tosŏ ch'ulp'an susŏwŏn.

Han'gŭl hakhoe. 1957. "Li" [unit of measurement]. In *K'ŭn sajŏn* [A Large Dictionary], vol. 2. Seoul: Ŭlyu munhwasa.

Harnish, David. 2001. "A Hermeneutical Arc in the Life of Balinese Musician, I Made Lebah." *World of Music* 43, no. 1:21–41.

Henderson, John S., and Patricia J. Netherly. 1993. "Introduction: Murra, Materialism, Anthropology, and the Andes." In *Configurations of Power: Holistic Anthropology in Theory and Practice*, edited by John S. Henderson and Patricia J. Netherly, 1–8. Ithaca: Cornell University Press.

Herskovits, Melville. 1965. *Economic Anthropology*. New York: Knopf.

Hesselink, Nathan. 1998a. "Han'guk ŭi t'aak, p'ungmul-esŏ ŭi kyosubŏp: Chŏgyong-kwa saengjon ŭi tu kaji sarye yŏn'gu" [Teaching Methodology in Korean Percussion Band Music (P'ungmul): Two Studies in Assimilation and Survival], translated by Pak Shin'gil. In *Che 2 hoe kukche ŭmakhaksul shimpojium* (Second International Symposium for Korean Musicology), 17–24. Seoul: Korean National University of Arts.

———. 1998b. "Of Drums and Men in Chŏllabuk-do Province: Glimpses into the Making of a Human Cultural Asset." *Korea Journal* 38, no. 3:292–326.

———. 1998c. "A Tale of Two Drummers: Percussion Band Music in North Chŏlla Province, Korea." Ph.D. diss., University of London, School of Oriental & African Studies.

———. 1999. "Two Sides of a Similar Coin: A Common Origin Hypothesis in Honam Region Percussion Band Music/Dance." *Tongyang ŭmak* 21:175–225.

———. 2001. *Contemporary Directions: Korean Folk Music Engaging the Twentieth Century and Beyond*, edited with an introduction by Nathan Hesselink. Korea Research Monograph 27. Berkeley: Institute of East Asian Studies, University of California.

———. 2002. "Modernization, Urbanization, and the Re-emergence of the Professional Korean Folk Musician." *Han'guk ŭmaksa hakpo* 29:717–46.

———. 2004. "*Samul nori* as Traditional: Preservation and Innovation in a South Korean Contemporary Percussion Genre." *Ethnomusicology* 48, no. 3:405–39.

Hesselink, Nathan, and Jonathan C. Petty. 2004. "Landscape and Soundscape: Geomantic Spatial Mapping in Korean Traditional Music." *Journal of Musicological Research* 23, no. 3–4:265–88.

Honam chwado p'ungmulgut. 1995. *Honam chwado P'ilbong maŭl p'ungmulgut ŭi hyŏngshik-kwa chŏngsŏ* [Form and Aesthetics in Chŏlla Province "Left Side" P'ungmul of P'ilbong Village]. Namwŏn: Honam chwado p'ungmulgut.

Hong Hyŏnshik. 1969. "Honam nongak sogo" [A Brief Explanation of Chŏlla Province *Nongak*]. *Munhwajae* 4:45–52.

Hong Hyŏnshik, Kim Ch'ŏnhŭng, and Pak Hŏnbong. 1967. *Honam nongak* [Chŏlla Province *Nongak*]. *Muhyŏng munhwajae chosa pogosŏ 33* [Intangible Cultural Asset Report of Investigation 33]. Seoul: Mun'gyobu munhwajae kwalliguk.

Howard, Keith D. 1983. "*Nongak,* the *Changgu* and Kim Pyŏng-sŏp's *Kaein Changgu Nori.*" *Korea Journal* 23, no. 5:15–31 and no. 6:23–34.

———. 1985. "Volksmusik." In *Korea: Einführung in die Musiktradition Koreas,* edited by Wolfgang Burde, 129–56. Mainz: Schott.

———. 1988. *Korean Musical Instruments: A Practical Guide.* Seoul: Se-Kwang Music.

———. 1990 [1989]. *Bands, Songs, and Shamanistic Rituals: Folk Music in Korean Society.* Seoul: Royal Asiatic Society, Korea Branch.

———. 1991. "Samul Nori: A Re-Interpretation of a Korean Folk Tradition for Urban and International Audiences." In *Tradition and Its Future in Music: Report of SIMS 1990 Osaka,* edited by Yoshijiko Tokumaru et al., 539–46. Osaka: Mita Press.

———. 1991–92. "Why Do It That Way? Rhythmic Models and Motifs in Korean Percussion Bands." *Asian Music* 23, no. 1:1–59.

———. 1993. "Sacred and Profane: Searching for the Shamanistic *Kukkŏri* and Rhythmic Cycle." *Han'guk ŭmaksa hakpo* 11:601–42.

Hsu, Francis L. K. 1973. "Prejudice and Its Intellectual Effect in American Anthropology." *American Anthropologist* 75:1–19.

Hughes, David W. 1989. "The Historical Uses of Nonsense: Vowel-pitch Solfège from Scotland to Japan." In *Ethnomusicology and the Historical Dimension,* edited by M. L. Philipp, 3–18. Ludwigsburg: Philipp Verlag.

———. 1991. "Oral Mnemonics in Korean Music: Data, Interpretation, and a Musicological Application." *Bulletin of the School of Oriental and African Studies* 54, no. 2:307–35.

Huhm, Halla Pai. 1980. *Kut: Korean Shamanist Rituals.* Elizabeth, N.J.: Hollym International.

Hwang, Mi-yon [Hwang Miyŏn]. 2004. "A Study of Musical Cultures in the Samhan Period." *Asian Musicology* 4:5–36.

Hwang Sŏnmyŏng, An Chino, Pae Yongdŏk, Shin Ch'ŏrho, Kim Nakp'il, and Ko Ŭn. 1983. *Han'guk kŭndae minjung chonggyo sasang* [Modern *Minjung* Religious Thought in Korea]. Seoul: Hangminsa.

Im, Dong-kwon [Im Tonggwŏn]. 1994. "Village Rites: A Rich Communal Heritage." *Koreana* 8, no. 1:6–11.

Jung, Carl Gustav. 1965 [1961]. *Memories, Dreams, Reflections.* Recorded and edited by Aniela Jaffé. Translated by Richard and Clara Winston. New York: Vintage Books.

———. 1997. *Selected Writings.* With an introduction by Robert Coles. New York: Book-of-the-Month Club.

Kartomi, Margaret J. 1990. *On Concepts and Classifications of Musical Instruments.* Chicago: University of Chicago Press.

Kendall, Laurel. 1987. *Shamans, Housewives, and Other Restless Spirits: Women in Korean Ritual Life*. Honolulu: University of Hawaii Press.

———. 1996. *Getting Married in Korea: Of Gender, Morality, and Modernity*. Berkeley and Los Angeles: University of California Press.

Killick, Andrew P. 2001. "The Traditional Opera of the Future? *Ch'anggŭk*'s First Century." In *Contemporary Directions: Korean Folk Music Engaging the Twentieth Century and Beyond*, edited by Nathan Hesselink, 22–53. Berkeley: Institute of East Asian Studies, University of California.

Kim, Chiha. 1977. "A Declaration of Conscience." *Bulletin of Concerned Asian Scholars* 9:8–15.

Kim Chiyŏng. 1987. "P'ilbong Nongak ŭi naeyong-kwa hyŏngt'ae-e kwanhan yŏn'gu" [A Study of P'ilbong Nongak's Form and Content]. Master's thesis, Ihwa Women's University.

Kim Chŏngho. 1984. "Sŏmin ŭi p'ungnyu nongak" [Elegant *Nongak* of the Common People]. In *Han'gugin ŭi ppuri* [The Roots of the Korean People], edited by Kim Chuyŏng. Seoul: Sahoe palchŏn yŏn'guso.

Kim, Chongsuh [Kim Chongsŏ]. 1993. "Eastern Learning: An Overcoming of Religious Pluralism." In *Reader in Korean Religion*, edited by Kim Chongsuh, 223–43. Sŏngnam: Academy of Korean Studies.

Kim, Duk Soo [Kim Tŏksu]. 1992. Author's introduction. In *Korean Traditional Percussion: Samulnori Rhythm Workbook I, Basic Changgo*, Korean Conservatorium of Performing Arts, SamulNori Academy of Music (Kim Duk Soo [Kim Tŏksu], Lee Kwang Soo [Yi Kwangsu], Kang Min Seok [Kang Minsŏk]), 7–11. Seoul: Sam-Ho Music.

Kim Hakchu. 1987. "Chwado yŏngsan karak-e taehan ŭmakchŏk koch'al—yŏngsan kut-ŭl chungshim-ŭro" [A Musical Examination of "Left Side" *Yŏngsan* Rhythmic Pattern: The Performance of *Yŏngsan*]. Master's thesis, Academy of Korean Studies.

Kim Hŏnsŏn. 1994 [1991]. *P'ungmulgut-esŏ samul nori-kkaji* [From *P'ungmulgut* to *Samul nori*]. Seoul: Kwiinsa.

———. 1995. *Kim Hŏnsŏn ŭi samul nori iyagi* [Kim Hŏnsŏn's Account of *Samul nori*]. Seoul: P'ulbit.

Kim Hyŏkche, ed. 1978. *Maŭi sangbŏp* [Hemp Clothing *Kwansang* Method]. Seoul: Myŏngmundang.

Kim Hyŏnsuk. 1987. "Honam chwado nongak-e kwanhan yŏn'gu: Imshil-kwa Chin'an ŭi p'an kut-ŭl chungshim-ŭro" [A Study of Chŏlla Province "Left Side" *Nongak*: The *P'an kut* of Imshil and Chinan]. Master's thesis, Seoul National University.

———. 1991. "Nongak-esŏ ch'aebo-wa punsŏk ŭi munje" [Problems of Transcription and Analysis with *Nongak*]. *Han'guk ŭmak yŏn'gu* 19:73–89.

Kim Iktu, No Poksun, Im Myŏngjin, Chŏn Chŏnggu, and Ch'oe Sanghwa. 1994. *Honam udo p'ungmulgut* [Chŏlla Province "Right Side" *P'ungmulgut*]. Chŏnju: Chŏnbuk taehakkyo Chŏlla munhwa yŏn'guso.

Kim Inu. 1993. "P'ungmulgut-kwa kongdongch'ejŏk shinmyŏng" [*P'ungmulgut* and Communal Spirit]. In *Minjok-kwa kut: Minjok kut ŭi saeroun yŏllim-ŭl wihayŏ* [Folk and Ritual: Toward a New Understanding of Folk Ritual], 102–44. Seoul: Hangminsa.

Kim Jong-ho [Kim Chongho]. 1977. *Saemaŭl undong-kwa chido inyŏm* [The New Village Movement and Its Guiding Ideology]. Suwŏn: Saemaŭl Leader's Training Institute.

Kim, Joo-young [Kim Chuyŏng], and Seung-u Park [Pak Sŭngu]. 2002. *On the Road: In Search of Korea's Cultural Roots.* Seoul: Korea Foundation.

Kim, Kwangil. 1988. "*Kut* and the Treatment of Mental Disorder." Translated by Suh Kikon [Sŏ Kigon] and Im Hyeyoung [Im Hyeyŏng]. In *Shamanism: The Spirit World of Korea,* edited by Chai-shin Yu and R. Guisso, 131–61. Berkeley: Asian Humanities Press.

Kim Kwangŏn and Kim Sunam. 1989. *Minsok nori* [Folk Entertainments]. Seoul: Taewŏnsa.

Kim, Mae-ja [Kim Maeja]. 1981. "The Characteristic of the Korean Traditional Dance in Shaman Rituals." *Han'guk ŭmak yŏn'gu* 11:77–80.

Kim Myŏnggon. 1994. *Han: Kim Myŏnggon ŭi kwangdae kihaeng* [*Han:* Kim Myŏnggon's Travels of the *Kwangdae*]. Seoul: Tosŏ ch'ulp'an sanha.

Kim Myŏnghwan. 1992. *Nae puk-e aenggil sori-ka ŏpsŏyo* [There Is No Voice That Can Match My Drum(ing)], edited by Kim Haesuk, Pak Chonggwŏn, Paek Taeung, and Yi Ŭnja. *Ppuri kip'ŭn namu minjung chasŏjŏn 11: Kosu Kim Myŏnghwan ŭi hanp'yŏngsaeng* (The Deep-rooted Tree Oral Histories 11: The Life of the *P'ansori* Drummer Kim Myŏnghwan). Seoul: Ppuri kip'ŭn namu.

Kim Okhŭi. 1985. "Honam nongak p'an kut ŭi chinpuri-e kwanhan yŏn'gu" [A Study of *P'an kut* Ground Formations in Chŏlla Province *Nongak*]. Master's thesis, Ihwa Women's University.

Kim Sŏngbae. 1998. "Kŭmjul." In *Han'guk minsok taesajŏn* [An Encyclopedia of Korean Folk Customs], 203–4. Seoul: Minjung sŏgwan.

Kim Sunam, Im Sŏkchae, and Yi Pohyŏng. 1986. *P'ungmulgut: Han'gugin ŭi nori-wa cheŭi* [*P'ungmulgut:* Play and Ritual of the Korean People]. Seoul: P'yŏngminsa.

Kim Sunam and Kim Misuk. 1986. *Homi ssishi: Han'gugin ŭi nori-wa cheŭi* [*Homi ssishi:* Play and Ritual of the Korean People]. Seoul: P'yŏngminsa.

Kim T'aegon. 1985 [1981]. *Han'guk musok yŏn'gu* [A Study of Korean Shamanism]. Seoul: Chimmundang.

Kim Tongwŏn. 2003. *Samul nori Uttari p'ungmul* [*Samul nori*'s Composition "Uttari P'ungmul"]. Taejŏn: Ch'ungch'ŏng namdo kyoyuk kwahak yŏn'guwŏn.

Kim Uhyŏn. 1984. *Nongak kyobon* [A Manual on *Nongak*]. Seoul: Segwang ŭmak ch'ulp'ansa.

Kim Ŭisuk. 1993. *Han'guk minsok cheŭi-wa ŭmyang ohaeng: Minsok cheŭi ŭi hyŏngsŏng iron* [Korean Folk Ritual and the Concepts of *Ŭm/Yang* and the Five Elements: A Formative Theory of Folk Ritual]. Seoul: Chimmundang.

Kim Wŏnho. 1999. *P'ungmulgut yŏn'gu* [A Study of *P'ungmulgut*]. Seoul: Hangminsa.

Kim, Yang-kon [Kim Yanggon]. 1967. "Farmer's Music and Dance." *Korea Journal* 7, no. 10:4–9 and 29.

Kim, Y. K. Kirk. 1977. "The Impact of Japanese Colonial Development on the Korean Economy." In *Korea's Response to Japan: The Colonial Period, 1910–1945,* edited by C. I. Eugene Kim and Doretha E. Mortimore, 85–100. Kalamazoo: Center for Korean Studies, Western Michigan University.

Kim, Yong-Choon [Kim Yŏngjun]. 1997. "Ch'ŏndogyo and Other New Religions of Korea." In *Religion and Society in Contemporary Korea,* edited by Lewis R. Lancaster and Richard K. Payne, 249–73. Korea Research Monograph 24. Berkeley: Institute of East Asian Studies, University of California.

Kim Yŏngt'ak. 2002. "Nongak-kwa p'ungmul ŭi ch'ai" [The Difference between *Nongak* and P'ungmul]. *Wŏlgan munhwajae* 5–6:5.

Kim Yŏngun. 1989. "Han'guk t'osok akki ŭi akkironjŏk yŏn'gu" [An Organological Study of Korean Folk Instruments]. *Han'guk ŭmak yŏn'gu* 17–18:31–77.

Kim, Yoon-shik [Kim Yunshik]. 1998. *Understanding Modern Korean Literature,* edited and translated by Jang Gyung-ryul [Chang Kyŏngnyul]. Seoul: Jipmoondang.

Kim Yunho, ed. 2000. *Kujŏn munhak: Chosŏn ŭi minsok chŏnt'ong* [Oral Literature: Folk Tradition of the Chosŏn Period]. Seoul: Taesan ch'ulp'ansa.

Knez, Eugene I. 1997. *The Modernization of Three Korean Villages, 1951–1981: An Illustrated Study of a People and Their Material Culture.* Smithsonian Contributions to Anthropology 39. Washington, D.C.: Smithsonian Institution Press.

Koo, Hagen. 1993. "The State, *Minjung,* and the Working Class in South Korea." In *State and Society in Contemporary Korea,* edited by Hagen Koo, 131–62. Ithaca: Cornell University Press.

Korean Conservatorium of Performing Arts, SamulNori Academy of Music—Kim Duk Soo [Kim Tŏksu], Lee Kwang Soo [Yi Kwangsu], Kang Min Seok [Kang Minsŏk]. 1992. *Korean Traditional Percussion: Samulnori Rhythm Workbook I, Basic Changgo.* Seoul: Sam-Ho Music.

Kunst, Jaap. 1973. *Music in Java: Its History, Its Theory and Its Techniques.* Vol. 1. Edited by E. L. Heins. The Hague: Martinus Nijhoff.

Kwak, Young-kwon [Kwak Yŏnggwŏn], Dong-won Kim [Kim Tongwŏn], and Suzanna Samstag Oh. 2003. *The Story of Samulnori: A Fairy Tale for Children.* Seoul: Sakyejul.

Kwon, Do Hee [Kwŏn Tohŭi]. 2003. "The Female Musicians' Activity since the Dissolution of *Gisaeng* Guilds." In *Korean Music Viewed from In and Out: Korean Music Research Methodologies between Native and Foreign Scholars,* 177–90. Seoul: Asian Music Research Institute.

Kwŏn Hŭidŏk. 1981. *Nongak, Sŏnye kut, Akki nori.* Seoul: Huban'gi ch'ulp'ansa.

———. 1995. *Nongak kyobon* [A Manual on *Nongak*]. Seoul: Seilsa.

Kwŏn Hyeryŏn (Donna Kwon). 2001. "Miguk-esŏ ŭi p'ungmul: Kŭ ppuri-wa yŏjŏng" (The Roots and Routes of *P'ungmul* in the United States). *Ŭmak-kwa munhwa* 5:39–65.

Lee, Bo hyung [Yi Pohyŏng]. "The Rhythmic Formation of the *Changdan's* Syntactical Structure in Music with an Underlying Deep Structure." In *A Search in Asia for a New Theory of Music,* edited by José S. Buenconsejo, 99–129. Quezon City: University of the Philippines Center for Ethnomusicology.

Lee, Byongwon [Yi Pyŏngwŏn]. 1987. *Buddhist Music of Korea.* Seoul: Jungeumsa.

———. 1993. "Contemporary Korean Musical Cultures." In *Korea Briefing, 1993: Festival of Korea,* edited by Donald N. Clark, 121–38. Boulder, Colo.: Westview Press.

Lee, Hyoung-kwon [Yi Hyŏnggwŏn]. 1997. "Brass Maker Yi Pong-ju." *Koreana* 11, no. 4:50–55.

Lee, Ki-baek [Yi Kibaek]. 1984. *A New History of Korea.* Translated by Edward W. Wagner, with Edward J. Schultz. Seoul: Ilchokak.

Lee Man-gap [Yi Man'gap]. 1973. *Han'guk nongch'on sahoe ŭi kujo-wa pyŏnhwa* [The Structure of Korean Rural Communities and Its Change]. Seoul: Seoul National University Press.

Lee, Namhee [Yi Namhŭi]. 1991. "The South Korean Student Movement: 1980–1987." In *Chicago Occasional Papers on Korea,* edited by Bruce Cumings, 204–45. Select Papers 6. Chicago: Center for East Asian Studies, University of Chicago.

Lee, Peter H. 1985. "Versions of the Self in the *Storytellers' Miscellany (P'aegwan chapki).*" In *The Rise of Neo-Confucianism in Korea,* edited by Wm. Theodore de Bary and JaHyun Kim Haboush, 473–97. New York: Columbia University Press.

———, ed. 1993. *Sourcebook of Korean Civilization,* vol. 1, *From Early Times to the Sixteenth Century.* New York: Columbia University Press.

———, ed. 1996. *Sourcebook of Korean Civilization,* vol. 2, *From the Seventeenth Century to the Modern Period.* New York: Columbia University Press.

Lee, Po-hyŏng [Yi Pohyŏng]. 1981. "The Genetic Relationship of Farmer's Music and Dance to Village Communal Shaman Rituals in Korea." *Han'guk ŭmak yŏn'gu* 11:69–70.

Lee, Sang Taek [Yi Sangt'aek]. 1996. *Religion and Social Formation in Korea: Minjung and Millenarianism.* Berlin and New York: Mouton de Gruyter.

Loewen, James W. 1995. *Lies My Teacher Told Me: Everything Your American History Textbook Got Wrong.* New York: New Press.

Loken, Christine. 1983. "Moving in the Korean Way: Movement Characteristics of the Korean People as Expressed in their Dance." In *Korean Dance, Theater and Cinema,* edited by the Korean National Commission for UNESCO, 72–80. Seoul: Si-sa-yong-o-sa.

Loken-Kim, Christine, and Juliette T. Crump. 1993. "Qualitative Change in Performances of Two Generations of Korean Dancers." *Dance Research Journal* 25, no. 2:13–20.

MacClancy, Jeremy. 2002. "Introduction: Taking People Seriously." In *Exotic No More: Anthropology on the Front Lines,* edited by Jeremy MacClancy, 1–14. Chicago: University of Chicago Press.

Maliangkay, Roald H. 1999. "Handling the Intangible: The Protection of Folksong Traditions in Korea." Ph.D. diss., University of London, School of Oriental & African Studies.

Malm, William P. 1959. *Japanese Music and Musical Instruments.* Rutland, Vt.: Charles E. Tuttle Company.

Merriam, Alan P. 1964. *The Anthropology of Music.* Evanston, Ill.: Northwestern University Press.

Ministry of Home Affairs [MOHA]. 1979. *Saemaŭl chonggyŏl* [An Overall Evaluation of the New Village Movement]. Seoul: Ministry of Home Affairs.

Minjok kut hoe [Folk Ritual Society]. 1993. *Minjok-kwa kut: Minjokkut ŭi saeroun yŏllim-ŭl wihayŏ* [Folk and Ritual: Toward a New Understanding of Folk Ritual]. Seoul: Hangminsa.

Mun Hyŏn. 1996. *Kaeryang kugakki chŏn* [An Exhibition of Improved Traditional Instruments]. Seoul: Kungnip kugagwŏn.

Munhwajae kwalliguk [Office of Cultural Assets]. 1995. *Chijŏng munhwajae mongnok* [A List of Designated Cultural Assets]. Seoul: Chushik hoesa kyemunsa.

Munhwajae yŏn'guhoe [Cultural Asset Research Society]. 1999. *Chungyo muhyŏng munhwajae 2: Yŏn'gŭk-kwa nori* [Important Intangible Cultural Asset 2: Theater and Folk Entertainment]. Seoul: Taewŏnsa.

Myers, Helen, ed. 1992. *Ethnomusicology: An Introduction*. Norton/Grove Handbooks in Music. London: Macmillan.

Nettl, Bruno. 1983. *The Study of Ethnomusicology: Twenty-nine Issues and Concepts*. Urbana: University of Illinois Press.

No Kwangil. 1985. "P'ungmul ŭi saeroun ihae" [A New Understanding of P'ungmul]. In *Munhwa undongnon* [A Discussion of Cultural Movements], edited by Chŏng Idam, 268–87. Seoul: Kongdongch'e.

No Poksun. 1994. *Nongak*. Chŏnju: Pongch'ŏn ch'ulp'ansa.

O Chongsŏp. 1989. "P'ungmulgut-esŏ ŭi kongdongch'e ŭishik-e kwanhan yŏn'gu" [A Study of Communal Consciousness in P'ungmulgut]. Master's thesis, Seoul National University.

Oh, Myung-Seok [O Myŏngsŏk]. 1998. "Peasant Culture and Modernization in Korea: Cultural Implications of Saemaŭl Movement in the 1970s." *Korea Journal* 38, no. 3: 77–95.

Paek Taeung. 1985. "Changdan." In *Han'guk yesul sajŏn* [A Dictionary of Korean Arts], vol. 3, *Han'guk ŭmak sajŏn* [A Dictionary of Korean Music], 326–27. Seoul: Taehan min'guk yesulwŏn.

Paek Yŏngja. 1994. *Chosŏn shidae ŭi ŏga haengnyŏl* [Royal Carriage Processions of the Chosŏn Period]. Seoul: Han'guk pangsong t'ongshin taehakkyo ch'ulp'anbu.

Pak Chongsŏl. 1991. "Minsogak changdan kujo-e kwanhan punsŏk yŏn'gu" [An Analytical Study of the Structure of Folk Music Rhythmic Patterns]. *Han'guk ŭmak yŏn'gu* 19: 41–65.

Pak Hŏnbong and Yu Kiryong. 1965. *Nongak shibich'a* [Twelve Sections or Movements of Nongak]. *Muhyŏng munhwajae chosa pogosŏ 9* [Intangible Cultural Asset Report of Investigation 9]. Seoul: Mun'gyobu munhwajae kwalliguk.

Pak Hŏnbong, Hong Yunshik, and Yu Kiryong. 1970. *Shinawi: Muhyŏng munhwajae chosa pogosŏ 76* [Shinawi: Intangible Cultural Asset Report of Investigation 76]. Seoul: Munhwajae kwalliguk.

Pak Hŭngsu. 1967. "Yijo ch'ŏkto-e kwanhan yŏn'gu" [A Study of Chosŏn Period Measurements]. *Taedong munhwa yŏn'gu* 4: 199–216.

Pak Hwang. 1974. *P'ansori sosa* [A Short History of P'ansori]. Seoul: Shin'gu munhwasa.

Pak, Ki-hyuk [Pak Kihyŏk], and Sidney D. Gamble. 1975. *The Changing Korean Village*. Seoul: Shin-Hung Press.

Pak Myŏngja, ed. 2000. *Kim Ki Chang*. Seoul: Gallery Hyundai.

Pak Sangguk, Kim Hohwan, Ch'ŏn Chin'gi, and Sŏ Hŏn'gang. 1996. *Chungyo muhyŏng munhwajae che 11-na ho P'yŏngt'aek Nongak* [Important Intangible Cultural Asset no. 11B P'yŏngt'aek Nongak]. Seoul: Kungnip munhwajae yŏn'guso.

Pak Sangguk, Yi Chongjin, Yi Chunsŏk, and Kim Chongok. 1999. *Imshil P'ilbong Nongak.* Seoul: Kungnip munhwajae yŏn'guso.

Pak Yongjae. 1992. *Kwangsan nongak* [*Nongak* of Kwangsan]. 2 vols. Kwangju: Kwangsan munhwawŏn.

Park, Chan E. 2001. "'Recycling' an Oral Tradition Transnationally." In *Contemporary Directions: Korean Folk Music Engaging the Twentieth Century and Beyond,* edited by Nathan Hesselink, 121–48. Berkeley: Institute of East Asian Studies, University of California.

Park, Chung-hee [Pak Chŏnghŭi]. 1979. *Saemaul: Korea's New Community Movement.* Seoul: Korea Textbook.

Park, Joo Won [Pak Chuwŏn]. 2005. "Poongmul Pae in the United States: Their Role and Function." http://plaza.ufl.edu/joowon/jwpoongmul.zip.

Park, Shingil [Pak Shin'gil]. 2000. "Negotiating Identities in a Performance Genre: The Case of *P'ungmul* and *Samulnori* in Contemporary Seoul." Ph.D. diss., University of Pittsburgh.

Pongch'ŏn norimadang. 1995 [1994]. *Minsok kyoyuk charyojip* [A Collection of Materials for Folk Education]. Seoul: Uri kyoyuk.

Pratt, Keith. 1987. *Korean Music: Its History and Its Performance.* Seoul: Jung Eum Sa.

Provine, Robert C. 1975. *Chŏnbuk nongak changgo changdan* (Drum Rhythms in Korean Farmers' Music). Seoul: Shinjin munhwasa.

———. 1984a. "Changgo." In *The New Grove Dictionary of Musical Instruments,* edited by Stanley Sadie, 1:337–38. London: Macmillan.

———. 1984b. "Ching." In *The New Grove Dictionary of Musical Instruments,* edited by Stanley Sadie, 1:355. London: Macmillan.

———. 1984c. "Kkwaenggwari." In *The New Grove Dictionary of Musical Instruments,* edited by Stanley Sadie, 1:443. London: Macmillan.

———. 1984d. "Nabal." In *The New Grove Dictionary of Musical Instruments,* edited by Stanley Sadie, 2:413. London: Macmillan.

———. 1984e. "Sogo." In *The New Grove Dictionary of Musical Instruments,* edited by Stanley Sadie, 2:735. London: Macmillan.

———. 1984f. "T'aep'yŏngso." In *The New Grove Dictionary of Musical Instruments,* edited by Stanley Sadie, 3:499–500. London: Macmillan.

———. 1985. "Drumming in Korean Farmer's Music: A Process of Gradual Evolution." In *Music and Context: Essays for John M. Ward,* edited by Anne Dhu Shapiro, 441–52. Cambridge: Harvard University Press.

———. 1988. *Essays in Sino-Korean Musicology: Early Sources for Korean Ritual Music.* UNESCO Traditional Korean Music Series 2. Seoul: Il Ji Sa.

P'ungmul/ch'ump'ae Kippal. 1994 [1991]. *P'ungmul kyoshil: Ch'oech'o ŭi ch'egyejŏgin nodongja p'ungmul kyogwasŏ* [P'ungmul Classroom: The First Systematic P'ungmul Textbook for the Working Man]. Seoul: Tosŏ ch'ulp'an minmaek.

Radano, Ronald M. 1993. *New Musical Figurations: Anthony Braxton's Cultural Critique.* Chicago: University of Chicago Press.

Ricoeur, Paul. 1981. *Hermeneutics and the Human Sciences: Essays on Language, Action and Interpretation,* edited and translated by John B. Thompson. Cambridge: Cambridge University Press.

Ringer, Alexander L. 1991. "One World or None? Untimely Reflections on a Timely Musicological Question." In *Comparative Musicology and Anthropology of Music: Essays on the History of Ethnomusicology,* edited by Bruno Nettl and Philip V. Bohlman, 187–98. Chicago: University of Chicago Press.

Robinson, Michael Edson. 1988. *Cultural Nationalism in Colonial Korea, 1920–1925.* Seattle: University of Washington Press.

"The Romanization of Korean According to the McCune-Reischauer System." 1961. *Transactions of the Korea Branch of the Royal Asiatic Society* 38 : 121–28.

Rutt, Richard. 1961. "The Flower Boys of Shilla (*Hwarang*): Notes on their Sources." *Transactions of the Royal Asiatic Society, Korea Branch* 28 : 1–66.

Ryu Muyŏl [Yu Muyŏl]. 1986. *Nongak.* Seoul: Minjok munhwa mun'go kanhaenghoe.

Scheper-Hughes, Nancy. 1987. "The Margaret Mead Controversy: Culture, Biology and Anthropological Inquiry." In *Perspectives in Cultural Anthropology,* edited by Herbert Applebaum, 443–54. Albany: State University of New York Press.

Shim Usŏng. 1978. *Minsok munhwa minjung ŭishik* [Folk Culture, People's Rituals]. Seoul: Taehwa ch'ulp'ansa.

———. 1994 [1974]. *Namsadangp'ae yŏn'gu* [A Study of *Namsadang* Troupes]. Seoul: Tosŏ ch'ulp'an tongmunsŏn.

Shin Chunho, ed. 1991. "Chambap mŏgigi." In *Han'guk minsok taesajŏn* [Korean Folk Encyclopedia], 2 : 1190. Seoul: Minjok munhwasa.

Shin Kinam. 1992. *Ŏttŏk'e hŏmŏn ttokttok hŏn cheja han nom tugo chugŭlkko?* [What Do I Have to Do to Get a Single Smart Disciple before I Die?], edited by Kim Myŏnggon. *Ppuri kip'ŭn namu minjung chasŏjŏn 3: Imshil "sŏlchanggu chaebi" Shin Kinam ŭi hanp'yŏngsaeng* (The Deep-rooted Tree Oral Histories 3: The Life of the Korean Drummer Sin Ki-nam). Seoul: Ppuri kip'ŭn namu.

Shin, Yongha. 1985. "A Social History of *Ture* Community and *Nongak* Music." *Korea Journal* 25, no. 3 : 4–17 and no. 4 : 4–18.

Small, Christopher. 1998. *Musicking: The Meanings of Performing and Listening.* Hanover, N.H.: Wesleyan University Press.

Sŏ Okkyu. 1988. "Nongak pokshik-e kwanhan yŏn'gu" [A Study of *Nongak* Attire]. Master's thesis, Ihwa Women's University.

Sŏ Taesŏk. 1997. *Kubi munhak* [Oral Literature]. Seoul: Haenam.

Sŏk Chusŏn. 1992 [1971]. *Han'guk pokshiksa* [A History of Korean Dress and Ornaments]. Seoul: Pojinje.

Son Kyŏngja. 1986. "Kokkal." In *Tonga wŏnsaek segye taebaekkwa sajŏn* [Tonga's Color World Encyclopedia], edited by Kim Hyŏnshik, 2 : 608. Seoul: Tonga ch'ulp'ansa.

Son Pyŏngu. 1988. "Nongak hyŏngshik-e issŏsŏ chinp'uri-e kwanhan yŏn'gu" [A Study of Form and Ground Formations in *Nongak*]. Master's thesis, Chungang University.

Song, Bang-song [Song Pangsong]. 1980. *Source Readings in Korean Music.* Seoul: Korean National Commission for UNESCO.

———. 2001. "An Aspect of Korean Traditional Music in the 1920s." *Review of Korean Studies* 4, no. 2 : 265–79.

Sŏng Chaehyŏng. 1984. "Chwado nongak-kwa udo nongak ŭi pigyo" [A Comparison of "Left Side" and "Right Side" *Nongak*]. Master's thesis, Hanyang University.

Song Chiyŏng, Son Sŏkchu, and Kim Shin'gyŏng. 1980. *Muak* [Shaman Music]. Seoul: Han'guk munhwa yesul chinhŭngwŏn.

Sŏng Kyŏngnin. 1985. "Han'guk muyongsa I" [A History of Korean Dance, part 1]. In *Han'guk yŏn'gŭk/muyong/yŏnghwasa* [A History of Korean Film, Dance, and Theater], edited by Yi Haerang, 293–440. Seoul: Taehan min'guk yesulwŏn.

Song Pangsong. 1993 [1982]. *Han'guk ŭmaksa yŏn'gu* [Studies in Korean Music History]. Kyŏngsan: Yŏngnam taehakkyo ch'ulp'anbu.

Song, Soo-nam [Song Sunam]. 1990. "*Shinmyŏng* in Korean Group Dance Performance." *Korea Journal* 30, no. 9:32–35.

Sorenson, Clark W. 1988. *Over the Mountains Are Mountains: Korean Peasant Households and Their Adaptations to Rapid Industrialization*. Seattle: University of Washington Press.

Suh, Doo Soo [Sŏ Tusu]. 1965. *Korean Literary Reader*. Seoul: Dong-A.

Sung, Ki-Ryun [Sŏng Kiryŏn]. 2001. "The *Pansori* Performance Culture in Colonial Korea: The Role of *Joseon-seongak-yeonguhoe.*" *Tongyang ŭmak* 23:193–200.

Takashi Ishikawa. 1986. *Kokoro: The Soul of Japan*. Tokyo: East Publications.

Thrasher, Alan R. 1984. "Suona." In *The New Grove Dictionary of Musical Instruments*, edited by Stanley Sadie, 3:474–75. London: Macmillan.

Tyler, Stephen A. 1986. "Post-modern Ethnography: From Document of the Occult to Occult Document." In *Writing Culture: The Poetics and Politics of Ethnography*, edited by James Clifford and George E. Marcus, 122–40. Berkeley and Los Angeles: University of California Press.

U Chwamiyangja. 1999. "Honam chwado p'ungmulgut-e kwanhan yŏn'gu: Imshil-kwa Kohŭng ŭi madang palki kut-ŭl chungshim-ŭro" [A Study of Chŏlla Province "Left Side" *P'ungmulgut:* With Regard to the Fund-raising Ritual Performance of Imshil and Kohŭng]. Master's thesis, Chŏnbuk University.

War History Compilation Committee. 1975. *History of U.N. Forces in Korean War*, vol. 4, *The United States Forces in the Korean War: June 1950–June 1951*. Seoul: Ministry of National Defense.

Whang, In-joung [Hwang Injŏng]. 1981. *Management of Rural Change in Korea: The Saemaul Undong*. Seoul: Seoul National University Press.

Williams, Sean. 2001. *The Sound of the Ancestral Ship: Highland Music of West Java*. New York: Oxford University Press.

Yang Chinsŏng. [1980?]. *Honam chwado: P'ilbong maŭl p'ungmulgut* [Chŏlla Province "Left Side" Style: *P'ungmulgut* of P'ilbong Village]. Namwŏn: Honam chwado p'ungmul p'an kut palp'yohoe shilmut'im.

Yang, Jongsung [Yang Chongsŭng]. 2003. *Cultural Protection Policy in Korea: Intangible Cultural Properties and Living National Treasures*. Seoul: Jimoondang.

Yi Chaesuk. 1979. *Kugak panjubŏp* [Accompaniment Methodology in Korean Traditional Music]. Seoul: Sumundang.

Yi Chongjin. 1996. "P'ungmulgut ŭi karak kujo-wa yŏktongsŏng: P'ilbong P'ungmulgut-ŭl chungshim-ŭro" [Rhythmic Structure and Kinetic Energy in *P'ungmulgut:* With Regard to P'ilbong P'ungmulgut]. Master's thesis, Andong University.

Yi Chŏngno. 1998. "Honam chwa-udo nongak ŭi hyŏngshik-kwa ch'um pigyo yŏn'gu: Imshil P'ilbong Nongak-kwa Iri Nongak-ŭl chungshim-ŭro" [A Comparative Study of Chŏlla Province "Left Side" And "Right Side" *Nongak*'s Form and Dance: With Regard to Imshil P'ilbong Nongak and Iri Nongak]. Master's thesis, Chungang University.

Yi Hogwan, Yi Chuyŏng, Chŏng Chun'gi, and Yi Pohyŏng. 1982. *Chŏlla pukto kugak shilt'ae chosa* [Research on the Actual State of Traditional Music in North Chŏlla Province]. Seoul: Munhwajae kwalliguk, Munhwajae yŏn'guso.

Yi Hyegu. 1973. "Chuakto II" [Illustration of Musical Performances 2]. *Konggan* 77 : 27–32.

———, ed. 1986. *Korean Music and Instruments.* Translated by Alan C. Heyman. Seoul: National Classical Music Institute of Korea.

———. 1987. *Chŏngganbo ŭi chŏnggan / taegang mit changdan* [*Chŏnggan, Taegang,* and *Changdan* of Korean Rhythmic Notation]. Seoul: Segwang ŭmak ch'ulp'ansa.

———. 1991. "Changdan ŭi kaenyŏm" [The Concept of *Changdan*]. *Han'guk ŭmak yŏn'gu* 19 : 11–33.

Yi Kyuwŏn and Chŏng Pŏmt'ae. 1997 [1995]. *Uri-ka chŏngmal araya hal uri chŏnt'ong yein paek saram* [One Hundred of Our Traditional Artists We Should Know]. Seoul: Hyŏnamsa.

Yi Man'gap. 1980. "Chŏnt'ongjŏk hyŏptong-kwa ch'ollak sahoe ŭi palchŏn" [The Development of Traditional Cooperation and Village Society]. *Han'guk ŭi sahoe-wa munhwa* 3 : 76–105.

Yi Pohyŏng. 1976. "Shindae-wa nonggi" [The Spirit Pole and the Farming Flag]. *Han'guk munhwa illyuhak* 8 : 59–66.

———. 1984. "Nongak-esŏ kilgut (kil kunak)-kwa ch'aegut" [*Ch'aegut* and *Kilgut* Rhythmic Patterns in *Nongak*]. *Minjok ŭmakhak* 6 : 31–47.

———. 1991. "Musok ŭmak changdan ŭi ŭmakchŏk t'ŭksŏng" [Musical Features of Shaman Music Rhythmic Patterns]. *Han'guk ŭmak yŏn'gu* 19 : 125–32.

———. 1992. "Han'guk minsok ŭmak changdan ŭi taegangbak (taebak), pak, punbak (sobak)-e taehan chŏnt'ong kiboronjŏk koch'al" [A Theoretical Investigation of Traditional Notation Regarding the Concepts of *Taegangbak (Taebak), Pak,* and *Punbak (Sobak)* Found in Korean Folk Music *Changdan*]. *Kugagwŏn nonmunjip* 4 : 23–56.

———. 1994. "Han'guk minsok ŭmak changdan ŭi ridŭmhyŏng-e kwanhan yŏn'gu: Chungjungmori, kukkŏri, t'aryŏng, salp'uri-wa kat'ŭn 3 sobak nŭrin 4 pakchahyŏng changdan-ŭl chungshim-ŭro" [Research on the Rhythmic Patterns of Korean Folk Music *Changdan: Chungjungmori, Kukkŏri, T'aryŏng, Salp'uri,* and Similar Triple-subdivision, Slow Four-beat Form *Changdan*]. *Minjok ŭmakhak* 16 : 39–70.

———. 1995. "Chŏnt'ong kiboron-esŏ pak ŭi chiphamnon-kwa punhallon ŭi hamnisŏng-kwa hyoyongsŏng" [The Logic and Usefulness of the Method of Grouping and Division of Beats Found in Traditional Music Notation]. *Minjok ŭmakhak* 17 : 19–40.

Yi Sangil. 1987. *Han'gugin ŭi kut-kwa nori* [Ritual and Play of the Korean People]. Seoul: Munŭmsa.

———, ed. 1988. *Nori munhwa-wa ch'ukche* [Play Culture and Festivals]. Seoul: Sŏnggyun'gwan taehakkyo ch'ulp'anbu.

Yi Sangjin. 2002. *Han'guk nongak kaeron* [An Introduction to Korean *Nongak*]. Seoul: Minsogwŏn.

Yi Sŏngjae. 1999 [1994]. *Chaemi innŭn kugak killajabi* [An Interesting Guide to Traditional Music]. Seoul: Seoul Media.

Yi Sora and Chŏng Sumi. 2000. *Iri Nongak*. Seoul: Hwasan munhwa.

Yi Yŏngbae. 2000. "P'ilbong P'ungmulgut ŭi kongyŏn kujo: Wŏlli-wa sahoejŏk ŭimi" [The Performance Structure of P'ilbong *P'ungmulgut:* Its Principles and Societal Meaning]. Master's thesis, Chŏnbuk University.

Yi Yonggu. 1995 [1994]. *Ching: Param ŭi sori, hanŭl ŭi sori* [*Ching:* The Sound of Wind, the Sound of the Heavens]. Pusan: Yujin p'ŏsŭk'om.

Yu Kiryong. 1975. "Nongak yongŏ haesŏl" [A Glossary of *Nongak* Terms]. *Konggan* 99:75–80.

Yu Kyŏngok. 1987. "Iri Nongak ŭi yŏn'gu: Ch'ae sangmo ch'um kaein nori-rŭl chungshim-ŭro" [A Study of Iri Nongak: The Individual *Ch'ae sangmo* Dance]. Master's thesis, Sungmyŏng Women's University.

Yu Pyŏngdŏk. 1985. *Han'guk minjung chonggyo sasangnon* [A Discussion of *Minjung* Religious Thought in Korea]. Seoul: Shiinsa.

Yun Chigwan. 1990. *Minjok hyŏnshil-kwa munhak pip'yŏng* [National Realities and Literary Criticism]. Seoul: Shilch'ŏn munhaksa.

Yun Myŏngwŏn. 1994. "Taech'wit'a ŭi kusŏng-e kwanhan yŏn'gu" [A Study of the Composition of Military Processional Music]. *Munhwajae* 27:157–94.

INDEX-GLOSSARY